1988

COLERIDGE AND THE INSPIRED WORD

Samuel Taylor Coleridge was the central figure in the dissemination of higher criticism, that analytical and historical study of the Bible begun in Germany in the late eighteenth century by Lessing, Herder, and Eichhorn. This movement radically revised the interpretation of the Bible as an "inspired" book, and also helped to redefine the inspiration attributed to poets, since many poets of the period, including Coleridge himself, wished to emulate the prophetic voice of biblical tradition. Coleridge's mastery of this new study and his search for a new understanding of the Bible on which to ground his faith are the focus of this book.

Beginning with an exposition of Coleridge's double role as theologian and poet, Harding analyses the development and transmission of Coleridge's views of inspiration—both biblical and poetic—and provides a history of his theological and poetic ideas in their second generation, in England especially in the work of F. D. Maurice and John Sterling, and in America in that of Ralph Waldo Emerson.

Harding argues that Coleridge's emphasis on the human integrity of the scriptural authors provided his contemporaries with a poetics of inspiration which seemed likely to restore to literature a "biblical" sense of the divine as a presence in the world. Coleridge's treatment of biblical inspiration is thus an important contribution to Romantic poetics as well as to biblical scholarship. His concept of inspiration is also linked directly to his literary theory and thus to the current debate over the reader's relation to text and author.

Anthony John Harding is Professor of English, University of Saskatchewan, and the author of *Coleridge and the Idea of Love*.

McGill-Queen's Studies in the History of Ideas

1 Problems of Cartesianism
Edited by Thomas M. Lennon, John M. Nicholas,
and John W. Davis

2 The Development of the Idea of History in Antiquity
Gerald A. Press

3 Claude Buffier and Thomas Reid:
Two Common-Sense Philosophers
Louise Marcil-Lacoste

4 Schiller, Hegel, and Marx:
State, Society, and the Aesthetic Ideal of Ancient Greece
Philip J. Kain

5 John Case and Aristotelianism in Renaissance England
Charles B. Schmitt

6 Beyond Liberty and Property:
The Process of Self-Recognition in Eighteenth-Century
Political Thought
J. A. W. Gunn

7 John Toland:
His Method, Manners, and Mind
Stephen H. Daniel

8 Coleridge and the Inspired Word
Anthony John Harding

COLERIDGE AND THE INSPIRED WORD

Anthony John Harding

McGill-Queen's University Press
Kingston and Montreal

ISBN 0-7735-1008-7
Legal deposit 3rd quarter 1985
Bibliothèque nationale du Québec
Printed in Canada

Canadian Cataloguing in Publication Data

Harding, Anthony John
Coleridge and the inspired word
Includes index.
Bibliography: p.
ISBN 0-7735-1008-7.
1. Coleridge, Samuel Taylor 1772–1834.
2. Inspiration. I. Title.
PR4484.H37 1985 821'.7 C85-098421-1

To My Mother
Vera Harding
and to the Memory of My Father
Cecil Harding

Contents

Acknowledgments

THE IDEA of this book has been with me in various forms for so long that to set down all my obligations to the work of others, and to those friends and colleagues with whom I have discussed the matters here raised, would itself be a formidable task. As an undergraduate at the University of Manchester in the late sixties I spent daytime hours discussing English literature with instructors who were always generous with their time and their ideas, while the rainy Manchester nights were usually occupied in discovering the nature of prophecy, and how to read the Bible, with the group of Christian radicals and radical Christians who made up the University of Manchester Student Christian Movement. At the prompting of Dr. David Pirie I read *Inquiring Spirit,* Kathleen Coburn's anthology of Coleridge's prose writings (first published in 1951). The immediate result was a sense of powerful curiosity and anticipation—something which other students of Coleridge will, I think, recognize. Professor Coburn's "presentation" of Coleridge seemed to indicate a way of healing the breach between the two halves of my life; or, more to the immediate point for the reader of this book, a way of finding out whether prophecy and literature were irredeemably divorced, or whether the reader of English literature did not need an understanding of biblical tradition at least as much as the reader of the Bible needed literary imagination and critical training.

I cannot pretend that this book answers these questions, even to my own satisfaction. It is not offered as an exhaustive treatment of the relationship between literature and biblical prophecy: the reader will find this relationship much more authoritatively investigated in the work of Joseph Anthony Wittreich, Jr., M. H. Abrams, and Northrop

Frye (to all of whom my work is indebted). My more limited aim here is to demonstrate the importance to Coleridge, and certain other English and American writers, of an idea that still figures occasionally in critical discourse: that of inspiration, particularly the inspiration of the Scriptures. I am aware that the book has numerous deficiencies even when measured against this more modest aim, and I ask the many people who helped, guided, and encouraged me along the way to forgive these defects and to share my wish that a better book on this subject may soon appear.

L. C. Knights, then King Edward VII Professor of English Literature in the University of Cambridge, and John Beer, Fellow of Peterhouse, Cambridge, fostered my first serious study of Coleridge, and have continued to give of their time and their friendship. For support and guidance in the early stages of the work I am also grateful to Dr. Howard Erskine-Hill, now Fellow of Pembroke College, Cambridge, Professor Lilian R. Furst, now at the University of Texas at Dallas, and Professor C. B. Cox, of the University of Manchester. Fr. J. Robert Barth, of the University of Missouri at Columbia, has been a selfless friend and a generous and constructive critic of my work for many years; he read the entire first draft of this book and made many valuable suggestions. Some parts of the draft were also read by Professor Stuart Curran, of the University of Pennsylvania, and Professor N. Merrill Distad, of University College, University of Toronto. I am grateful to them both for their thoughtful, challenging comments.

Many of my friends and colleagues have allowed me to talk Coleridge with them, sometimes at strange hours or in strange places: in particular Athelyn and Graham Haydon, William and Camille Slights, Craig Miller, Raimonda Modiano, Vincent Sherry, Kathleen Wheeler, and Douglas Wilson. For invaluable help in obtaining vitally necessary leaves, grants, and fellowships, I am indebted to Professors J. Keith Johnstone, Robert L. Calder, and Claud A. Thompson, of the University of Saskatchewan, and to Dr. John Beer, Dr. Howard Erskine-Hill, and Professor William R. Robbins. Miss Molly Lefebure, Mr. Richard Wordsworth, Dr. Molly Klapper, Dr. David Jobling, Dr. John Flynn, Miss Prudence Tracy, and Dr. Judith Williams helped in important ways.

Professor Kathleen Coburn kindly made the resources of the Coleridge collection at Victoria University Library, Toronto, available to me. I am grateful for her help and for the gracious and hospitable manner in which she made a pilgrim from the West feel at home in Victoria College. I also wish to thank Mr. J. S. Ritchie, Keeper of Manuscripts at the National Library of Scotland, and his staff, and the staff of the British Library, London, Cambridge University Library, the University of Washington Library, the Guy W. Bailey Library at the University of Vermont, the Library of Trinity College, Cambridge, and the University of Saskatchewan Library.

I am grateful to Mrs. Joan Coleridge and Mrs. Priscilla Coleridge Needham for permission to use materials from unpublished manuscripts of S. T. Coleridge; to the Master and Fellows of Trinity College Cambridge for permission to quote from the Whewell-Hare correspondence in Trinity College Library; and to Mr. W. Knowlton Hall for permission to quote from a manuscript of James Marsh in the Guy W. Bailey Library, University of Vermont. My efforts to trace the present owner of copyright in the manuscripts of John Sterling have not been successful.

The President of the University of Saskatchewan awarded me two grants from the President's Fund which facilitated the early stages of the research. In 1980–81 the Social Sciences and Humanities Research Council of Canada honoured me with a Sabbatical Leave Fellowship, and the University of Saskatchewan gave me a year's sabbatical leave.

This book has been published with the help of a grant from the Canadian Federation for the Humanities, using funds provided by the Social Sciences and Humanities Research Council of Canada.

Part of chapter 1 appeared in the *The Wordsworth Circle* 13 (1982), and part of chapter 5 in *Victorian Studies* 26 (1983). I am grateful to the editors of these journals for allowing republication of this material.

Professors Kerry McSweeney and David Norton of McGill-Queen's University Press have been the most positive and encouraging editors an author could wish for.

The unfailing cheerfulness, patience, and good sense of my wife, Patricia Williams, kept me working at this book many times when but for her I should have given it up. I wish these pages could be a more adequate expression of my love and gratitude.

Abbreviations

AmS	Ralph Waldo Emerson, "The American Scholar," in *Nature, Addresses, and Lectures*
BL	Samuel Taylor Coleridge, *Biographia Literaria*
C&S	Coleridge, *On the Constitution of the Church and State*
CL	Coleridge, *Collected Letters*
CM	Coleridge, *Marginalia*
CN	Coleridge, *Notebooks* (references to entry numbers, not to page numbers)
CW	Coleridge, *Complete Works*
DSA	Emerson, "An Address delivered before the Senior Class in Divinity College, Cambridge, July 15, 1838," in *Nature, Addresses, and Lectures*
E&T	John Sterling, *Essays and Tales . . . Collected and Edited, with a Memoir of His Life, By Julius Charles Hare*
EESS	Emerson, *Essays* [and] *Essays: Second Series*
EL	Emerson, *Letters*
EP	Emerson, *Poems*
Friend	Coleridge, *The Friend*
JMN	Emerson, *Journals and Miscellaneous Notebooks*
KofC	[John Frederick Denison Maurice,] *The Kingdom of Christ . . . In Letters to a Member of the Society of Friends. By a Clergyman of the Church of England*
Lects 1795	Coleridge, *Lectures 1795 on Politics and Religion*
LS	Coleridge, *Lay Sermons*
LSA	Emerson, *Letters and Social Aims*
N	Emerson, *Nature*, in *Nature, Addresses and Lectures*
NT	New Testament

OT	Old Testament
PMLA	*Publications of the Modern Language Association*
PW	Coleridge, *Complete Poetical Works*
TT	Coleridge, *Table Talk and Omniana*

COLERIDGE AND THE INSPIRED WORD

And when the crowds saw what Paul had done, they lifted up their voices, saying in Lycaonian, "The gods have come down to us in the likeness of men!" Barnabas they called Zeus, and Paul, because he was the chief speaker, they called Hermes. And the priest of Zeus, whose temple was in front of the city, brought oxen and garlands to the gates and wanted to offer sacrifice with the people. But when the apostles Barnabas and Paul heard of it, they tore their garments and rushed out among the multitude, crying, "Men, why are you doing this? We also are men, of like nature with you, and bring you good news, that you should turn from these vain things to a living God who made the heaven and the earth and the sea and all that is in them."

Acts 14:11–15 (*RSV*)

Introduction

IN THE "Melchester" section of Thomas Hardy's *Jude the Obscure*, Sue Bridehead, Jude's well-read and unconventional cousin, offers to help him in his study of the Bible by making for him a "*new* New Testament," similar to one she used to read. The books of the New Testament would be separated one from the other and rearranged in their order of composition, so that Thessalonians would come first, then the other Epistles, then the Gospels. Sue's idea strikes Jude as rather sacrilegious, and to most modern readers who are not biblical scholars the thought of a "rearranged" New Testament is still a little shocking. A lingering reverence for the written word seems to demand that the traditional order be adhered to.

In fact, of course, a strictly chronological edition of the New Testament (much more one of the whole Bible) would be impossibly complex to produce, entailing the rearrangement not only of the books themselves but of chapters within the books, verses within chapters, and even phrases within verses. Sue's radical proposal is meant to indicate her modernity relative to Oxford and the Victorian church. But by 1894—the date *Jude* began serialization in *Harper's*—it would already have been a familiar and rather simplistic notion as far as serious biblical scholars were concerned. Critical study of the Bible according to modern historical methods was initiated by J. G. Eichhorn's *Einleitung in das Alte Testament*, 1781; but, as Hans Frei points out in *The Eclipse of Biblical Narrative*, the idea of a unitary *meaning* to be found in the Bible had begun to show the first signs of weakness as early as the mid-seventeenth century, with the work of Spinoza and Cocceius and Richard Simon.[1]

1. Hans Frei, *The Eclipse of Biblical Narrative* (New Haven: Yale University Press, 1974), pp. 7, 17, 42–50. See also Ernst Cassirer, *The Philosophy of the Enlightenment*,

It would be wrong, however, to reason that as generally accepted notions of the unity of the Bible were progressively undermined by historical scholarship, its significance, for either faith or literature and literary criticism, must have progressively declined. Literary critics know that a work very often becomes much more important and interesting when they can go behind the apparently seamless fabric of the received text and explore the fragments, drafts, cancelled pages, and other materials among which an author or editor thought he or she saw sufficient unifying elements to make a complete book. (In a similar way, Sue Bridehead tells Jude that reading the New Testament chronologically makes it "twice as interesting as before, and twice as understandable.") The discovery of neglected manuscripts can bring about a revolution in our sense of an author's development, achievement, and continuing significance. Interpretations long accepted as definitive often must be revised or even jettisoned. A completely new approach to the author in question may have to be worked out.

Something like this happened with the Bible in the eighteenth and nineteenth centuries. A growth of historical awareness among scholars and the general public meant that the Bible could no longer be read as some of the Reformers had read it (not Luther himself, but many Lutherans of the sixteenth century and later): as equally and fully inspired in every word, and therefore inerrant.[2] Herder even based a *defence* of biblical poetry against the scepticism of other Enlightenment writers, such as Voltaire, on the argument that a biblical text must always be read with full imaginative grasp of the historical context that originally gave it meaning. Such an approach often helped to rescue biblical poetry from the dead hand of literalism and to recover something of the imaginative richness of biblical texts that literalism had concealed. Yet many Christian believers felt there was a "danger"—as the American scholar James Marsh put it—"of turning

---

trans. Fritz C. A. Koelln and James P. Pettegrove (Princeton, N.J.: Princeton University Press, 1951), p. 185. On the formation of the biblical canon, see George A. Buttrick, ed., *The Interpreter's Dictionary of the Bible*, 4 vols (New York and Nashville: Abingdon Press, 1962), and Supplement (1976), arts. "Canon of the OT" and "Canon of the NT."

2. See Frei, *Eclipse of Biblical Narrative*, p. 37, and Robert M. Grant, *A Short History of the Interpretation of the Bible*, rev. ed. (London: Adam and Charles Black, 1965), p. 104.

all our religion to poetry."[3] Part of what Marsh meant was that the Bible had to be interpreted as more than just an anthology of beautiful "poetic" passages. It formed a canon of sacred writings with a single message, despite the fact that individual parts of the canon were written many hundreds of years apart. Whatever other texts were permitted to remain fragmentary, the requirements of exegesis meant that some way must be found to preserve the sacred meaning of the Bible: to prevent the biblical canon from being completely disintegrated by historicism.

The literary study of biblical texts initiated by Lowth and continued by Herder also brought into focus, however, some features of the poetry of the Hebrews which accorded very well with the literary tastes of the late eighteenth century. Intensity, conciseness, metrical flexibility: these qualities, frequently to be found in Hebrew poetry, appealed to the age of Collins, Smart, and Blake. Since the opposite qualities—elaboration, urbanity, etiolation—were associated in many people's minds with an over-refined, exhausted civilization, it was natural to associate the emotional intensity of Hebrew poetry with its origin in what was taken to be the first dawning of history, or "infancy of the human race." There was a prevailing assumption that the most ancient Jewish writers were closer to the sources of divine inspiration than writers of later times, paralleling the assumption that the child was closer to the well-springs of creative genius than the adult. It even became possible, then, to speak of the earliest parts of the Bible as "inspired" in a higher degree than later parts.

Yet this inspiration was not seen by Romantic writers as simply the manipulation of passive human instruments by an all-powerful godhead that completely obliterated the individuality of the prophet. The Romantics insisted on the uncompromised humanity of the prophet: indeed, in the inspired state he or she was held to be most fully human.

Besides upholding against Voltairean sceptics the claim of divine inspiration for at least parts of the Bible, this view also provided the Romantics with an answer to the fears of orthodox Christians that once the unity of the biblical canon was undermined, nothing would

3. [James Marsh,] "*Intorno all'ingiustizia di alcuni guidizii letterarii Italiani. Discorso di Lodovico Arborio Gattinara di Breme, figlio* . . . 1816" (a review, running titles: "Ancient Literature of Italy," "Ancient and Modern Poetry"), *North American Review* 15 (1822): 131.

be left but a collection of beautiful pieces of literature. The most urgent summons of the prophetic voice, Romantic commentators argued, could still be heard in the nineteenth century. The historical distance between the biblical prophets and the modern student of the Bible was of comparatively little significance when they could meet at the level of their common humanity. Such an emphasis on the comparative unimportance of mere chronological remoteness, and belief in the possibility of a meeting of minds across the millennia, also enabled the Romantics to overcome a difficulty which the thinkers of the Enlightenment, even Herder, had not dealt with: the tendency of the historicist approach to neutralize the impact of a biblical text on the reader, even while that reader was in theory admiring the text's literary qualities.

At the same time, Romantic so-called primitivism, which is more accurately seen as a desire to re-establish contact with universal human values—"the primary laws of our nature," in Wordsworth's phrase—led many poets to imitate the spareness and emotional intensity they found in biblical poetry. For such poets, the fact that the Bible was traditionally treated as a canon was arguably less important than the discovery that it was nevertheless open not only to imitation but to reinterpretation, if all imitation is not in fact a form of reinterpretation. The English Romantics began to see the Bible as Emerson was to describe it in the "Divinity School Address," as an inspired but unfinished epic, *still in the process of composition*, and capable of being added to by the inspired writings of later times.

Blake strikes the distinctive note here, when in *The Marriage of Heaven and Hell* (plate 12) he has Isaiah say: "as I was then perswaded, & remain confirm'd; that the voice of honest indignation is the voice of God, I cared not for consequences but wrote."[4] Though naturalistic in his terminology at this point, Blake shares with Schleiermacher and Coleridge the conviction that we cannot assume a stance of knowing superiority towards the Bible. His very earthy portrayal of Isaiah and Ezekiel has the same broad intention as Schleiermacher's hermeneutic: to show that what the Bible records is the human voice—a voice of honest indignation, of pain, despair, hope, or triumph—expressing God's living presence and action. (And the evident corollary of this

4. William Blake, *The Poetry and Prose*, ed. David V. Erdman, commentary by Harold Bloom (Garden City, N.Y.: Doubleday and Company, 1965), p. 38.

view was that prophetic utterance was still possible, for the individual who would dare to be honest.)

For Schleiermacher, to interpret, or to exercise the "art of understanding" on a text, is to place oneself in a dialogical relationship with the author; and the interpreter's job is to reconstruct not merely the historical circumstances surrounding the production of the text but the mental life of the author, which that text expresses.[5] Coleridge, too, saw that to recognize the historical distance between author and reader was only a first step. What had to be recovered was the authentic ("honest") claim of one whole human being addressing another whole human being. Coleridge's own experience of biblical study convinced him that, so far from destroying the authority of the Bible and ending its role as witness to the sacred, recognition of the human individuality that lay behind each verse of Scripture would remove an unnecessary obstacle between the Bible and its readers and place in a much clearer light the true challenge of scriptural prophecy.

Coleridge responded to the Bible not only as a religious thinker, however, but as a poet. As a poet, he participated in the late eighteenth-century rediscovery of the oracular poetic voice, which was closely linked with the rediscovery of Hebrew poetry as well as with the revaluation of Greek oracular poets such as Pindar and of prophetic poets in the English tradition such as Spenser and Milton.[6] For the creation of a poetry of prophetic dignity and strength, "An Orphic song indeed" (*PW* 1: 406), the attempt to comprehend the mystery of inspiration was obviously crucial. Coleridge's imagination was more imbued with Hebrew literature, imagery, and thought-forms than that of any other English poet of the time except Blake, and he found in Hebrew poetry the exemplary instance of Imagination, the "*modifying*, and *co-adunating* Faculty" (*CL* 2: 866).

However, this exceptionally close relationship with Hebrew literature could not shield Coleridge from the anxieties attendant upon the poet in a remote time and a strange land who tries to emulate the

5. See Richard E. Palmer, *Hermeneutics: Interpretation Theory in Schleiermacher, Dilthey, Heidegger, and Gadamer* (Evanston, Ill.: Northwestern University Press, 1969), p. 86.

6. See Joseph Anthony Wittreich, Jr., " 'A Poet Amongst Poets': Milton and the Tradition of Prophecy," in J. A. Wittreich, Jr., ed., *Milton and the Line of Vision* (Madison: University of Wisconsin Press, 1975), p. 98. On the oppressive ("baleful") aspects of Milton's influence on the Romantics see Harold Bloom, *The Anxiety of Influence: A Theory of Poetry* (London: Oxford University Press, 1973), p. 35 and *passim*.

poets of ancient Israel. Indeed, these anxieties were already vividly present in Jewish literature written after the subjugation of Jerusalem by the Babylonians in 587 B.C., Psalm 137 being the most notable instance:

> By the rivers of Babylon, there we sat down, yea, we wept, when we remembered Zion.
> We hanged our harps upon the willows in the midst thereof.
> For there they that carried us away captive required of us a song; and they that wasted us required of us mirth, saying, Sing us one of the songs of Zion.
> How shall we sing the Lord's song in a strange land?
>
> (Verses 1–4)

Every Romantic (which is to say, post-Enlightenment) poet experienced the modern equivalent of this exile; and like all other Romantics Coleridge had to confront the fear expressed most starkly in Collins's "Ode on the Poetical Character": that perhaps all the ancient sources of inspiration were now inaccessible, that as a latecomer he was disqualified from entry into the ghostly circle of true poets. More than other Romantics, Coleridge had to deal with the specifically biblical poetic heritage—in both its liberating and its anxiety-producing aspects.

We should be prepared to recognize, then, important connections between Coleridge's ventures into Biblical scholarship and his poetics. It will be found that the two constantly interpenetrate. My argument is that the new sense of the Bible propagated by historical scholarship, and the significant Romantic reaction to historicism, contributed in a major way to the Romantic poetics of inspiration, and that Coleridge was a central figure in the spread of this new sense of biblical inspiration in the English-speaking world.

This involves bringing into prominence a work often neglected by students of Coleridge's literary criticism, his "Letters on the Inspiration of the Scriptures." (The work was curiously mistitled *Confessions of an Inquiring Spirit* when it was published by Coleridge's nephew, Henry Nelson Coleridge, several years after Coleridge's death. I propose to use the title by which Coleridge himself most often referred to the work, since that title more accurately describes its form and subject-matter.) In the "Letters," as in all Coleridge's writings about the Bible, his emphasis on the human integrity of the authors of Scripture provided his contemporaries with a poetics of inspiration which for a time seemed likely to restore to literature a "biblical" sense of the human word as a response to the omnipresent divine creative power, and an affirmation of humankind's "responsibility" or accountability before its God. Coleridge's distinctive contribution to the understanding of Scripture in the English-speaking world is his development in the "Letters" of the Romantic perception that the prophets and witnesses whose words are recorded in the Bible remain human—only become, in fact, most fully human—when God moves them to speak. When we read Judges 5, Coleridge argues, is it better to see in Deborah the passive instrument of an infallible Intelligence, speaking words not her own, or "the impassioned, high-souled, heroic woman in all the prominence and individuality of will and character" (*CW*, 5: 592–93)? In one of his notebooks, Coleridge remarks on the curiously different, but complementary, human qualities of St. John and St. Paul; yet obviously he does not feel that their humanness made them less effective as apostles (*CN* 3560). The same point recurs in a *Table Talk* entry for 31 March 1832:

> There may be dictation without inspiration, and inspiration without dictation: they have been and continue to be grievously confounded. Balaam and his ass were the passive organs of dictation; but no one, I suppose, will venture to call either of those worthies inspired. It is my profound conviction that St. John and St. Paul were divinely inspired; but I totally disbelieve the dictation of any one word, sentence or argument throughout their writings. Observe, there was revelation. . . . Revelations of facts were undoubtedly made to the prophets; revelations of doctrines were as undoubtedly made to John and Paul;—but is it not a mere matter of our very senses that John and Paul each dealt with those revelations, expounded them, insisted on them, just exactly according to his own natural strength of intellect, habit of reasoning, moral, and even physical temperament? (Pp. 152–53)

Coleridge would certainly have agreed with Frederick Denison Maurice's argument that the "dictation" theory of biblical inspiration is, in fact, "wholly at war with the idea of Inspiration" and that "holy men could not speak as they were moved by the Holy Ghost . . . if they acted as amanuenses, not as men."[7] Despite differences in their terminology (and theology), for Maurice, as for Blake and Coleridge, the human

7. [John] Frederick Denison Maurice, *Sequel to the Inquiry, What is Revelation? In a Series of Letters* . . . (Cambridge and London: Macmillan, 1860), p. 51. See also J. Robert Barth, S.J., *Coleridge and Christian Doctrine* (Cambridge, Mass.: Harvard University Press, 1969), p. 84.

integrity of the prophet and the apostle is our guarantee of the meaning of the texts which record their words.

In this respect, the "Letters" develop the famous definitions of primary and secondary Imagination found in chapter 13 of *Biographia Literaria*. Primary Imagination according to Coleridge is "the living Power and prime Agent of all human Perception, and . . . a repetition in the finite mind of the eternal act of creation in the infinite I AM." Secondary Imagination is "an echo of the former, co-existing with the conscious will, yet . . . identical with the primary in the *kind* of its agency, and differing only in *degree*, and in the *mode* of its operation" (*BL*, 1: 304). The "Letters" share with these definitions two important features: the Hebraic sense of the ultimate dependence of all things human on the divine eternal act of creation, and the equally important stress on the integrity of the human witness, evident in the definition of secondary Imagination as "an echo of the former, *co-existing with the conscious will*." By questioning the simplistic but widespread belief that the Scriptures were "throughout dictated, in word and thought, by an infallible Intelligence" (*CW*, 5: 591), Coleridge showed himself not only to be broadly on the side of contemporary biblical scholarship and its findings but also convinced that a person who read the Bible with "free and unboding spirit" (*CW*, 5: 617)—free of exaggerated reverence for the *letter* of the text—would come away with a far livelier sense of the efficacy of Scripture, as the work of many women and men "actuated by . . . one Spirit, working diversly" (*CW*, 5: 591-92). This formulation is indeed more conservative theologically than the definitions of primary and secondary Imagination in *Biographia Literaria*. Not only does it have an obviously Trinitarian basis, but it limits itself to the canonical Scriptures, where the earlier work had carried the more universalist and "Emersonian" implication that *every* product of the secondary Imagination reflects the creative activity of the Word. The continuities between *Biographia* and the "Letters" are important, however, and should not be ignored. They indicate that however far Coleridge may have deviated from Christian orthodoxy in the periods of his life when he was attracted to other systems of belief, the deeper ground of his thought, and the perspective from which he interpreted and weighed all other systems, remained essentially a biblical one.

Any claim that Coleridge's approach to the question of biblical inspiration remains of interest to modern students has to be made in the expectation that the Coleridgean position will attract criticism from at least two groups of readers. Formalist and post-structuralist literary critics are extremely hostile to the notion that our knowledge of an author's "mind" or "human qualities" is in any way relevant to the reading of a given text. Even the rather more defensible argument that it is always necessary, when reading a text, to hypostatize authorial "intention" simply as a step towards attributing meaning to that text—the view put forward most studiedly by E. D. Hirsch, Jr., in *Validity in Interpretation*—has met with considerable opposition. Coleridge, I shall argue in my second chapter (focusing upon *Biographia Literaria*), has provided some valuable warnings against the total expulsion of the author or "author's mind" from the text. While Coleridge's arguments were formulated in response to some of the tendencies of German philosophical idealism and not, of course, to structuralism and post-structuralism, they are still worth careful re-examination, especially since the structuralists are in some respects the progeny of Schelling and of Hegel and since Coleridge has been blamed (by Geoffrey Hartman) for failing in *Biographia Literaria* to consummate the marriage of a German-style "philosophical" criticism with British practicality and empiricism.[8]

A reader who is familiar with the developments in interpretation theory that are commonly grouped under the heading "The New Hermeneutic" may see in certain features of Coleridge's thought (for instance, the idea that a biblical text, properly read, will "marry with" the impulses of the reader, though not all readers of the Bible will respond to the same texts) an anticipation of Heideggerian and Bultmannian emphasis on the historically circumscribed nature of each act of interpretation, and the use of interpretation as a movement towards "self-understanding." In other respects, however, Coleridge adopts elements of Romantic hermeneutics which the Heideggerians reject as no longer tenable. Probably the most important of these is the belief, which he shared with Schleiermacher, that the reader's task, ideally described, is to relive the mental processes that were

8. Geoffrey H. Hartman, *Criticism in the Wilderness: The Study of Literature Today* (New Haven: Yale University Press, 1980), p. 47. It is interesting to note that a generation ago Herbert Read praised Coleridge because he *did* make criticism philosophical: *Coleridge as Critic* (London: Faber and Faber, 1949), p. 18. For strictures upon E. D. Hirsch, Jr.'s, *Validity in Interpretation* (New Haven: Yale University Press, 1967), see, among others, Palmer, *Hermeneutics*, pp. 62–65, and Louise M. Rosenblatt, *The Reader: the Text: the Poem: The Transactional Theory of the Literary Work* (Carbondale, Ill., and London: Southern Illinois University Press and Feffer and Simons, 1978), pp. 109–13.

experienced by the author of a text, not only comprehending what the author chose or was able to say—his or her "understanding"—but also seeing why that author might *not* have said something else—his or her "ignorance."

The use of the term "human integrity" in connection with the authors of Scripture may also invite criticism from those who wish to defend the authority of the Bible by emphasizing its special status as the unchanging Word of God, and who feel that nothing is to be gained, and much may be lost, by treating the authors of Scripture as anything other than the chosen instruments of revealed truth. I would ask such readers to consider carefully the discussion centred on the "Letters" in my third chapter. Though methodical textual analysis of the Bible was often feared and reviled in England and America during the nineteenth century, it is possible to argue that its effect on the faith of those who engaged in it was by no means always so devastating as has usually been assumed. It was realized quite early in the nineteenth century that a conception of "inspiration" which went no further than ascribing inspiration to the original author of the words recorded was quite inadequate for a book so complex in its textual history as the Bible. Schleiermacher argued persuasively in his *Critical Essay on the Gospel of St. Luke* that the work of the Spirit must also be recognized in the amanuensis or transcriber of the words uttered, in the editors who assembled the written accounts into a connected narrative, and in the faith community which preserved and studied the received texts. C. F. Evans describes this new perspective accurately and concisely, as it applies to the New Testament:

> The critical analysis of the Scriptures, as it is pressed further and deeper, leads at every point—and this is a truth still unwelcome to some—to the Church, to the people of God, as the sphere within which the language of revelation has worked and continues to work. . . . The Gospels, it is now seen, are not biographies, but compositions, more poetically subtle than was imagined, out of stories and traditions which already had a history behind them in the faith and worship of the Church, out of which they came, and which they existed to serve.[9]

Such a view of inspiration is surely a far more vital one than the view which would confine the work of the Spirit rigidly to one

9. C. F. Evans, "The Inspiration of the Bible," *Theology* 59 (1956): 16.

inspired person writing—or speaking—a sequence of words, as if from dictation.

In fact, as Walter J. Ong has pointed out, the whole notion of being inspired to *write* is rather misleading in the context of biblical studies, because the Bible emerged from a culture which—even in New Testament times—was still predominantly oral. Further, "the Bible often incorporates into itself lengthy passages previously pretty well shaped up elsewhere either by formalized oral tradition or in writing," and this is one reason why its textual history is so complex.[10] The Song of Miriam, the Song of Deborah, Joshua's "Appeal to the Sun and Moon," and Samson's Riddles are examples of utterances which are known to be far older than the narratives in which they now find themselves (Exodus 15:21; Judges 5:2–31; Joshua 10:12; Judges 14:14, 18). Scholars have also isolated certain confessions or creedlike narratives, such as those contained in Deuteronomy 26:5–9 and Joshua 24:2–13, which probably originated in cultic activity rather than in the mind of a single person. In early Jewish tradition, too, a clear distinction was drawn between the actual spoken words of a prophet—which might be regarded as divinely inspired—and the written record, which for some centuries was not accorded the same authority.[11]

In the New Testament, too, scholars point to considerable evidence of an "oral substratum," comprising liturgical, credal, catechetical, and homiletic materials which were formulated and passed down in an oral tradition for some decades before being incorporated in the gospel narratives. The notion that only the apostles and evangelists themselves were actually inspired obviously needs careful re-examination in the light of such evidence.

A third group of readers who do not share the concerns of either of the first two groups may still be doubtful about the usefulness of combining literary theory with the study of so unfamiliar a subject as biblical inspiration. Even if the two subjects were intimately connected

10. Walter J. Ong, S.J., *The Presence of the Word: Some Prolegomena for Cultural and Religious History* (Minneapolis: University of Minnesota Press, 1981), p. 184.

11. By the sixth century B.C., when the Deuteronomic editor combined the Deuteronomic Code with the two narratives known to biblical scholarship as J and E, the notion of divine inspiration had been extended to include the written accounts. Later still, the books of the Former and Latter Prophets, and writings other than prophecies—the three "poetic" books for instance (Psalms, Proverbs, Job)—were accorded the status of "inspired" writings. See Buttrick, *Interpreter's Dictionary of the Bible*, art. "Canon of the OT."

for Coleridge, is that any reason for us to follow his example? But—quite apart from the intrinsic historical interest of the subject—biblical scholarship in general, and Coleridge's in particular, has some surprising and useful things to teach the literary critic. To give one not altogether irrelevant example: when Stanley Fish claims (in *Is There a Text in This Class?*) to have discovered the role of "interpretive communities" in general hermeneutics, he is arguably just delivering a secularized version of what was already hoary orthodoxy for Schleiermacher's pupils in the 1820s. On the other hand, in Northrop Frye's fascinating and compendious *The Great Code: The Bible and Literature* there is little said about the assumed position of *our* "interpretive community" with regard to the Bible. Thus Frye can at some moments appeal to an assumed liberal-humanist consensus as to what constitutes literary excellence, or literariness itself ("The Bible . . . is as literary as it can well be without actually being literature," "the Bible taken as a poem is so spectacularly bad a poem that to accept it all as poetry would raise more questions than it solves," "the dreary chess problem of 'theodicy' "), and at other times choose to defend the Bible's strange preoccupation with witnessing to God's presence in history ("The Christian Bible is a written book that points to a speaking presence in history, the presence identified as Christ in the New Testament . . . ; from this point of view it makes good sense to call the Bible and the person of Christ by the same name").[12]

For the student of Romanticism, however, the most clearly significant point of contact between the contemporary understanding of biblical inspiration and the poetic theory and practice of the Romantics is in the extremely problematic Romantic rediscovery of the oracular and prophetic voice.[13]

This rediscovery was fraught with difficulties, not only because of the "belatedness" of the Romantic poet with regard to biblical and classical poetry but also in part because the Romantics lived in a literate and (to use Ong's term) "alphabetized" culture and had to wrestle

12. See Stanley Fish, *Is There a Text in This Class? The Authority of Interpretive Communities* (Cambridge, Mass.: Harvard University Press, 1980), pp. 303–21, and Northrop Frye, *The Great Code: The Bible and Literature* (Toronto: Academic Press Canada, 1982), pp. 62, 114, 47, 76–77. Frye seriously misrepresents the aims of the "demythologizers," too (pp. 41–42).

13. See Max F. Schulz, *The Poetic Voices of Coleridge* (Detroit: Wayne State University Press, 1963), pp. 27–28, and Murray Roston, *Prophet and Poet: The Bible and the Growth of Romanticism* (London: Faber and Faber, 1965), pp. 104, 157.

with the problem of transmitting the poem as spoken word to the printed page without giving up its oracular power. Wordsworth's story of how he composed the hundred and sixty lines of "Tintern Abbey" during a walk of four or five days from Tintern, without writing any of it down until he reached Bristol, is well known, but Wordsworth did not always find the transition so easy to make. Coleridge in particular found the transition from oral to written composition difficult, and he was also keenly aware that the printed text had to be in some way re-animated by the reader before it could begin to communicate the poet's voice and vision. In *The Creative Mind in Coleridge's Poetry*, Kathleen Wheeler argues persuasively that "Kubla Khan," "The Rime of the Ancient Mariner," and some of the conversation poems contain not only the record of visionary experience but also a "negative interpretive model," which the alert reader recognizes as *inadequate* to the vision contained within the poem. The gloss to "The Ancient Mariner," for example, offers such a negative interpretive model, and in rejecting it as an interpretation of the poem the reader learns to participate in the fully creative, imaginative activity which is the poem's ultimate aim and subject-matter.[14] One can agree with the general thrust of Wheeler's argument, I think, without giving up the point that the gloss is an essential part of the poem only within the conditions imposed by its existence as printed text. It is not only that "The Ancient Mariner" may work best when orally (and aurally) interpreted (and of course one cannot aurally register the gloss and the text simultaneously) but that the Mariner himself stands in the tradition of the illiterate, travelling story-teller; his experience of being seized by a power not his own ("My frame was wrenched with agony") and forced to begin his tale is an unmistakable reference to the prophet's traditional reluctance to speak and sense of being physically overpowered (compare Numbers 23:5–12, Jeremiah 1:4–9, Ezekiel 3:12–14). The printed text offers itself as the surviving record of an essentially oral-aural experience, and the gloss is of course part of this elaborate fiction, added by Coleridge as he began to understand the nature of the fiction he had created and the limitations of the printed text within which it achieved permanence.

Inspiration—and a type of inspiration that has strong biblical overtones—is also a theme in "Kubla Khan" and in "Christabel." "Kubla

14. Kathleen M. Wheeler, *The Creative Mind in Coleridge's Poetry* (Cambridge, Mass.: Harvard University Press, 1981), pp. 51–64.

Khan" in particular has frequently been cited as—for better or worse—*the* poem of Romantic inspiration. C. M. Bowra, for example, finds in this poem an instance of "inspiration in its ideal, least restricted, most disembarrassed and most disembodied form."[15] The poem has also been used as a stalking-horse for those who want to denigrate Romanticism as largely self-indulgent fancifulness. The arguments of such critics usually turn out to be circular: the poem means nothing because it refers to the experience of being supernaturally inspired, and we know that the poet's so-called inspiration is valueless because the poem means nothing. A third view is also possible, however: that the poem does genuinely address the question of inspiration, but far from describing it in its "ideal" form, exhibits the trauma of the seer who attempts to mediate between the eternal realm figured forth by the Abyssinian maid and the transitory world of language, history, and the poet's own self-conscious mind. As a recent article by Donald Pearce suggests, "Kubla Khan" can be read as a poem about interruption, about suspended powers.[16] However, the matter goes deeper than the inability of a notoriously self-doubting poet, on one particular occasion, to prolong or preserve a particular moment of vision. The understanding of supernatural inspiration within Judaeo-Christian tradition provides the essential elements of Coleridge's specific crisis: "Christabel" sets out the crisis in parabolic form.

Like the Ancient Mariner and the seer in "Kubla Khan," Geraldine shows unmistakable signs of possession. She faints at Sir Leoline's threshold, and again when Christabel lights the lamp; her eye glitters; she rolls her eyes; she utters a spell over the reclining Christabel. Possessed herself, she passes on her strange powers to the innocent Christabel, whose better mind is now at war with whatever it was Geraldine awoke in her.

> "Sure I have sinn'd!" said Christabel,
> "Now heaven be praised if all be well!"
> And in low faltering tones, yet sweet,
> Did she the lofty lady greet
> With such perplexity of mind
> As dreams too lively leave behind.
>
> *PW*, 1:228

15. C. M. Bowra, *Inspiration and Poetry* (London: Macmillan, 1955), p. 8.

16. Donald Pearce, " 'Kubla Khan' in Context," *Studies in English Literature 1500–1900* 21 (1981): 581.

In this story of an unprotected girl whose innocence appears to be threatened by a power at once internal and external, we can see Coleridge following up some of the more sinister implications of the inspiration-myths offered in "The Ancient Mariner" and "Kubla Khan." There is possession by evil forces, as well as by divine powers. Christabel's "perplexity" is the perplexity of the inexperienced human who cannot *know* whether the "lofty lady" who shared her bed—and her mind—is an embodiment of good or of evil. What Christabel suffers should not be conflated with popular conceptions of demonic possession drawn from Hollywood film scripts. If Christabel *knew* Geraldine to be wholly evil, there would be no "perplexity." Christabel's position is analogous to that of the poet-hermeneut, unsure whether to ascribe his own high-sounding utterance to pseudo-poetic madness or to the *furor divinus*.

A similar ambivalence runs through "The Rime of the Ancient Mariner." It has usually been assumed, both by Coleridge's critics and by his defenders, that the Mariner's vision of a universe animated by love, in which the Mariner himself participates through blessing the watersnakes, is meant to be a benign vision, in the sense that it helps the Mariner's audience, the Wedding Guest, to understand the human condition and to recognize human responsibility towards other living creatures and towards the divine presence within the universe. But that is a judgment on our part. Nothing in the poem absolutely guarantees that the Mariner's vision is benign, "true," or angelic rather than diabolical. Many episodes in the poem, it is true, suggest that a power of love and grace is at work in the Mariner's world; and often these episodes involve imagery of music, wind, rain, and the moon, though sometimes, too, the moon presides over scenes of death and the cursing of the Mariner. We do not "know" that it was the Virgin Mary who sent the rain to assuage the Mariner's thirst, nor do we "know" that the Polar Spirit loved the albatross, who loved the Mariner: the only authority we have for these interpretations is the Mariner himself. In this way, too, "The Ancient Mariner" is faithful to the tradition of prophetic utterance. Like the Wedding Guest, we must make up our own minds about whether the Mariner's inspiration is by a good spirit or (as the Pilot's Boy plainly thinks) an evil one. The fact that the Mariner shows many of the symptoms of being supernaturally possessed does not *in itself* guarantee the truth of his utterance. Many others have been in states of ecstasy besides the prophets of the Lord. As Walter Ong observes, inspiration in the stricter theologian's sense as a term recognizing the supernatural authority of certain utterances, "is not necessarily conscious. It is recognized by its acceptance in the Church, not by its writer's assertion, gratuitous or even accompanied by proofs, that he writes under divine inspiration."[17]

We confront here the problem and paradox that lie close to the core of Romanticism as a movement, as well as to Coleridge's own poetic endeavour. Romantic poets saw themselves as the inheritors of a prophetic tradition. They aspired to the condition of the seer, visionary, or prophet; and they claimed that divine truth could in some sense be intuited by the poet in an inspired state. Yet at the same time they had to act as their own normative tradition, their own "church," in judging the fitness of their work to be received into the canon of inspired utterance. The point is that this divided consciousness changes the way the vision is received and interpreted: it does not merely assert itself when the vision is over. Wordsworth, reliving, moderating, and reinterpreting his own youthful ecstasies in successive versions of *The Prelude*; Shelley, crying out and clasping his hands as the shadow of Intellectual Beauty falls on him; and Keats, confronting the stern figure of Moneta in *The Fall of Hyperion*—all are interpreting, constructing their own normative traditions, at the same time as they assume the prophet's stance and the seer's fervour. To have been inspired is not trivial, but it is not everything. What is much more important is *to decide what it means to have been inspired.* With Coleridge, the inspired state itself seems to coexist with the desire to be extending and not subverting the normative tradition he chose (or which chose him). Such a desire is not antagonistic to Coleridge's poetic gift: it is part of it. This at any rate is what is suggested by Coleridge's paraphrase and reinterpretation of Chapman, in one of his notebooks.

> Two kinds of Madness—the Insania pseudo-poetica, i.e. nonsense conveyed in strange and unusual language, the malice prepense of vanity or an inflammation from debility—and this is *de*generate/the other the Furor divinus, in which the mind ~~in a~~ by infusion of a celestial Health supra hominis naturam erigitur et in Deum transit—and this is Surgeneration, which only the Regenerate can properly appreciate. (*CN* 3216)

17. Ong, *Presence of the Word*, p. 184. Compare William James, *The Varieties of Religious Experience* (1902; reprint ed., London: Longmans, Green and Co., 1928), p. 20: "the problem how to discriminate between such messages and experiences as were really divine miracles, and such others as the demon in his malice was able to counterfeit . . . has always been a difficult one to solve."

Coleridge's concern in this passage, I suggest, is with the situation of the oracular and sibylline poet who wishes to be able himself to distinguish between the two states. It is a question not of a fiery creative impulse being reined in by a nervous devotion to self-censorship but rather of the very conditions under which the "ecstatic" state is approached in the post-Enlightenment period, the period immediately following that which Kant described as "man's emergence from his self-inculpated tutelage."[18] Pure, uninterpreted, unmediated experience is no longer possible for the Romantic, a latecomer in the history of prophetic utterance. Romantic irony comes into play, creating a poetry that is always *becoming* and never *in being*, as Schlegel expressed it; a poetry in which "*mythoi* can be used, but never believed."[19]

Harold Bloom has taught us to look for evidence of the poet's anxiety in poems of the Romantic period which centre on the sources of inspiration:

> Poetic anxiety implores the Muse for aid in divination, which means to foretell and put off as long as possible the poet's own death, as poet and (perhaps secondarily) as man. The poetry of any guilt culture whatsoever cannot initiate himself into a fresh chaos; he is compelled to accept a lack of priority in creation, which means he must accept also a failure in divination, as the first of many little deaths that prophesy a final and total extinction. His word is not his own word only, and his Muse has whored with many before him.[20]

One may accept as both valid and enriching this perception about the probable existence within the poet of an awareness of his own insufficiency and still question the terms in which Bloom expresses it as dangerously one-dimensional and limiting. Bloom's language excludes a priori the possibility of an escape from the personal, the individual. To implore the Muse for aid, Bloom says, "means" to foretell and put off one's death; to take what is inevitably a secondary place in creation "means" to accept "the first of many little deaths that

18. Quoted in Hans Küng, *On Being a Christian*, trans. Edward Quinn (n.p.: Collins, 1978), p. 81.

19. Janice L. Haney, " 'Shadow-Hunting': Romantic Irony, *Sartor Resartus*, and Victorian Romanticism," *Studies in Romanticism* 17 (1978): 313. Also pertinent is Kenneth R. Johnston's remark: "It was always a potentially traumatic problem for Jewish sacred writing to close its canon, and the possibility of further 'existential' revelation poses the same trauma for the Romantic epic of self-consciousness" (" 'Home at Grasmere': Reclusive Song," *Studies in Romanticism* 14 [1975]: 25–26).

20. Bloom, *Anxiety of Influence*, p.61.

prophesy a final and total extinction." These meanings—Bloom's meanings—invite comparison with the meaning given to inspiration within biblical tradition itself. But most of Bloom's successors have kept biblical traditions at arm's length in dealing with this question. For example, in *Romantic Origins*, Leslie Brisman sees poetic anxiety in psychoanalytic terms: transcendental entities such as "Spirit" and "Muse" are metaphors for the elements of imaginative creative power which lie beyond or beneath the poet's conscious control. The Absolute Other posited by the Romantic poet is the product of a defensive reaction, prompted by the poet's awareness of his own solitude.[21] Brisman's book is a brilliant investigation of the phenomenon of inspiration within the terms suggested by the modern myth of psychoanalysis. In writing about the Romantics, however, it seems arbitrary if not wilful to take one's interpretive tools from modern psychoanalytical theory when the Romantics themselves were so much closer to biblical traditions. Coleridge, like Wordsworth, Emerson, Carlyle, and Margaret Fuller, endeavoured to uphold the unity of the human personality against the fragmenting tendency of Humean and Rousseauan thought and, we might add, against the fragmented nature of his own experience. For us, as Eugene Goodheart observes, "the very idea of an integral humanity has become severely problematic."[22] But if we apply to Coleridge's work a heuristic method that is moulded by the *presupposition* that the human personality is a fragmented thing, we risk screening out too much of what Coleridge attempted to say. At the very least, we need to comprehend better than I think we do the thought-world which led Coleridge to affirm so emphatically the idea of an integral humanity: to "understand his understanding," that is, as well as his ignorance.

The nature of Coleridge's task as an oracular and sibylline poet may best be approached by looking first at what the Enlightenment writers had achieved. It was the writers of the late Enlightenment period, Herder, Lessing, and Eichhorn, who brought biblical texts to the attention of the literary world as possible models for poetic imitation by stressing the specific historical situation of the authors of the Scrip-

21. Leslie Brisman, *Romantic Origins* (Ithaca, N.Y.: Cornell University Press, 1978), p. 167.

22. Eugene Goodheart, *The Failure of Criticism* (Cambridge, Mass.: Harvard University Press, 1978), p. 114.

tures, therefore their humanity, and therefore too, in a way, their closeness to contemporary poets; and yet at the same time these writers were conscious of the historical distance between Old Testament times and eighteenth-century Europe. Indeed, part of the defence of Old Testament literature against the scepticism of Voltaire and the Encyclopaedists was to consist in the argument that Old Testament texts must be read with full imaginative grasp of their historical setting, of what later came to be called their "Sitz-im-Leben," including the ancient belief in divine inspiration. Contrary to Rousseau's suggestion in *Du contrat social*, the prophets and patriarchs were not cunning manipulators of public opinion. As Blake remarked with characteristic bluntness: "The Ancients did not mean to Impose when they affirmd their belief in Vision & Revelation Plato was in Earnest. Milton was in Earnest. They believd that God did Visit Man Really & Truly. . . ."[23]

Coleridge could hardly have shrugged off this view of Scripture: indeed, he shared it during the 1790s when, as a student at Cambridge, a political pamphleteer and lecturer, and a Unitarian preacher, he moved in the circles that were most influenced by German Enlightenment thought. At the same time, too, he shared in the Enlightenment habit of adopting a "cosmic" point of view towards history—of placing the "ground of intelligibility" of events not in the events themselves, as a modernist would, but in a timeless order of things. For both the Enlightenment rationalist and the Romantic, as Richard Palmer points out, history is not "really historical," but only "the raw material for deducing an atemporal truth or an atemporal *Geist*."[24] If the Enlightenment affirms humankind's right to think about everything, "all thinking things, all objects of all thought," from the viewpoint of atemporal Reason, Coleridge was in that respect an Enlightenment thinker, pursuing universals through particulars.

The paradoxical double motion of historicism, in which biblical language comes to seem more "human," more universal, and more accessible to us as its historical origins are more imaginatively grasped, is clearest in the first dialogue of Herder's *Vom Geist der Ebräischen Poesie*. Euthyphron, the spokesman for Herder's "imaginative com-

23. Blake, *Poetry and Prose*, p. 647.

24. Palmer, *Hermeneutics*, p. 79. On links between Enlightenment and Romantic notions of the "ground of intelligibility" of events, see Gerald L. Bruns, "The Formal Nature of Victorian Thinking," *PMLA* 90 (1975): 905.

prehension" approach to Scripture, proposes to consider the language of the Bible "as a human language, and its contents as merely human." But in order to form a proper judgment on the poetry of a nation, "we must live in their time, in their own country, must adopt their modes of thinking and feeling, must see, how they lived."[25] So, quoting part of Psalm 119, Herder points out how difficult it is for moderns, who have no national festivals, songs of public rejoicing, or national temple, to sympathize with the spirit of that psalm: "How spiritless is all this, when severed from its original connexions and relations! But how apposite, when these praises are considered as the jubilant expressions of a free people, to be ruled only by the fixed and determinate laws of God."[26]

Alongside this plea for sympathetic, imaginative consideration of the historical setting of biblical texts, and sometimes running oddly counter to it, is the characteristically Herderian argument that Hebrew poetry is to be valued because of its *universality*. It emerges from the first dawn of human intelligence, while the human race was in its infancy. In biblical poetry, therefore, "the earliest Logick of the senses, the simplest analysis of ideas and the primary principles of morals . . . are brought before our eyes."[27] So, the description of Paradise in the Book of Genesis is defended as a poetic, imaginative description of the childhood of each race and of the human race as a whole, even while Herder also wishes to embrace the euhemeristic view that the widespread occurrence of paradise-myths among ancient peoples suggests a corresponding reality in primeval experience as the source of such "fables." The implication seems to be that some actual historical experience, preserved in folk-memory, was the origin of the Genesis story; but now it should be valued chiefly as a poetic representation of the infancy of the human race, speaking to a perpetual human sense of total dependence on God. Likewise Abraham's covenant

25. Johann Gottfried von Herder, *The Spirit of Hebrew Poetry*, trans. James Marsh, 2 vols. in 1 (1833; reprint ed., Naperville, Ill.: Aleph Press, 1971), 1: 27, 18. German text: Herder, *Sämmtliche Werke*, ed. B. Suphan, 33 vols (Berlin: Weidmannsche Buchhandlung, 1877–1913), 11 (1879): 225, 226. Rabbinic tradition recognized only *three* books of poetry, in the strict sense, in the Hebrew Bible: Psalms, Proverbs, and Job. The Song of Solomon was one of the "Five Scrolls." Herder's understanding of Hebrew "poetry" is obviously much more inclusive. Compare the essay "Hebräer" in Johann Wolfgang von Goethe's *West-oestlicher Divan* (Stuttgart: Lottaischer Buchhandlung, 1819), p. 248, where Goethe remarks that a great part of the OT, because it was written with exalted mind, belongs to the category of poetry.

26. *Spirit of Hebrew Poetry*, 2: 101; *Werke*, 12 (1880): 88.

27. *Spirit of Hebrew Poetry*, 1. 46; *Werke*, 11: 242.

with God in Genesis 15 and 17 is to be read, Herder says, not in theosophical and mystical terms, but as expressive of a pristine sense of personal relationship, friendship, and responsibility between man and the Supreme Being. With well-placed irony, Herder's persona argues, "let us not turn to ridicule the genuine beauties in the poetry of ancient nations, because they understand not our systems of natural philosophy and metaphysics."[28]

Behind this respect for the actual experience of an author and the primary sense ("Ursinn") of that author's words lies a scholar's interest in uncovering something of the purpose of the author, by painstaking philological research.[29] This marks the limits of Enlightenment hermeneutic generosity, however, and the point where Romantic hermeneutics has to take over. Herder leaves us free, of course, to decide in the end that *our* "systems of natural philosophy and metaphysics" are still best. The unanswered question here is whether such an attitude does not leave the modern reader still so comfortably swathed in his or her own moral and metaphysical assumptions that the full existential impact of the biblical author's words is softened to the point where it is barely discernible. Historical criticism can reach a point where everything of substance in the text is explained away as a product of this or that socio-cultural force acting on the individual author. Historicist critics, as Schleiermacher complained in *The Hermeneutics*, "tend to explain everything in the light of available concepts and forms."[30]

Schleiermacher's answer was the adoption of a hermeneutic principle of imitation or reconstruction ("Nachbildung"), dissolving the time-gap that intervened between reader and author and enabling a reader to share the author's utterance at the level of their common humanity.[31] This was the other side of the question of biblical inspiration, the side Coleridge touched on when he observed that, practically speaking, biblical inspiration was really a matter of whether this or that passage was "inspired . . . *for* you" (*CN* 3440). Herder believed it possible to separate what he chose to call the primary or original sense ("dem simpeln Ursinn") from the religious or mystical senses

28. *Spirit of Hebrew Poetry*, 1: 95; *Werke*, 11: 293–94.

29. See Isaiah Berlin, *Vico and Herder: Two Studies in the History of Ideas* (New York: Viking Press, 1976), p. 169.

30. Friedrich Daniel Ernst Schleiermacher, "*The Hermeneutics*: Outline of the 1819 Lectures," trans. Jan Wojcik and Roland Haas, *New Literary History* 10 (1978–79), no. 1 (Autumn 1978): 5.

31. See Frei, *Eclipse of Biblical Narrative*, p. 290, and Palmer, *Hermeneutics*, p. 86.

("mystischen Sinne") later found in some passages. He did not deny that the mystical senses were actually there, however: that an inspired speaker might say "more than perhaps he means to utter."[32] Herder was of course writing a literary man's critique of biblical poetry, not a manual of practical religion. But Herder's postulation of an *Ursinn*, or original sense, raises problems that are of concern both to the biblical scholar and to the literary critic. He appears to assume that the *Ursinn* is equally accessible to anyone who has the right linguistic preparation and that it is a stable, empirically measurable entity. He implies, too, that the original sense may be built on by successive interpreters, but that like the foundation of a building it remains essentially unaltered by what is put on top of it. The *Ursinn* is the author's sense; other meanings are, as it were, optional.

Coleridge and Schleiermacher both saw the inadequacies of this view and, in similar ways, advanced beyond it. Both give considerable weight to the interpreter's attainment of sympathy with an author. Schleiermacher, whose particular interest was in the emergence of the New Testament from an already-existing body of Christian tradition, testimony, and liturgy, posited two complementary steps as essential to the interpretation of a text: the divinatory, understanding a writer so intimately that one *becomes* that writer, grasping his or her meaning from the inside; and the comparative, "viewing the work . . . in light of others like it."[33] Schleiermacher's divinatory approach differs from Herder's in the sense that in order to begin the work of interpretation the interpreter must submit to being changed in nature, must become open to the mind of the author in a sense never envisaged by Herder. Schleiermacher seems to admit that a text (specifically the New Testament) cannot be comprehended from "outside" (outside the tradition from which it emerged and to which it was addressed). Coleridge's approach equally stressed the interpreter's willingness to be changed by a text: the Scriptures are not inspired "*for* you," he wrote, "unless the truth, they contain, enter your understanding & marry with your desires & impulses" (*CN* 3440). (This corresponds closely to Calvin's view that the *text* of Scripture is not to be regarded as "inspired": it is the reader who is or hopes to be inspired.)[34] But Coleridge also held that the text coheres and speaks

32. *Spirit of Hebrew Poetry*, 2: 27; *Werke*, 12:23.
33. Schleiermacher, "*Hermeneutics*: Outline of the 1819 Lectures," pp. 14–15.
34. Frei, *Eclipse of Biblical Narrative*, p. 21.

to the interpreter only by virtue of being the product of a mind, even if the actual identity of the author is unknown. That is why he insisted, in the "Letters," that any utterance claimed by its author to represent the divinely inspired Word of God must be so received. (We are here dealing strictly with canonical writings, so the utterance would already have passed the Church's test of canonicity.) To do otherwise, Coleridge held, would be to fragment the human integrity of that particular biblical author and remove ourselves from the position of willing listeners to that of insulated, self-sufficient critics.

The same scrupulousness led Coleridge to reject the then frequent pietistic device of "rewriting" Scripture by juxtaposing a verse from one book with another from a different book, often far removed from it in time, and treating the resultant collage as a meaningful utterance (*CN* 2908). Still more significantly, Coleridge most vehemently attacked Schleiermacher's argument that the evangelists themselves might have permitted some obviously fictional passages to be combined with factual narrative in the synoptic Gospels.[35] He was certainly prepared to consider the possibility that parts of the Gospels might be fictional or based on traditionary stories rather than on eye-witness accounts of actual events. But he refused to accept that Matthew or Luke might themselves have combined fiction with fact in their narratives, without leaving any clue to which was which. The hermeneutic notion of the evangelists' own human integrity must be preserved, even if it meant recognizing that the Gospels were not unities and were not wholly apostolic.

Clearly, Coleridge's idea of the coherence and integrity of the human personality is not available to us in any straightforward way as a hermeneutic tool, for that idea itself demands critical interpretation. In the following pages I have tried to suggest why, despite its obsolescence, it should continue to engage us and why reinterpretation of it might be considered necessary. Though Coleridge strove to uphold against Hume and others the idea of the unity of the human personality, his impulse towards integration and harmonization was frequently threatened by an equally powerful awareness of fragmentation and disunity, as Thomas McFarland has shown in *Romanticism and the*

35. See Schleiermacher, *A Critical Essay on the Gospel of St. Luke* [trans. Connop Thirlwall,] (London: John Taylor, 1825), p. 51. Coleridge's criticism of Schleiermacher is contained in his margin annotations of a copy of the *Critical Essay* now in the British Library, London, shelfmark C.126.h.9 (pp. 51–55).

Forms of Ruin; and it is that awareness of fragmentation which predominates, perhaps, in the modern literary consciousness. Hartman observes that "The modern poet has committed himself to the task of understanding experience in its immediacy. He has neglected the armature of the priest—the precautionary wisdom of tradition—and often, the inculcated respect for literary models."[36] Still more bluntly: "modern literature," says Eugene Goodheart, "deliberately refuses wisdom for truthtelling, the witnessing of chaos."[37] Recognizing this we can recognize also the need to understand how it came to be that "wisdom" and "truthtelling" presented themselves as mutually exclusive alternatives. At what point did inspiration cease to be regarded as the expression of a voice that originated in (or at least was guaranteed by) a transcendent order and begin a newly demythologized existence as a metaphor for the intense alertness of the senses to the purely physical actuality that lies around one or for unusual rapidity of thought and impulse that leads unhesitatingly to full expression? For all her Comtism, and her rejection of Christian belief in a transcendent order, George Eliot still has to say of her Methodist preacher, Dinah Morris, "do we not all agree to call rapid thought and noble impulse by the name of inspiration? After our subtlest analysis of the mental process, we must still say, as Dinah did, that our highest thoughts and our best deeds are all given to us."[38] What was lost in the exchange, and what was gained?

The figure who most clearly patterns out for us this transition is, I believe, Emerson. His early orations, the "Divinity School Address" and "The American Scholar," mark a joyful affirmation of each individual's right to drink in the universal sources of inspiration. To adapt the phrase which Hazlitt used of Wordsworth: Emerson exhorts every member of his audience to "take a personal interest in the universe." The American people will be the first true nation on earth, Emerson says, when Americans speak their own minds and "each believes himself inspired by the Divine Soul which also inspires all men" (*AmS*, p. 115). Not a select group of prophets, nor even a faith

36. Geoffrey Hartman, *The Unmediated Vision: An Interpretation of Wordsworth, Hopkins, Rilke, and Valéry* (New Haven: Yale University Press, 1954), p. 164.

37. Goodheart, p. 11. See also Thomas McFarland, *Romanticism and the Forms of Ruin: Wordsworth, Coleridge, and Modalities of Fragmentation* (Princeton, N.J.: Princeton University Press, 1981), intro., pp. 3–55, *passim.*

38. George Eliot, *Adam Bede*, ed. Stephen Gill, Penguin English Library (Harmondsworth: Penguin Books, 1980), p. 158.

community as understood by Schleiermacher, but an entire nation will believe itself inspired, or so Emerson prophesies; and this "inspiration" is a kind of guarantee of one's full humanity, one's personhood. In *Nature,* Emerson attempts to hold physical actuality and divine power in balance by stressing that Nature is constantly shaped and permeated by Spirit. All of Nature, in other words, is inspired—a return to the ancient biblical sense of breath, or *rûaḥ,* as the breath of life (Genesis 2:7, 6:17)—though Emerson does not distinguish, as the writer of Genesis did, between animate beings and inanimate ones. The pine tree and the clod of clay, for Emerson, share the spirit bestowed on birds, beasts, and human beings, a view which arguably brings him closer to Hinduism than to Judaism.[39] The inspired individual, this view suggests, is simply one who is in a high degree open to the constant presence of the divine within and around each human being. In all this Emerson speaks as a kind of radical Unitarian prophet, one expressing the universalist vision of Christianity which is found in the latitudinarian John Sterling and in the radical Hegelian biblical critic David Friedrich Strauss. Opposed to the "cult" of the person of Jesus, which is to him a form of idolatry, Emerson sees himself as propagating instead the liberating truth which Jesus brought: that God exists within each of us.

Later, in the poem "Musketaquid" and in the 1853 essay "Inspiration," Emerson's early trumpet-calls are muted, and the state now held out before us as the desirable one for humankind is no longer a state of intoxication with the omnipresent Spirit, the Deity within, but one in which a distinctively human order can be cultivated. This "human order" is not to be read out from Nature in any direct way, because Nature's signals are baffling, sometimes pointing towards harmony but frequently also indicating discord and disunity. A sense of universal harmony can still be achieved, and the poet can still from moment to moment express it, but Emerson now locates this sense within the human realm, not within the objective world. It is a symptom of psychic and spiritual health in the individual, rather than a permanent gift of the universal Spirit: a cherishing of one's better (more innocent) moments, in the full and even tragic awareness of everything that rises up to contradict them. Emerson is close here to the spirit of

39. See Protap Chunder Mozoomdar, "Emerson as seen from India," in F. B. Sanborn, ed., *The Genius and Character of Emerson* (1885; reprint ed., Port Washington, N.Y.: Kennikat Press, 1971), p. 368.

Thoreau's "To perceive freshly, with fresh senses, is to be inspired": it is the American equivalent of what Geoffrey Hartman calls, in the context of European Romanticism, "second naiveté"—not a primitivistic return to a hypothetical state of nature, but the willed, mature choosing of a healed and redeemed consciousness, of participation in the world rather than flight from it.[40] Second naiveté of course has to be a highly vulnerable state. The writer virtually chooses to be humanized by distress, to make himself vulnerable: "I am a willow of the wilderness," writes Emerson, "loving the wind that bent me" (*EP*, p. 126). By stepping outside (and reinterpreting) his self-made paradise, by immersing himself in the destructive element, the poet risks not his inspiration (because like other things inspiration can be demythologized and relocated in actuality, as Emerson relocates it in his 1853 essay and as Whitman relocates it in "Song of Myself") but his sense of coherence, both internal and external. "Truthtelling" replaces "wisdom." The privileged viewpoint is voluntarily renounced.

We know, however, that this did not mean the end of poetry, despite the gloomy prognostications of some nineteenth-century commentators such as Alfred Austin.[41] It could be that poets have found in the voluntary recognition and embracing of human suffering and limitation a tragic knowledge superior to that expressed in the more stable, apodictic, and harmonious fictions of the past, as Paul judged the "folly" of the crucifixion story superior to all the wisdom of the Greeks. If so, criticism cannot divorce itself from the poets' experience, even in the interests of a neoclassical or humanistic or Romantic tradition, because no tradition, as Emerson and others tell us, is ever closed. The canon of secular literature, like the canon of sacred literature, is perpetually open to reinterpretation and continuation, because its meaning demands constant retranslation into significance, meaning-for-us, and what interprets its significance in the last analysis is no one privileged point of view, but our own complex, continuing human experience.

40. Geoffrey Hartman, *Beyond Formalism* (New Haven: Yale University Press, 1970), p. 300.

41. "We have no concord, intellectual, moral, social, or vital; and accordingly, we waste our puny individual or sectional efforts in letting off a series of small fireworks": Alfred Austin, *The Poetry of the Period* (London: Bentley, 1870), p. 288.

I

Beyond Mythology: Coleridge and the Legacy of the Enlightenment

GREAT AS WAS Herder's service to biblical studies, his very achievement in rendering the Bible more accessible, because more historical and "human," set an almost insoluble problem for the development of a Romantic poetics of inspiration. On the one hand, Herder denied that any poet or prophet had direct apprehension of what was in the mind of the Divine Being. Language was a divine gift, poetic language pre-eminently so, but "whatever was given to the most godlike men, even through a higher influence, to feel and experience in themselves, was still human."[1] On the other hand, the true poet was one who could perceive "connexion, order, benevolence and purpose" in Nature, and whose work embodied this perception in a true "cosmos" of its own.[2] The particular excellence of the Jewish poets consisted in the fact that, more than any Greek or Roman poet, they responded to the one great plan of Nature and gave it human utterance. Herder in this manner accounted for the human defects of some parts of the Old Testament (the factual inaccuracies, the sentiments we have to consider unworthy of a divine author), while continuing to affirm the divine origin of the poets' language—though in the more limited sense that he held poetic language in general, not the specific *words* uttered by David or the author of the Book of Job, to be the gift of God.

A modern poet who desired to emulate the Old Testament poets' achievement, however, could not hope to do so without sharing in some degree their exalted comprehension of Nature's holy plan, her "connexion, order, benevolence and purpose." By showing how

1. Herder, *Spirit of Hebrew Poetry*, 2:6; *Werke*, 12:6.
2. *Spirit of Hebrew Poetry*, 1:97; *Werke*, 11:296.

"human" the Bible was, Herder had brought within reach, it seemed, a perfect model of the universal, progressive poetry that was the aim of Romantic art as Friedrich Schlegel defined it, a poetry that would be "a mirror of the whole world."[3] Yet this exhilarating challenge of giving human expression to the divine unity must be undertaken without supernatural aid. The romantic poet was guaranteed no more assistance than any other human being who undertook a sacred task.

Coleridge, of all the English Romantics, exhibited the tensions of this ambivalent inheritance most acutely, though (despite the praise accorded to Herder in chapter 11 of *Biographia Literaria*) he was no unqualified admirer of Herder's work. Herder's scepticism about the ability of the human finite to transcend Nature and have direct intuition of the divine was anathema to Coleridge, who (in his copy of Herder's *Briefe das Studium der Theologie betreffend*) commented scornfully that Adam had a better source for his knowledge of the meaning of love than the rutting of the beasts he saw around him in the Garden of Eden.[4] Yet the poetic agenda set by Herder's *Vom Geist der Ebräischem Poesie* and by the Schlegels' *Athenäum* was similar in both its liberating scope and its suggestion of poetic *hubris* to the agenda set by Coleridge, first for himself, and then for his fellow prophet of Nature, Wordsworth.

> Wordsworth complains, with justice, that Southey writes *too much at his ease*—that he seldom "feels his burthened breast
>
> Heaving beneath th'incumbent Deity."
>
> . . . I am fearful that [Southey] will begin to rely too much on *story* and *event* in his poems, to the neglect of those *lofty imaginings*, that are peculiar to, and definitive of, the poet. . . . Observe the march of Milton—his severe application, his laborious polish, his deep metaphysical researches, his prayers to God before he began his great poem, all that could lift and swell his intellect, became his daily food. I should not think of devoting less than 20 years to an Epic Poem. (*CL*, 1: 320)

The model with which Coleridge rather unfairly compared Southey's recent work here was of course *Paradise Lost*. In this great poem Milton

3. Friedrich Schlegel, *Charakteristiken und Kritiken I*, ed. Hans Eichner, Kritische Friedrich-Schlegel-Ausgabe (Munich: Verlag Ferdinand Schöningh; Zurich: Thomas-Verlag, 1959—), 2 (1967): 182 (*Athenäum*, no. 116).

4. See G. A. Wells, "Man and Nature: an Elucidation of Coleridge's Rejection of Herder's Thought," *Journal of English and Germanic Philology* 51 (1952): 321.

had combined in one epic sweep the three types of poetry described in Sir Philip Sidney's *Apology*: poetry that represents "what may be, and should be"; poetry that deals with moral philosophy, natural science, or history; and—the "chief" kind, "both in antiquity and excellency"—poetry that "imitate[s] the inconceivable excellencies of God," such as the Psalms of David, the Book of Job, and the Song of Solomon. Coleridge wished to claim for the poetry of his own age the same ambitious scope, and it was for this reason that, as John Coulson has pointed out, his account of poetic language was ultimately an account of religious language.[5] But it was no longer quite so clear what religious language truly was. The Renaissance certainties, especially concerning the unitary meaning of the Bible, had evaporated by Coleridge's time. Even Milton, in many respects, had had to construct his own understanding of the Bible's "unifying principle." Now it was more than ever doubtful whether, for example, the Song of Solomon, which Sidney confidently treated as descriptive of the "inconceivable excellencies of God," could still be received in this sense, when the more acute historical perception of the eighteenth century had seen it as an Oriental love poem, which later tradition had reinterpreted according to different criteria of meaning.

To Coleridge, the Hebrew poets possessed in exemplary form the imaginative power, the sense of the "one Life" (*CL*, 2: 866). The modern poet who wished to emulate the biblical poets was faced, however, with the immense task of being, like Milton, his own normative tradition. Biblical criticism had begun to show that there may be a considerable lapse between the utterance or composition of a hymn, poem, or narrative and its recognition as consonant with divine truth. An utterance may be judged to have religious significance because it is ascribed to a religious leader (Moses, David, Jesus). Or, as some biblical critics would prefer to argue, it may be that because an utterance is judged to have religious significance, it is ascribed, after the fact, to a religious leader. It may even emanate from a person with no pretensions to holiness or even to virtue. In each case, it is the attestation of later tradition that counts, not the state of mind of the speaker at the time the utterance was made. For a poet such as Coleridge, the conflict arising from this necessary suspension of judg-

5. John Coulson, *Newman and the Common Tradition* (Oxford: Clarendon Press, 1970), p. 22.

ment was acute. Since the attestation of later tradition was not immediately available, he was forced to be his own "later tradition" and exercise judgment on his own inspired utterance. Shelley's solution—to make the composition of poetry an activity quite distinct from the exercise of conscious judgment[6]—was not available to Coleridge, for whom the poetic faculty or secondary Imagination coexisted with the conscious will (*BL*, 1: 304). It was exactly as if the two moments of religious language—oracular utterance, followed (after some years or centuries) by the judgment that such utterance was consonant with divine truth, that "holy men of God spake as they were moved by the Holy Ghost" (2 Peter 1:21)—had become telescoped into a single moment. They could not be separated again, Coleridge saw, without surrendering something he prized at least as much as he prized inspiration: human freedom.

As M. H. Abrams has shown, Coleridge shared with Shelley and Wordsworth a particular fondness for the image of the breeze or breath as metaphor for the creative impulse. Citing Coleridge's "Dejection: An Ode," "The Eolian Harp," and "To Matilda Betham," Shelley's "Ode to the West Wind," and the first book of Wordsworth's *Prelude*, Abrams links the "correspondent breeze" awakened within these poets by the blowing of a physical, palpable breeze to the breath of life, which is called *anima* in Latin, πνεῦμα in Greek, and *rûaḥ* in Hebrew.[7] As "The Eolian Harp" shows, the idea of inspiration as an irresistible impulse from without, which stirs the poet's mind to give voice to sweet harmony, was an attractive one for Coleridge, and it was supported by Plato's descriptions of the poet as the instrument of a greater power, moved by a mighty external force:

> All good epic poets . . . compose all those lovely poems of theirs not by their own skill but in a state of inspiration and possession.

6. See "A Defence of Poetry," in Percy Bysshe Shelley, *Complete Works*, ed. Roger Ingpen and Walter E. Peck, 10 vols. (London and New York: The Julian Editions, 1926–30), 7: (1930), 135.

7. M. H. Abrams, "The Correspondent Breeze: A Romantic Metaphor," in M. H. Abrams, ed., *English Romantic Poets: Modern Essays in Criticism (*1960; reprint ed., London: Oxford University Press, 1960), p. 44.

When a poet takes his seat on the Muse's tripod, his judgment takes leave of him. He is like a fountain which gives free course to the rush of its waters. . . .[8]

Neo-Platonism was an influence on some of the early Christian writers and the neo-Platonic term for the state of being divinely inspired, Θεόπνευστος , was taken up by the writer of 2 Timothy and applied to the Scriptures as a whole (2 Timothy 3:16); so it might appear to have the sanction of the early Christian church as a term of approbation for inspired utterance.

The two traditions, Hebrew and Greek, did not, however, combine quite so readily as this suggests. The occurrence of Θεόπνευστος in 2 Timothy is a misleading instance. Other New Testament writers, as well as the authors of the Septuagint, studiously avoided using the term, which had connotations of pagan vaticination and ecstatic seizure. Sir Philip Sidney, in the blithely syncretistic manner of the Renaissance, applied the Latin term *vates* to David; but it is clear from several texts that for the Hebrews there was no *necessary* connection between being inspired and speaking truth. "Possession" did not necessarily mean that the words one pronounced were inspired of God. The Hebrew word *nābî*, which the Septuagint translated as προφήτης or (when applied to a "false" prophet) Ψευδοπροφήτης, meant simply an ecstatic and it was quite as possible for an ecstatic to utter falsehood as truth (see for instance Ezekiel 13:2, 14:9, and Hosea 9:7).[9] The term *rûaḥ* (like the Greek πνεῦμα in one of its meanings) meant chiefly "the breath of life," possessed by every living thing—by Cain and the serpent, as well as by Adam and Eve. It did not connote wisdom or insight, evidently, since animals possessed it as well as human beings; yet it was the gift of God, for every living creature drew its life-spirit from the one divine source. The Holy Spirit (τὸ πνεῦμα τό Ἅγιον) —which, according to Acts 1:16, Acts 3:18, 2 Peter 1:21, and other New Testament passages spoke "through the mouths" of David and the Prophets—belonged, as a theological concept, to a much later period of Jewish history. While some commentators, it is true, were inclined to treat the *whole* of Scripture as if directly authored or dictated by the Holy Spirit (Philo Judaeus, for example), others very

8. Plato, *Ion*, trans. Michael Oakley, in *Symposium and Other Dialogues* (London: Dent; New York: Dutton, 1964), p. 68; *The Laws*, trans. A. E. Taylor (London: Dent, 1934), p. 103.

9. Fr. Bruce Vawter, *Biblical Inspiration* (London: Hutchinson; Philadelphia: Westminster, 1972), pp. 8–12.

quickly became aware of the difficulties involved in such an approach. These, from Origen in the third century to Schleiermacher in the nineteenth, had to reason that since prophets could evidently err, even when in a state of inspiration or possession, the action of the Holy Spirit must be allowed to be operative not only in the original speaker, his or her amanuenses and witnesses, and his or her editors, but also in the tradition that judges and approves their utterances and admits some writings to the canon while excluding others.[10]

When Coleridge interrupts his visionary outpourings in "The Eolian Harp," then, and (in the person of the "heart-honour'd Maid") interprets them as "shapings of the unregenerate mind" (*PW*, 1: 102), he can be seen as in one sense imitating in a highly condensed form the centuries-old pattern of inspired utterance followed by the devout sifting of the results to determine whether what they contained was true doctrine or specious. The poem makes most critics uneasy, of course, because it is unusual to come across a poet who decides to be in such an overt manner his own interpreter or hermeneut. But the tension made explicit here between inspiration and the normative tradition of Christianity provides a key to his lifelong search for a Christian poetic. To attribute the censorious words Coleridge puts into his fiancée's mouth merely to the poet's sense of intellectual impotence, as Albert Gérard does,[11] is to falsify this peculiarly Coleridgean dilemma, which characterizes his relationship with neo-Platonism as a whole, as well as with the particular neo-Platonic concept of divine inspiration we have been discussing. Neo-Platonism represented for Coleridge the possibility of bringing diversity in phenomena into a connected, unified whole—the direct intuition of that "connexion, order, benevolence and purpose" in the universe of which Herder wrote[12]—while obeying the injunction of Micah 6:8 to "walk humbly with thy God." What Coleridge called in 1810 "the groves & enchanted Islands" of Plato, Proclus, and Plotinus had the valuable property of rendering the mind "lofty," "generous," and "*abile*": they furnished "no unbecoming Symbols—Counters at least—of moral Truth." Yet

10. Vawter, pp. 14, 26. See also, on the "heilsgeschichtliche Schule" of Johan Albrecht Bengel, Gottfried Menken, etc., Frei, *Eclipse of Biblical Narrative* pp. 173–81.

11. Albert Gérard, "The Systolic Rhythm: The Structure of Coleridge's Conversation Poems," *Essays in Criticism* 10 (1960): 313.

12. See Bishop C. Hunt, Jr., "Coleridge and the Endeavor of Philosophy," *PMLA* 91 (1976): 832–33.

these groves and islands were salubrious only for one whose mind already acknowledged "the practical Reason" (*CN* 3820). Even neo-Platonism, that is, must submit to judgment by the normative tradition. This had been the process that took place over centuries of Christian history; Coleridge found, as he grew from the "inspired charity-boy" of Lamb's famous description to the author of *Biographia Literaria* and *Aids to Reflection*, that the same process has to be repeated an infinite number of times with in the compass of a single lifetime.

Some time before his adoption of an overtly Trinitarian faith, which we can place with some certainty between October 1803 and February 1805 (by comparing *CN* 1543 with *CN* 2444 and 2448),[13] Coleridge for one brief period associated himself with the Unitarian position, holding Jesus to be simply a gifted prophet and the Holy Spirit to be a sublime metaphor. Yet, as we shall see, even Coleridge's Unitarianism had to leave room for his belief in the possibility of the direct intuition of divine truth.

It was Coleridge the Unitarian thinker who in 1796 wrote to John Thelwall describing Jesus as a teacher merely, though one possessing unusual qualities of intellect: "I allow, and rejoice that *Christ* appealed only to the understanding & the affections. . . .' (*CL*, 1: 281). It was Coleridge the Unitarian preacher that Hazlitt trudged many miles to hear in the winter of 1798. But on both occasions the somewhat dry, cool light of Priestleian rationality was at odds with the enthusiastic poet's powerful apprehension of the sublimity, imaginative richness, and revelatory significance of Scripture. Convinced that revealed religion was not opposed to Reason, but was rather its major source, as comets were believed to feed the sun (*CN* 88), the Coleridge of the 1790s had to confront the problem of reconciling the obviously poetic and inspired character of many parts of the Bible with the need to demonstrate to sceptics who had read their Voltaire and their Gibbon that a rational man could be a believer.

The sceptics had derided as obvious impostures the wonders performed by biblical prophets and found the hyperbolical style of much sacred scripture to be repugnant to a modern sensibility. They also

13. This is not to deny that before 1805 Coleridge used certain formulae that are suggestive of Trinitarianism. See J. B. Beer, *Coleridge's Poetic Intelligence* (London: Macmillan, 1977), pp. 45–46, and Owen Barfield, *What Coleridge Thought* (London: Oxford University Press, 1972), p. 249, n. 5.

attacked the authority of Scripture on ethical grounds, pointing to the barbarity and inhumanity of the laws supposedly revealed to the Old Testament prophets: this was a point stressed by Voltaire in his *Dictionnaire philosophique* (see for example the articles "Moïse," "Ezéchiel"). Herder's stress on the *human* character of the Old Testament writings enabled him to turn aside many of the sceptics' objections. Herder argued that as the Divine Being chose to work through human agents, he must necessarily have allowed them to retain their human imperfections: "It is no valid objection to the wisdom of Providence, that it carries forward its work by instruments, and attains its divine purposes by human means."[14] Admitting, too, that passages such as the Garden of Eden story, and the descriptions of Behemoth and Leviathan in the Book of Job, were fabulous and not factual narratives, Herder argued that, like other ancient writings, these must be understood in the context of their times and that Oriental poetry was composed for audiences which possessed a high degree of imaginative power.[15] Without himself supporting the orthodox view of inspiration, Herder agreed that those biblical characters who spoke in the name of God *believed* themselves to be inspired and that this belief should not be ridiculed but accepted as part of the cultural milieu in which they lived: "Miriam, Deborah, and others were Prophetesses, because they had a poetical inspiration, and inspired, especially sacred poetry, was always deemed of supernatural and Divine origin."[16]

Together with this respect for the cultural assumptions of an earlier, pre-scientific age went the belief, characteristic of Enlightenment thought, that the human race exhibited a progression from the equivalent of infancy, in which firm leadership and colourful, imaginative fable were essential to its proper government, to a maturity in which scientific reasoning and an internalized moral arbiter took over. Herder, in defending the child-like and perhaps simplistic language of the early representations of God in the Pentateuch, argued that discriminating analysis was the privilege of the adult. The child, and the human race during its childhood, needed a language more expressive of wonder and awe, a figurative rather than a scientific language.[17]

14. *Spirit of Hebrew Poetry*, 1:269; *Werke*, 11:451.
15. *Spirit of Hebrew Poetry*, 2:16–20; *Werke*, 12:15–20.
16. *Spirit of Hebrew Poetry*, 2:51; *Werke*, 12:47.
17. *Spirit of Hebrew Poetry*, 2:9–13; *Werke*, 12: 8–12.

The most influential statement of this notion, however, was Gotthold Ephraim Lessing's *Die Erziehung des Menschengeschlechts*. Lessing was a man of the Enlightenment in that he felt that the Judaeo-Christian scriptures should be open to scholarly and critical investigation, and his publication of the notoriously acerbic "Wolfenbüttel Fragments" of Hermann Samuel Reimarus was intended not as endorsement of Reimarus's views but as a contribution to informed debate. In *Die Erziehung des Menschengeschlechts*, however, Lessing defended Scripture with the argument that there was a perceptible element of progress in religious ideas. The Old Testament traced the development of Jewish religious thought from the cruder legalisms of the Mosaic dispensation to the more ideal religion of later prophets, and the New Testament contained the purest realization of those same moral and religious ideas.[18] On this view, as Ernst Cassirer has pointed out, there need no longer be any opposition between the historical nature of religion—its origins in the primitive—and the dry light of eighteenth-century rationalism. It is only *within* history, indeed, that the rational can come into being.[19] Something of the sense of liberation with which Lessing must have contemplated this new perception of the value of perpetual development can be inferred from his statement in *Eine Duplik*: "If God held enclosed in His right hand all truth, and in His left hand the ever-living striving for truth, although with the qualification that I must for ever err, and said to me 'Choose,' I should humbly choose the left hand and say 'Father, give! Pure truth is for Thee alone!' "[20]

The Scriptures remained significant for Lessing, therefore, as the documents of an earlier, vital stage in our progress towards spiritual maturity, though the claim that the Scriptures were divinely inspired was not one that Lessing could accept. Of the crucial belief that the four evangelists were divinely inspired, Lessing wrote despairingly that it was "the foul gaping chasm" over which he could not leap.[21]

18. See Frei, *Eclipse of Biblical Narrative*, p. 172.

19. Cassirer, *Philosophy of the Enlightenment*, p. 195.

20. John Passmore, *The Perfectibility of Man* (London: Duckworth, 1970), p. 48; German text: *Lessings Werke*, ed. G. Witkowski, 7 vols (Leipzig and Vienna: Bibliographisches Institut, n.d.), 7:102.

21. Quoted from Lessing's "Über den Beweis des Geistes und der Kraft" by Elinor Shaffer, *"Kubla Khan" and The Fall of Jerusalem: the Mythological School in Biblical Criticism and Secular Literature* 1770–1880 (Cambridge: Cambridge University Press, 1975), p. 45.

The doctrines which were thought to stand or fall by the authority of the four Gospels could be for Lessing no more than a human creed which lacked divine sanction.

Coleridge shared with the Enlightenment thinkers their respect for science and scholarship and their trust in the ability of the human race to develop from infancy to maturity. As Elinor Shaffer has demonstrated, it was through the dissenting milieu in which he moved in the 1790s that Coleridge was early admitted into considerable knowledge of the work of Herder, Reimarus, Lessing, Michaelis, and Eichhorn, even before his visit to Germany in 1798–99.[22] From these writers, by way of their English adherents such as Thomas Beddoes, Coleridge derived a creed that could appeal to the progressivist assumptions of the age of Wilkes and Paine. In an outline of a "Sermon on Faith," Coleridge asserted that faith "has always been given when it was wanted—so as to assist & carry on, not to contradict or confute our perceptions & deductions." He went on to identify a three-stage process in Revelation: first, the revelation of "deity & his attributes," then "the revelation of laws & morals by Moses," and lastly "the Revelation of Immortality by Jesus Christ" (*CN* 6)—a pattern that remarkably resembles Lessing's own three-stage scheme of Revelation. The best proof of how completely Coleridge at this point had adopted the progressivist stance, however, occurs in the 1795 *Lectures on Revealed Religion*:

> The World has its Ages as well as Individuals. Its infancy, and its Childhood and its Youth.
>
> We find that independently of the Pleasures to which we change, every act of changing is itself a pleasure—so that the Sum of Happiness is twice as great to a Being who has arrived at a certain point by gradual progressiveness as it would be to him who was placed there in the first step of his Existence. . . . in short, it is impossible for us to conceive Happiness that does not result from Progressiveness. (*Lects 1795*, pp. 113, 109)

Unexpectedly, perhaps, the same series of lectures shows that Coleridge took a far more positive view than Lessing and Herder of the possibility that God could impart knowledge directly to human minds.

> A prophet among the Jews was one who had received communication from

22. Shaffer, pp. 28–29.

> the Deity. These communications consisted sometimes of Admonitions and moral Precepts, but more frequently contained annunciations of future Events. To determine whether these annunciations were accidental guesses, or imparted Rays of the divine Foreknowledge we must again adopt that mode of reasoning by which we proved the existence of an intelligent First Cause, namely the astonishing fitness of one thing to another not in single and solitary instances which might be attributed to the effects of Chance, but in the combination and Procession of all Nature. (*Lects 1795*, pp. 149–50)

The point here is that our comprehension of Nature's processes is a progressive thing, just as is our moral and religious being. What seems a miracle to one age is to a later age simply part of that unending miracle which is the development of life in the universe, so that Moses' striking water from a rock, though miraculous to the eyes of his people, shows only that he possessed a larger share of "the divine Foreknowledge" than they. Biblical accounts of miracles can never be the ground of faith, therefore, but once a person embraces Christian faith the miracles take their place in the unfolding of the divine economy. Nature is governed and has always been governed by a divine Word or Intelligence (which is one with God, and not an emanation from him), and in particular instances this Intelligence has been imparted by direct Inspiration to human beings.

Quoting part of the first chapter of St. John's Gospel, Coleridge interprets it as meaning that though Jesus was truly a man like us (not, as the Gnostics asserted, a supra-angelic being in a human body), he was chosen to receive the divine Intelligence in a still greater degree than Moses and the Prophets.

> The texts, "It was in the World and the World was made by it, and the World knew it not" and "it was made Flesh and dwelt among us" imply—that the divine Intelligence never ceased to govern the world which it had created, though almost all mankind worshipped blind and senseless Deities; and that this same Intelligence was imparted by immediate Inspiration to the man Jesus, who dwelt among us. These passages were written to condemn the doctrine of the superangelic nature of Jesus. St John here asserting that the same intelligential Energy which operated in Jesus had been in the World before his existence, teaching the Law to Moses and foreknowledge to the Prophets. (*Lects 1795*, p. 200)

The passage avoids a difficulty in the "Unitarian" interpretation of John 1 by simply passing over it in silence; for Coleridge saw, even in 1795, that St. John was no Unitarian and that he held Jesus to be the incarnate Word of God, not merely a man to whom that Word had been communicated by "immediate Inspiration." Coleridge represents John as saying only that the Word or Intelligence of God "operated in" Jesus.

Even this, however, was a good deal more than Herder or Lessing would have wished to claim. Coleridge evidently felt it important to rescue the concept of miracle, and especially of miraculous inspiration, from the limbo into which it had been cast by the Enlightenment thinkers. Of course it was difficult to understand in everyday commonsense terms how certain men and women could enjoy some particle of divine Omniscience, "Rays of the divine Foreknowledge." The explanation might well lie, however, not in some quality of the miraculous event itself but in "our limited Nature as Percipients" (*Lects 1795*, p. 151). Many wonders were related as having occurred, and not only in biblical times, which future generations would come to understand as part of God's provision for the world, and the mind of faith while awaiting this fuller knowledge would be content to trust the narrative and look for the spiritual illumination contained within it.

This early optimism about the ability of the human mind to progress in spiritual knowledge, through its response to the appearances of Nature, throws into sharp relief Coleridge's later distrust of all that comes from merely natural objects, those objects which "(*as* objects) are essentially fixed and dead" (*BL*, 1: 304). The troublesome change of direction in the concluding lines of "The Eolian Harp" suggests that, as early as 1795, Coleridge was inclined to doubt whether every notion that natural powers called up within the mind was necessarily benign. Yet the general argument that Nature is empowered by God to call up within our minds the powers that are necessary to comprehend not only Nature herself but the presence of divine creative activity within Nature is a repeated theme of the poems of this period. It is a version of the well-known argument that God's presence is revealed to human minds in the "book of Nature" as well as in Scripture, but Coleridge's enthusiastic handling of the theme revives the rather exhausted theological argument and touches it with new visionary power. "The Destiny of Nations," though intended to include an account of the supernatural voices heard by Joan of Arc (*PW*, 1: 140–44), also contains the most explicit statement of

Coleridge's belief that Nature itself can teach us to raise our eyes to "bright Reality":

> all that meets the bodily sense I deem
> Symbolical, one mighty alphabet
> For infant minds . . .
>
> (*PW*, 1: 132)

More firmly grounded in an actual scene is the visionary climax of "This Lime-Tree Bower My Prison":

> So my friend
> Struck with deep joy may stand, as I have stood,
> Silent with swimming sense; yea, gazing round
> On the wide landscape, gaze till all doth seem
> Less gross than bodily; and of such hues
> As veil the Almighty Spirit, when yet he makes
> Spirits perceive his presence.
>
> (*PW*, 1: 180)

At such moments—and there are parallel examples in "Reflections on having left a Place of Retirement," "Frost at Midnight," and other "conversation poems"—the poet invites us to trace the inspiration of the lines chiefly to the influence of the natural scene, although it is not so much a Wordsworthian sense of *place* that Coleridge seems to experience as a sense of *occasion*, the moment of interpenetration between the earthly and the celestial (Keats's "heaven's bourne").[23] At these points Coleridge reaffirms the promise of Milton's archangel to Adam before his departure from Eden:

> thou knowst Heav'n his, and all the Earth,
> Not this Rock only; his Omnipresence fills
> Land, Sea, and Air, and every kind that lives,[24]

a speech which Coleridge surely had in mind when he composed the central, visionary lines of "Reflections": "It seem'd like Omnipresence!" (*PW*, 1: 107). The theme of departure from Eden was almost

23. See Earl R. Wasserman, *The Finer Tone* (1953; reprint ed., Baltimore: Johns Hopkins University Press, 1967), pp. 15–16.

24. John Milton, *Paradise Lost*, Book 11, lines 335–37; in *Poems*, ed. B. A. Wright (1962; reprint ed., London: Dent; New York: Dutton, 1966), p. 363.

a commonplace of English Romantic poetry, of course, but the Coleridge of the conversation poems was exceptional in his ability to reaffirm the perpetual presence of a wider Eden in the world around him, antedating in this respect the Wordsworth of *The Prelude*. Through prayer, joy, or the visionary powers of childhood it was possible to behold the world which was the world of all of us as a Temple of God ("Reflections"), another Eden ("The Eolian Harp"), or as a hornbook setting out the living alphabet of God's language ("Frost at Midnight").

Except for the troublesome case of "The Eolian Harp," none of the conversation poems refers directly to poetic inspiration. The technique throughout is mimetic, with the important qualification that the world the poet imitates is always seen as a unity, imbued with the divine presence, not as a "mass of *little things*" (*CL*, 1: 354). The "goodly scene" the poet describes is but an image of the "World" ("Reflections"; *PW*, 1: 107), where "Omnipresence," not aesthetic richness or atmosphere, is the salient quality. Though the aesthetic categories of the landscape tradition are often present to the poet's mind,[25] the fine distinctions of a Gilpin are swallowed up in the joyful apprehension of unity. More important still, there is no sense that language is an unreliable medium for the expression of this quality of "Omnipresence." The blissful certainty with which the poet utters his conviction that the earth is the Lord's and the fulness thereof suggests that the locodescriptive genre has here taken into itself some of the characteristics of the hymn. This certainty reaches its apotheosis in "Frost at Midnight," in which the poet's unequivocal use of language is made the type of God's relationship to Nature. The human poet's affirmative language is sanctioned, ultimately, by the divine provision of an eternal, living language through which God expresses his own being:

> But *thou*, my babe! shalt wander like a breeze
> By lakes and sandy shores, beneath the crags
> Of ancient mountain, and beneath the clouds,
> Which image in their bulk both lakes and shores
> And mountain crags: so shalt thou see and hear
> The lovely shapes and sounds intelligible
> Of that eternal language, which thy God
> Utters, who from eternity doth teach
> Himself in all, and all things in himself.
>
> (*PW*, 1: 242)

25. See Anne K. Mellor, "Coleridge's 'This Lime-Tree Bower My Prison' and the Categories of English Landscape," *Studies in Romanticism* 18 (1979); 253–70.

The poet is addressing his infant son Hartley, of course, and this fact introduces a small but important note of qualification into the affirmative climax of the poem. Hartley will have a better chance to learn the shapes and sounds of God's "eternal language" than the poet himself did, and while the tone remains one of joy and not of pathos or regret, it is all the same poignantly clear that the Hartley-figure in this poem is being placed in the role of future interpreter of Nature to his poet-father. Like Dorothy Wordsworth as she is represented in "Tintern Abbey," he will be closer to the "sweet sounds and harmonies" of Nature than the poet himself, his experience of it fresher and more immediate. "Frost at Midnight" is the richest of the conversation poems because, while still touching the hymn-like strain of the earlier poems, it raises the whole question of the interpretation of Nature—whether, if Nature is a language, its utterances are received better by some individuals, children for example, than by others, and whether, if so, the poet who draws on Nature for inspiration stands in need of a mediator, a hermeneut, who will interpret Nature's forms to him better than he can interpret them himself. The true importance of the earlier conversation poems may lie in the possibility that they are among the last works in which the Romantic poet claims in his own person the ability to interpret Nature as unambiguously benign. Wordsworth's Wanderer, in book 1 of *The Excursion*, is described as able to "read" the eternal language of God:

> He looked—
> Ocean and earth, the solid frame of earth
> And ocean's liquid mass, in gladness lay
> Beneath him:— Far and wide the clouds were touched
> And in their silent faces could he read
> Unutterable love. Sound needed none,
> Nor any voice of joy; his spirit drank
> The spectacle: sensation, soul, and form,
> All melted into him; they swallowed up
> His animal being; in them did he live,
> And by them did he live; they were his life.[26]

The Wanderer is not Wordsworth, however; and moreover, his faith is questioned by the Solitary and "corrected" by the Pastor. It is presented, that is, as one point of view in a dramatized debate, not simply

26. William Wordsworth, *Poetical Works*, ed. E. de Selincourt and Helen Darbishire, 5 vols (Oxford: Clarendon Press, 1940–49), 5 (1949): 15.

as a moment of illumination which invites the reader's whole-hearted assent. And the love that the Wanderer reads in the silent faces of the clouds is itself unutterable, beyond the power of human language to articulate. The Wanderer corresponds not to the inspired seer who interprets Nature in "The Eolian Harp" or "Reflections" but to Hartley in "Frost at Midnight" and Dorothy in "Tintern Abbey": innocent mediators between Nature and the poet, whose very mediation necessarily keeps the poet himself from a pristine, univocal affirmation of his own faith.

The point is reinforced by comparing any of Coleridge's conversation poems with Shelley's "Mont Blanc," in which the equivocation of Shelley's language mirrors the equivocation Shelley perceives in nature herself. The argument from design underwent Kant's searching criticism long before the publication of *The Origin of Species*. In Coleridge's lifetime, it seems Nature ceased to be transparent and become ambiguous, untrustworthy, and even malign to the subjective onlooker. To Shelley, the analogy between Nature as God's language and poetry as the human emulation of that language was no longer so self-evident.

In the so-called daemonic group of poems, Coleridge moved much closer to a Shelleyan scepticism about the extent to which humanity can "read" divine love in the face of Nature. Nature's signs are ambiguous, and the poems invite us to doubt whether the human mind has, or ever will have, the key to unlock her ambiguities. No amount of human progress, it seems, is likely to make the Mariner's story innocuous. Near the turn of the century, as Robert Sternbach has shown, Coleridge's faith in the built-in power of the human race to progress to spiritual and political maturity suffered a blow from which it never recovered, and the blithe hopes of "The Destiny of Nations" had to be tempered, in later versions of the poem, by an unsparing depiction of the present sufferings of humanity.[27] It would be wrong, of course, to imply that Coleridge suddenly abandoned the conversation poem at this juncture, turning immediately to genres less personal in tone. "Frost at Midnight," "Fears in Solitude," and "The Nightingale" all date from 1798, while "The Rime of the Ancient Mariner" and "Christabel" were both begun in 1797, and "Kubla Khan" may belong to the earlier year as well.[28] Even in these later

27. Robert Sternbach, "Coleridge, Joan of Arc, and the Idea of Progress," *ELH* 46 (1979): 259.

28. E. H. Coleridge prints "Kubla Khan" among poems of 1798, even though Coleridge's prose preamble assigns 1797 as its date of composition (*PW*, 1: 295, n. 2).

conversation poems, however, we can see the beginnings of the idea that the benevolent or malevolent appearance of natural phenomena may depend much more on the beholder's state of mind than on any objective quality of Nature herself—the idea that was to be expressed with such potent force in "Dejection: An Ode." The first published version of "Frost at Midnight," for example, contained these lines:

> But still the living spirit in our frame,
> That loves not to behold a lifeless thing,
> Transfuses into all its own delights,
> Its own volition, sometimes with deep faith
> And sometimes with fantastic playfulness.
> (*PW*, 1: 240n)

Here, in deceptively simple form, is the Berkeleian proposition that underlines the complex preternatural machinery of "The Rime of the Ancient Mariner," the pervasive sense of loss in "Kubla Khan" and "Dejection: an Ode," and the nightmarish isolation of Christabel in the second part of the poem that bears her name. Objective Nature, whether as *natura naturata* or *natura naturans*, fails to reassure, fails to provide the poem with a convincing analogue to his own affirmative use of language. If, in the visionary climaxes of the conversation poems, the harmony praised by the poet in the goodly scenes he surveyed had been, in fact, a projection from his own "deep faith," then, in different circumstances, other internal states could also be projected—guilt, fear, despair, terror.

The difference of genres must be kept in mind. The alternately confiding and psalmic tone suitable for a blank verse meditation would have been inappropriate in an extended ballad, an epyllion, or a metrical tale. Nevertheless, as, in the conversation poems, we are invited to extrapolate from the poems to their inspirational sources in external Nature, so the daemonic group also invites enquiry into its sources of inspiration. Images of possession, bewitchment, and frenzy abound. The prose preambles to the 1816 version of "Kubla Khan" and the 1817 version of "The Rime" offers elaborate and misleading "clues" to the origins of these poems, as if Coleridge wished to build a protective fence around them. Our fascination with these

---

For the view that 1797 may after all be the right date see *CL*, 1: 348–49; and for the view that the poem may date from 1799 or later, see Elisabeth Schneider, *Coleridge, Opium and "Kubla Khan"* (Chicago: University of Chicago Press, [1953]).

bizarre diversionary tactics, coupled with a habit inherited from nineteenth-century biographical sketches of seeing Coleridge as the haunted *poète maudit,* has given rise to a host of bizarre explanations of the three poems. These range from the ultra-Jungian (the daemonic group is the purest anthology of archetypal images in English verse and originates therefore in the collective unconscious) to the simplistic (opium alone was Coleridge's source of inspiration). The common premise of all such explanations, especially of those that treat the poems as originating in a pathological condition of some kind, is that Coleridge, in one sense or another, did not know what he was doing when he wrote them. By taking the poems away from Coleridge, in effect, we drain them of nine-tenths of their meaning and leave them vulnerable to such destructive attacks as that of Richard Hoffpauir, an adherent of the New Criticism.[29] What the evidence suggests is that, far from having been helpless in the grip of the collective unconscious, oedipal fixation, or opium-induced hallucinations, Coleridge was fully aware that he was now capable of handling myth in an entirely new way.

It cannot be too much emphasized that "The Rime of the Ancient Mariner" is meant not as a historical narrative of certain events, to which an exotic colouring is given by the addition of a few archaic terms, but as a demonstration of the inseparability of event and witness, and as such, it represents a radical critique of the nature poetry Coleridge had written up to 1797. This poetry had been based, as we have seen, on the belief that by observing the forms God has disposed around us in the natural world, we may learn God's language and, through the analogy of the mundane world with the transcendent, grow in the understanding of his benevolence. Inspiration, in the conversation poems, is therefore simply the working of Nature's forms on the mind—the wind passing over the eolian harp. If, however, "the living spirit in our frame" is capable of transfusing "into all its own delights"; if, that is, our very experience of Nature is untrustworthy, owing more to our own powers of projection than to any

29. Richard Hoffpauir, " 'Kubla Khan' and the Critics: Romantic Madness as Poetic Theme and Critical Response," *English Studies in Canada*, 2 (1976): 402–22. In *Validity in Interpretation,* Hirsch argues—convincingly, I think—that the notion of authorial will is a prerequisite for the analysis of verbal meaning, even though it is sometimes impossible to be certain whether an author was conscious of a particular meaning (pp. 19–23, 51–57).

coherence or educative power in the external world—then the Christian poet must turn to a source of inspiration that is less subject to the ambiguities of natural phenomena.

The Mariner is often spoken of as a passive and colourless figure, in whom "all consciousness of personality is gone."[30] While it is true that he is given few significant physical acts other than that of killing the albatross, this should not obscure the fact that he is constantly active in mythologizing the world around him. Everything is anthropomorphized: the albatross is "a Christian soul," the sun is "God's own head," the storm-blast is "tyrannous and strong," the ship is moved by a spirit, sleep is a gift sent by the Virgin Mary, the ocean is an eye looking at the moon.[31] The Mariner responds to the sights and sounds around him not with the sophisticated man's detached and self-conscious judgment but with the instantaneously mythologizing imagination of a pre-scientific age. It is as useless to enquire what "really happened" to the Mariner as it would be to enquire what "really happened" when the sun appeared to stand still in Gibeon, and the moon in the valley of Ajalon (Joshua 10:13). The poem is designed to baffle interpretation if read with a sceptical hunger for objective fact, and the addition of a gloss, in the 1817 version, may be partly intended to enhance the feeling that we are deciphering an ancient text demanding a peculiar effort of *Verstehen*, imaginative comprehension.[32]

Drawing our attention to a passage in "The Destiny of Nations" in which Fancy is described as "the power / That first unsensualises the dark mind," leading to the eventual enthronement of Reason (*PW*, 1: 134), John Beer argues that for Coleridge, "the workings of superstition . . . [acted] as an intermediary between the world of firmly-organised sense-experience and buried awareness of—or capability of awakening to—further, more profound forces." What these profounder forces might be is suggested by the similarity between the Mariner's language at the point where he blesses the watersnakes—"A spring of love gushed from my heart" (*PW*, 1: 198)—and the

30. Lamb made this observation in 1801, in a letter to Wordsworth: Charles and Mary Anne Lamb, *Letters*, ed. Edwin W. Marrs, Jr. (Ithaca and London: Cornell University Press, 1975—), 1: 266.

31. *PW*, 1: 189, 190, 188, 201, 198, 202.

32. I owe this observation to Professor Maurice Elliott, of York University, Toronto.

vocabulary of religious conversion in, for instance, *The Pilgrim's Progress*.[33] The Mariner becomes aware for the first time of divine love welling up from *within* his own being, not taught from without. At some level, on this view, the poem describes the experience of religious conversion. The Mariner's tale suggests that there are two essential stages in the process. First, the imaginative powers, already present in even the least developed mind, mythologize the appearances of Nature so that the slightest wilful act (killing a bird, for instance) appears to bring down a terrible vengeance. (Browning's Caliban has reached this point at the end of "Caliban Upon Setebos.") Then, at the moment of greatest hopelessness, the presence of divine love within humankind itself is revealed—as if to emphasize that the appearances of the natural world, no matter how they are mythologized by the inventive mind of humanity, will not of themselves lead to knowledge of God, whose dealings are with the still small voice of spirit, not with the sense (1 Kings 19:9–12). The Mariner returns to carry the tale of his sufferings to those who are in need of the warning they contain and to recommend pious observance of conventional forms of worship.

If this represents in any sense the "plan" of Coleridge's poem, it is evidently a good deal too optimistic as a final interpretation. Empson, Bostetter and others have pointed out the difficulties that beset any "rigidly logical religious interpretation," such as that of Robert Penn Warren.[34] The dice game, the cruel and arbitrary liquidation of four times fifty living men, and the haunted state of the Mariner as he passes, like night, from land to land suggest the dislocated worlds of Dostoevsky, Kafka, and Sartre rather than the world of John Bunyan and the Quaker John Woolman, in which true repentance is followed by release from the burden of sin and assurance of heavenly reward.[35] This conclusion remains essentially the same, whether or not we re-

33. Beer, *Coleridge's Poetic Intelligence*, pp. 158, 160. A similar interpretation is offered by Edward E. Bostetter, "The Nightmare World of The Ancient Mariner," *Studies in Romanticism* 1 (1961–62): 241–54; see pp. 243–44.

34. William Empson, "The Ancient Mariner," *The Critical Quarterly* 6 (1964): 298–319; Bostetter, "Nightmare World of the Ancient Mariner," p. 245, uses the phrase "rigidly logical religious interpretation." Robert Penn Warren's famous essay "A Poem of Pure Imagination" first appeared in *Kenyon Review* 8 (1946): 391–427.

35. The example of John Woolman is cited by Beer, *Coleridge's Poetic Intelligence*, pp. 160—61. Lilian R. Furst, in *Romanticism in Perspective* (1969; reprint ed., London: Macmillan, 1972), p. 250, compares the Mariner's world with that of Franz Kafka.

gard the dice game and the death of the crew as having really happened; whether the world of the Polar Spirit and the troop of spirits blest is *discovered* by the Mariner or *constructed* by him as an explanation for the psychic changes that have taken place within him. The Mariner, moreover, is at certain times possessed—"wrenched / With a woful agony" (*PW*, 1: 208)—but the nature of this possession is left ambivalent. Despite its pious conclusion, his tale claims no divine sanction, and it is left to the interpreter (the Wedding-Guest, in the first instance) to decide whether the Mariner's words are prompted by a good or an evil daemon, much as it is left to Hamlet to decide whether the spirit that appears to him in his father's form is a good spirit or a fiend. The Wedding-Guest, at first convinced that the Mariner intends no good to him, is compelled to hear him out, but at the end we are told only that the tale left him "stunned," a response that surely has more to do with the bewildering ambivalence of the tale itself than with the nightmare images the Mariner has called up.

For if the Mariner begins as the representative of a pre-scientific age, untouched by the self-knowledge which his mythologizing capacities can bring him, he ends as the representative of an age very like our own. His condition is, in important respects, post-mythological. He has experienced the terror of a world without God, almost (in the 1798 and 1800 versions of the poem) without Christ: "And Christ would take no pity on / My soul in agony" (*PW*, 1: 196n). The spring of love that flowed within him seems to start a redemptive process of some kind, but this process brings no assurance of future bliss, and certainly no direct knowledge of God. When, at the end of the poem, the Mariner affirms that "the dear God who loveth us, / He made and loveth all" (*PW*, 1: 209), most critics who do not find this statement utterly absurd agree that it represents at best a highly precarious, vulnerable faith, not in any sense a triumphant Q.E.D. rounding off a theological "proof." The Mariner's world remains one of doubts and mysteries, its mythology unstable and full of contradictions.

It should not surprise us, I think, that Coleridge took up a mythology only to permit it to disintegrate within the confines of a single poem. The Enlightenment was already in an important sense a post-mythological age. Lessing, in his *Die Erziehung des Menschengeschlechts,* had hinted and more than hinted that the ultimate goal of humanity might be a third age, in which one will "do the Right because it *is* right, not because arbitrary rewards are annexed to it, which formerly were intended simply to fix his unsteady gaze, and to strengthen it to recognize the inner, better rewards of well-doing."[36] This "new, eternal Gospel" was destined to fulfil and transform the New Testament, just as that had fulfilled and transformed the Old, and the doubts and fears provoked by the higher criticism, as it revealed the mythological content of the Bible, would be swallowed up in the conviction that the essential promise of the New Testament, the perfectibility of humankind, remained valid. "The self-same road by which the Race reaches its perfection, must every individual man—one sooner, another later—have travelled over."[37]

Lessing's prophecy is rather too self-assured, however. Mythology does not relinquish its hold quite as readily as he appeared to expect. As a present-day student of myth, Joseph Campbell, has suggested, if we perceive mythology as providing humankind with a "second womb," we still have to recognize that healthy emergence from this womb is not guaranteed: "Misbirth is possible from the mythological womb as well as from the physiological: there can be adhesions, malformations, arrestations, etc. We call them neuroses and psychoses."[38] The Mariner's emergence into the post-mythological era has been a traumatic one, and his psychic scars remain with him. Though he has unselfconsciously created the mythology which brought him self-knowledge and a degree of freedom, he is not yet master of it. He remains the unwilling object of daemonic possession, a wounded θεῖος α'νήρ, limping along the road to the Enlightenment vision of perfected humanity.

"Kubla Khan" presents us with a similarly ambivalent portrait. The first thirty-six lines of the poem encapsulate the mythic constructs of the Orient: neither haphazard antiquarianism nor an unprecedented attack of the collective unconscious can be credited with responsibility for this narrative.[39] After Elinor Shaffer's lucid demonstration of the ferment of syncretistic thought that lay behind "Kubla Khan," it should

36. Gotthold Ephraim Lessing, *The Education of the Human Race*, trans. F. W. Robertson (London: Kegan Paul, Trench, Trubner, 1896), p. 70. German text: *Lessings Werke*, 7:448.

37. *Education of the Human Race*, p. 75; *Werke*, 7:449.

38. Joseph Campbell, "Bios and Mythos: Prolegomena to a Science of Mythology," in John B. Vickery, ed., *Myth and Literature: Contemporary Theory and Practice* (1966: reprint ed., Lincoln, Neb.: University of Nebraska Press, 1969), p. 22.

39. Shaffer, chaps. 1–4 *passim*.

no longer be possible to take seriously explanations of the poem based on pathology or associative psychology; nor, more important still, should we continue to refer to Coleridge's mind as consisting of a pagan half which possessed all the creativity and a Christian half which acted as his "orthodox censor."[40]

As a Christian in an age which already stood outside mythology, which looked back on it as on a road previously travelled (or, to use Campbell's metaphor, as the womb from which it had emerged), Coleridge understood that the poet's task must now be to survey mythology from above: to claim it as a dynamic heritage, not as the exhausted fictions derided by Voltaire. "Coleridge's transcendental enterprise was to lay bare the source of mythology, the sense for a God in the human race."[41]

While Shaffer is surely right to summarize in this way the impulse from which "Kubla Khan" sprang, we have to recognize that her work has raised in acute form all the problems associated with demythologization and its close relative in literary criticism, secularization. Modern humanistic scholarship sometimes tends to overlook the fact that at the very centre of Christian tradition lies the most potent of all images for the overthrow of hieratic religion and the release of the sacred into common experience: the rending of the veil of the temple. For the Christian poet there are grounds for believing that any barriers which once existed between the sacred and the profane have been thrown down. The Atonement or reuniting (at-one-ment) of God and humankind implies that (in Frye's words) "a channel of communication between the divine and human is now open."[42] Yet such a statement at once involves the recollection of a historical event—and therefore of the poet's own position in historical time, his fallibility and his finitude. A disturbing infiltration of the anagogical into the historical, thoughts of the end of all things into the image of an existing realized perfection, is an undeniable feature of "Kubla Khan," as it is of the thirteenth chapter of *Biographia Literaria*, in which the primary Imagination is held to be a repetition, in the finite mind, of the eternal, divine act of creation and is echoed by the secondary Imagination or

40. The phrase is used by Harold Bloom; see "Coleridge: The Anxiety of Influence," in Geoffrey H. Hartman, ed., *New Perspectives on Coleridge and Wordsworth: Selected Papers from the English Institute* (New York and London: Columbia University Press, 1972), p. 261.

41. Shaffer, p. 144.

42. Frye, p. 134.

poetic power, which coexists with the conscious will. Here, too, the process of recreating and unifying sometimes appears to be threatened by a counter-tendency within the secondary Imagination itself towards dissolution: "It dissolves, diffuses, dissipates, in order to re-create; or where this process is rendered impossible, yet still at all events it struggles to idealize and to unify" (*BL*, 1: 304).

Lawrence Kramer notes the same pattern of dissolution followed by recreation in "Kubla Khan": the woman wailing for her demon-lover, for erotic possession by an unknown primal other, and who thus personifies the "daemonic" aspect of Coleridgean imagination, is transmuted and taken up into the healing, idealized figure of the Abyssinian maid. Kramer's purpose in pointing out the similarity is "to link the daemonic imagination . . . with the romantic imagination of the *Biographia Literaria*," arguing that "the daemonic, in Romantic poems, rarely appears without generating a later appearance of its romantic contrary, which then proceeds to transcend, transform, or evade the daemonic vision."[43] While Kramer's interpretation of the wailing woman of the chasm as the Abyssinian maid's dark double or alter ego does highlight one reason for the peculiar fascination "Kubla Khan" holds for many readers, his suggestion about the woman of the chasm (the daemonic imagination) "generating" the later manifestation of the bright, inspirational maid (the romantic, or secondary Imagination) is wrong, I think, in so far as it gives one figure priority over the other, a causative function. The fact that the Abyssinian maid does not appear until the second part of the poem should not necessarily mean for us that her appearance is called up ("generated") by that of the lonely woman, or is dependent on the woman's erotic cry. Rather, the two figures embody alternative visions of the experience of inspiration, neither of which can entirely cancel out the other. "The poetry," as Kramer says, "idealizes the romantic imagination, as romantic theory does; daemonic vision tests fiercely the imagination's capacity to sustain the idealization."[44] The speaker is not permitted to know whether his words are of divine or daemonic origin. It is part of the peculiar honesty of this poem that this ambiguity about the true source of inspiration—divine, or daemonic—should be so carefully preserved.

43. Lawrence Kramer, "That Other Will: The Daemonic in Coleridge and Wordsworth," *Philological Quarterly* 58 (1979): 300.

44. Kramer, p. 318.

"Kubla Khan" reaffirms the sense for the divine in the human race but does not subsume or secularize it, if by that we mean that the sense for the divine is emptied of its content. Coleridge's seer, like St. John, prophesies the overthrow of a kingdom, and more than that, its transmutation from temporal construct into spiritual reality. Kubla's *hortus conclusus* embraces all Asia; but, as Shaffer argues, the already highly syncretic geography of Xanadu is transmuted by the seer into a "sacred geometry," a vision of paradise that is liberated at last from the trammels of spatiality and realizes the cabbalists' dream of the *aleph*, a place that is all places simultaneously.[45] (As Shelley put it, "A poet participates in the eternal, the infinite, and the one; as far as relates to his conceptions, time and place and number are not.")[46] Max Schulz, relating Kubla's artificial Eden or *hortus conclusus* to other Edenic images in Coleridge's poetry, and to the Renaissance and classical traditions of the earthly paradise, sees "Kubla Khan" as the supreme instance of the eighteenth-century search for an "extended Eden," including not only the whole earth but the cosmos itself.[47] Like the cosmos of "The Rime of the Ancient Mariner," however, the cosmos of "Kubla Khan" is hard to "read." Images of beneficence in Nature, seen in the sacred river and the fertile ground where Kubla plants his gardens, are countered by images of death and sterility (lifeless ocean, icy cavern). The chasm itself is both life-giving—it is the source of the fountain—and terrifying—"a savage place." Kubla's tenancy of this ambiguous microcosm seems to be destined to be brief, his "decree" merely a momentary stay against confusion. Unlike the Mariner, however, the seer of "Kubla Khan" has been granted, in the vision of the Abyssinian maid, an interpreter, a Beatrice who appears to promise divine guidance to the poet in his ascent to Paradise, or a moon-goddess, a Queen Isis, promising redemption and wholeness to the bard Osiris-Coleridge, and bringing ancient wisdom from the dark caves in which it had been hidden.[48] Through the inspiration which she imparts, the seer would be able to realize in his own imagination Kubla's paradise and even communicate this inspiration to others:

45. Shaffer, p. 165.

46. Shelley, "A Defence of Poetry," p. 112.

47. Max F. Schulz, "Coleridge and the Enchantments of Earthly Paradise," in W. B. Crawford, ed., *Reading Coleridge: Approaches and Applications* (Ithaca and London: Cornell University Press, 1979), p. 119.

48. Schulz, p. 151; J. B. Beer, *Coleridge the Visionary* (London: Chatto and Windus, 1970), pp. 255, 262.

Could I revive within me
Her symphony and song,
To such a deep delight 'twould win me
That with music loud and long,
I would build that dome in air,
That sunny dome! those caves of ice!
And all who heard should see them there . . .
(*PW*, 1:298)

The external world would be made internal, the seer and his audience become inheritors of many thousands of years of history in a single moment of vision. The apocalyptic language of Jewish tradition was first applied to the conduct of an individual life by Paul and other Apostles (Hebrews 12:18–29; 2 Peter 3:10–15), but Enlightenment thought carried still further the liberating idea that it was possible for one person's life to recapitulate the whole of human history. "The enthusiast often casts true glances into the future, but for this future he cannot wait. He wishes this future accelerated, and accelerated through him. That for which Nature takes thousands of years is to mature itself in the moment of his existence. For what possession has he in it if that which he recognizes as the Best does not become the best in his life time?"[49]

Though Lessing was writing of the thirteenth- and fourteenth-century Christian mystics, there are few better summaries of the difficulties faced by any Romantic poet. For Coleridge's seer evidently desires this telescoping of time, the realization in the present moment of a Paradise that is both past and to come. He transcends Schiller's distinction between the naive (or objective) poet and the sentimental (or subjective) poet, since he imitates the outward world solely as a step towards the transformation of the inner world.[50] He is also, however, conscious of a past and a present: "In a vision once I saw." Inevitably, therefore, the inspiration represented by the Abyssinian maid is time-conditioned—not, perhaps, in the sense that the seer had a vision of her and some hours, days, or years later recalls it, but in the sense that, for the modern, self-conscious mind, *any* event registered by the consciousness already belongs to a historical past. The significance of the past tense in line 38 of the poem is not to be

49. *Education of the Human Race*, p. 73; *Werke*, 7: 449.
50. Shaffer, p. 77.

confused with the Wordsworthian recollection of past years—"The things which I have seen I now can see no more"—nor even with Shelley's principle that "when composition begins, inspiration is already on the decline."[51] The difference of time represented by that small word "once" is a matter not of chronometer time but rather of two wholly different orders of time: the realm of the Abyssinian maid and that of the reflecting, self-conscious poet, whose aspiration towards the condition of Θεῖος ἀνήρ is perpetually doomed to frustration, because vision is not possession. We do not even give wholehearted assent, Coleridge observes, to our *dreams*—much less to any experience of our waking minds: "even in dreams of Sleep the Soul never *is*, because it either cannot or dare not be, any ‹ONE› THING; but lives in *approaches*—touched by the outgoing pre-existent Ghosts of many feelings—" (*CN* 3215).[52]

Having brought the whole sweep of human history into one brilliant image, therefore, Coleridge, in the second "moment" of "Kubla Khan," bravely makes the transition into the condition of post-mythological humanity. It is not that the post-mythological poet enjoys some promising visions which are blotted out by an orthodox censor jangling his keys in some dark dungeon of the mind: the truth is very far from either the farce or the pathos suggested by that reductive explanation. Nor is it exactly a matter of the imagination gaining control over its own content, at the cost of the vividness or freshness of an original experience.[53] It is rather than the humanist and Enlightenment drive to bring ever more areas of human experience under the hegemony of our matured consciousness—an endeavour in which Coleridge himself was fully engaged[54]—interposed the thinnest but most impenetrable of veils between one area of mental activity and another, and in place of naive impulse put the "outgoing pre-existent Ghosts of

51. Shelley, "A Defence of Poetry," p. 135.

52. See the comments by Kathleen Coburn on this passage: *Experience into Thought* (Toronto: University of Toronto Press, 1979), pp. 18–19.

53. For the phrases "gaining control," "original experience," see Jean-Pierre Mileur, *Vision and Revision: Coleridge's Art of Immanence* (Berkeley: University of California Press, 1982), p. 27. On the contrary, the poem itself tells us that "control" is itself a precondition of human experience—an integral part of the experiencing self—in modern times. Mileur's assumption that the poem is meant to refer to an "original experience" of Coleridge's seems to me inconsistent with his view (which I share) that we should treat the prose "Preface" as a fiction (p. 26).

54. A point made by Kathleen Coburn, *The Self Conscious Imagination* (London: Oxford University Press, 1974), pp. 22–23.

many feelings." "Kubla Khan" dramatizes this shared, communal (not personal) condition at the highest level of artistry. The fact that many poets at the end of the eighteenth century felt themselves to be the successors of Isaiah and Ezekiel, as well as of Homer and Pindar, could not seal them from the spiritual climate of their time, least of all in that most sensitive battleground of the artist's striving, the sense of self. The seer of "Kubla Khan" lost his power to revive within him the maid's symphony and song at the very instant when he recognized the maid as distinct from himself, when he became, that is, *conscious* of her. The truly possessed or inspired conjuror of a daemon has no notion, while he is in his trance, that the daemon is not himself. The Abyssinian maid withdraws into silence the instant she is recognized by the seer's conscious mind (just as Christabel, confronted with an imperious alter ego who usurps her dead mother's place in her mind and bed, is bewitched into spellbound silence).[55] This experience of loss, the withdrawal of the Beatrice-figure, the mediator between full knowledge and the conscious, history-bound, verbalizing mind of the poet, is surely the true subject of "Kubla Khan," rather than "inspiration in its ideal, least restricted, most disembarrassed and most disembodied form" (C. M. Bowra's phrase).[56] Coleridge creates a seer who precisely exemplifies the "loneliness and fixedness" of the post-mythological poet, one who in emulation of the biblical prophets courts the "state of inspiration and possession," but finds that he cannot transcend his time-bound self. As with John Keats's momentary glimpses of the region he called "heaven's bourne," it is not the vision that fails the poet, but the other way round. Remaining conscious of time and of mortality, the poet-surrogate surrenders his vision by reasserting his own humanity.

Coleridge's seer even pictures himself as a spectator, as it were *ab extra*, of what would have been his own transfiguration, had he really achieved the state of daemonic possession: "Weave a circle round him thrice . . ." (*PW*, 1: 298). As is surely sufficiently clear, if we give proper attention to the mood of the verbs, ("Could I revive . . . ," "And all should cry . . ."), these lines are not spoken in the character of the possessed bard, but, more subtly, in that of the bard who knows what it is to be possessed and knows, too, that this inspired state has now

55. See Anthony John Harding, "Mythopoeic Elements in 'Christabel,' " *Modern Language Quarterly* 44 (1983): 49–50.

56. Bowra, *Inspiration and Poetry*, p. 8.

left him, that the poem is written out of the memory of the inspired state rather than out of the inspired state itself. The most notable virtue of Coleridge's poem, after its dense mythological allusiveness and its hypnotic cadences, may be, unexpectedly, its startling honesty.

II

Beyond Nature: Naturphilosophie *and Imagination*

ALL OF Coleridge's mature writing on inspiration was marked by the conviction that inspiration, being—whatever else it may be—an eminently human state, must always be viewed in relation to the human context in which it is experienced. Coleridge was attracted by Schelling's philosophy and by its high a priori explanation of the nature of inspiration. Nevertheless, there runs through Coleridge's middle period (say 1802–20) and beyond into the "Letters" the deepseated belief that a person reading a text, especially and pre-eminently the Bible, is first and foremost a human being called into relationship with another human being. Where idealist criticism tended always to muffle the human pulse that animates all parts of Scripture and to translate the original writers' passionate declarations into pallid imitations of themselves, Coleridge stressed as energetically as any revivalist the human and therefore exemplary nature of the Scripture history.

As long as I have the image of Deborah before my eyes, and while I throw myself back into the age, country, circumstances, of this Hebrew Bonduca in the not yet tamed chaos of the spiritual creation;—as long as I contemplate the impassioned, high-souled, heroic woman in all the prominence and individuality of will and character,—I feel as if I were among the first ferments of the great affections—the proplastic waves of the microcosmic chaos, swelling up against—and yet towards—the outspread wings of the Dove that lies brooding on the troubled waters. So long, all is well,—all replete with instruction and example. . . . in the self-oblivion of these heroes of the Old Testament, their elevation above all low and individual interests,—above all, in the entire and vehement devotion of their total being to the service of their divine

Master, I find a lesson of humility, a ground of humiliation, and a shaming, yet rousing, example of faith and fealty. (*CW*, 5: 92–93)

For this reason, Coleridge could never accept the theory of verbal dictation, which would ascribe every word of Scripture directly to the Holy Spirit and render the human vehicle a mere passive instrument, manipulated by a "superhuman . . . Ventriloquist" (*CW*, 5: 593). Yet, as we have seen, Coleridge rejected the Enlightenment position of Herder and Reimarus, that the miracle of inspiration by the Holy Spirit was part of the pre-scientific cultural matrix of the Bible that must now, in a more rational age, be treated as a mere relic of primitive culture, just as he firmly contradicted Herder's argument that God and humankind have nothing in common and that humanity can reach knowledge of God only from the observation of Nature. In the "Letters on the Inspiration of the Scriptures," Coleridge's position was that where the scriptural authors themselves claimed to have recorded the directly revealed Word of God, the corresponding text must be received "with full belief":

Have I not declared—do I not begin by declaring—that whatever is referred by the sacred Penman to a direct communication from God, and wherever it is recorded that the Subject of the history had asserted himself to have received this or that command, this or that information or assurance, from a super-human Intelligence, or where the writer in his own person, and in the character of an historian, relates that the *Word of the Lord came* unto priest, prophet, chieftain, or other individual—have I not declared that I receive the same with full belief, and admit its inappellable authority? (*CW*, 5: 589)

The important consequence of this theologically rather conservative position was that it preserved intact the integrity of the scriptural authors, avoiding the rationalists' tendency to explain away or belittle their claims as the results of self-deception or imposture. Coleridge's mature belief was that the fundamental veracity of the scriptural writers must be respected.

This belief derived not so much from a pious veneration for the text as from Coleridge's experience as a reader, critic, and apologist for literature. More than most readers, he was (to use Kathleen Coburn's phrase) "keenly alive" to the independently thinking minds revealed in the books he constantly and omnivorously consumed.[1] Where many

1. Coburn, *Experience into Thought*, p. 29. A useful discussion of the idea of an authorial will, to which I am indebted, is Hirsch, *Validity in Interpretation*, chaps. 1 and 2.

modern critics focus exclusively on the text, Coleridge demanded of the reader a wider hermeneutic vision, which would at least attempt to grasp something of the authorial presence behind the text and sympathize with its aims, setting down as his "*golden rule*"—at any rate in the study of philosophy—the famous maxim "*until you understand a writer's ignorance, presume yourself ignorant of his understanding*" (*BL*, 1: 232). Rarely if ever, did Coleridge consider a book neutral as regards the moral good or moral harm it could do, and the moral character of a book was naturally affected by that of the person who wrote it. A notebook entry of 1807 suggests that, to Coleridge, even genius, the gift of heaven, could not achieve much unless it was fed with the appropriate fuel of the moral being: "Tho' Genius, like the fire on the Altar, can only be kindled from Heaven, yet it will perish unless supplied with appropriate fuel to feed it—or if it meet not with the virtues, whose society alone can reconcile it to earth, it will return whence it came . . ." (*CN* 3136).

The passage is a comment on a quotation from Strabo, in which the state of religious ecstasy was compared with the inspired utterance of the prophet. Strabo's principle (quoted by Jonson in the dedication to *Volpone*) that without being a good man, no one could be a good poet, was axiomatic for Coleridge; it was noted down as early as 1801, reappeared in a lecture of 1818 and in a *Table Talk* entry for August 1833 (see *CN* 1057 and n), and informed the whole discussion of the character of genius in the second chapter of *Biographia.* Few critics have argued more consistently than Coleridge that both the creation and the enjoyment of poetry are activities in which one's whole being—moral, intellectual, and aesthetic—is freely involved.

In the middle years of his life, however, Coleridge was deeply attracted to a way of thinking which threatened to explode this belief entirely. Pantheism made the poet's individuality almost superfluous: the mind of the poet was emptied of all the affections, powers, values, and particular experiences that belonged to the poet as individual and became a mere hollow chamber in which the Objective was fused as in a crucible with the Subjective, and the Intelligence striving to express itself in Nature finally reached articulate form through human agency.

> The revelation which the natural philosopher makes artificially for himself is original and natural for Art. What we call Nature is a poem that lies enclosed in a wondrous secret scripture. Yet the riddle can be solved. . . . Each masterly

> picture originates equally in the annulling of the invisible barrier which separates the actual and ideal worlds, and is simply the opening through which emerge fully those forms and aspects of the ideal world, which glimmer half-seen through the actual world . . . it is Art alone . . . that is able with universal validity to render objective what the philosopher can only demonstrate subjectively.[2]

Thus Schelling, who admitted that his system could be interpreted as a form of pantheism. Thomas McFarland is evidently right in his judgment that "pantheism, of all ontological schemes, is the one most favourable, on the level of abstract justification, to the poet's art,"[3] because it seems to encourage the direct channelling into art of the poet's joy in the completeness of the world around him or her. Yet pantheism denied free will and with it the whole meaning of the Christian faith. It perpetually threatened to swallow up the individual self, both by denying the personëity of God, which in Jewish tradition is the ultimate ground of human individuality, and by turning human consciousness into a mere temporary modification of the one eternal Substance. In Schelling's hands, however, this austere philosophy became an intoxicating description and justification of all art as the rending of a veil between the ideal and actual worlds, as, indeed, the highest philosophy: "Art . . . is to the philosopher the highest of things."[4]

This praise of art as "the highest of things" took its place in a long tradition, reaching back to the *Enneads* of Plotinus, that linked the artist as creator with the divine creative power. Where Schelling differed from his predecessors, however, was in the bold monism of his system, a monism that proved almost irresistible to a mind such as Coleridge's which ached for the unification of knowledge, some way to close the immense gap that had opened up between the ideal and actual worlds. Such knowledge, Schelling affirmed, was possible: the objective, unconscious world, or Nature, and the subjective, conscious world, or the Self, met and fused in a moment of recognition which transcended "object" and "subject." Humanity, in this moment, was

2. Friedrich Wilhelm Joseph von Schelling, *Sämmtliche Werke*, ed. K. F. A. Schelling, 14 vols (Stuttgart and Augsburg: J. G. Cotta, 1856–1861), 3: 628–29. Translation is my own.

3. Thomas McFarland, *Coleridge and the Pantheist Tradition* (Oxford: Clarendon Press, 1969), p. 112.

4. Schelling, *Werke*, 3: 628.

Nature arrived at self-consciousness, Nature become aware for the first time of its own existence. That the individual human mind—the impassioned, the high-souled, the heroic—became, in this system, a mere modification of the one existing Substance, possessing no separate identity, did not trouble Schelling, to whom that loss of individuality was a small price to pay for the discovery that knowledge of the thing-in-itself was, after all, possible. Schelling liked to claim that freedom was the *ne plus ultra* of his philosophy, yet—as McFarland observes—his thought preserves freedom only in a formal, philosopher's sense, not in the practical sense upheld by Coleridge.[5]

Despite the spectre of Spinozism that lurked behind it, and the concomitant threat of final collapse in the key Kantian idea of freedom ("If appearances are things-in-themselves," Kant had written, "freedom cannot be saved"),[6] the *Naturphilosophie* swept all before it in the early decades of the ninteenth century. The goal of unifying scientific and philosophical knowledge in a single, all-explaining system was perhaps most boldly announced by Wilhelm Nasse, professor of technology at the St. Petersburg Academy of Sciences, in 1809: "There is but one Knowledge: it is the recognition of Unity, the simultaneous identity of the productive power and the product."[7] Schelling's *System des transzendentalen Idealismus*, first published in 1800, set out the philosophical underpinnings of the movement from the subjectivist, idealist side; but Henrik Steffens's theory that "Nature is the first step towards mind," a key scientific notion for *Naturphilosophie*, was published the same year and elaborated in *Beytrage zur innern Naturgeschichte der Erde* (1801). The latter work spoke of an "animalizing and vegetizing tendency in Nature."[8] It was Steffens's aim to "demonstrate that Magnetism is the first step in the evolution of all forms in our world, and hence to elevate it into the principle of a theory of evolution."[9]

The choice of magnetism as the key to unlock all Nature's evolutionary mysteries, to us rather an arbitrary one, is ultimately less important here than the problem which Steffens saw as controlling all

5. McFarland, *Pantheist Tradition*, p. 152.

6. Quoted (and translated) by R. D. Miller, *Schiller and the Ideal of Freedom* (Oxford: Clarendon Press, 1970), p. 1.

7. Quoted by H. A. M. Snelders, "Romanticism and Natur-Philosophie and the Inorganic Natural Sciences 1797–1840: An Introductory Survey," *Studies in Romanticism* 9 (1970): 197. Translation is my own.

8. Quoted by Snelders, p. 210. Translation is my own.

9. Quoted by Snelders, p. 210. Translation is my own.

his scientific effort, that of explaining the evolution or development of forms (*Bildungen*). The doctrine that there existed an abiding, substantial One, from which the Many proceeded and to which they returned, was of no scientific value unless it could be shown *how* the primordial Substance developed out of itself the many different forms of things which impinge on our consciousness. There must be, it seemed, some power in nature which made for individuation, the development of various finite forms out of the one original Substance.

In Blumenbach's course of lectures, which Coleridge attended at Göttingen in 1799, the term used for this phenomenon, a kind of entelechy, would have been *nisus formativus* (in German, *Bildungstrieb*). (Blumenbach's *Institutiones physiologicae*, in which the term *nisus formativus* is used, was the textbook for the course.)[10] Blumenbach was careful to emphasize that *nisus formativus* was merely a heuristic concept, not to be thought of as having real existence; a mere name for the scientist's perception that in such-and-such an animal, a particular function (that of vision, say) had apparently been perfected. Blumenbach clearly wished it left to the theologians to ascribe this or that phenomenon to design or intelligence in Nature (see *CM*, 1: 535–36).

Nevertheless, other thinkers, including Coleridge, saw in the concept of a *nisus formativus* something more than a scientist's convenient categorization of a series of phenomena as displaying progression to a finishing point. Understood as a creative impulse, or a striving towards form, that *actually existed* in Nature herself, the *nisus formativus* seemed to constitute evidence that Nature was not a mere mass of atoms, lacking cohesion and purpose, nor yet a machine, never varying from its limited, pre-planned set of motions, but a living being, in which the very process of creation could be observed. Still more important for Coleridge, such a creative impulse provided an external analogue for his own creative processes. The ideas of a striving towards form was (to borrow John Beer's terms) one of the "speculative instruments with which to approach the processes of creation as they could be observed not only in the mind of the creative artist but in the organic processes of nature itself."[11]

The attraction of *Naturphilosophie*, then, was not merely that it promised to bring all knowledge into a unified whole but that one of its key ideas, that of *Bildungstrieb*, seemed to endow Nature with the same

10. See *CN* 3744n; and Snelders, p. 196.
11. Beer, *Coleridge's Poetic Intelligence*, p. 40.

purposive function as the poet knows when conceiving and composing a poem. This exciting possibility lay behind a note of March, 1810: "I wish much to investigate the connection of the Imagination with the Bildungstrieb—Imaginatio = imitatio vel repetitio *Imaginis*—per motum? ergo, et motuum—The Variolae—generation—Is there not a *link* between physical Imitation & Imagination?" (*CN* 3744).[12]

Since the time of Plato, of course, the artist's action had been defined as that of imitation (mimesis), in one sense or another. Plato's *Republic*, book 10, contained a famous attack on poetry and art as merely counterfeiting the outward appearance of the world and ignoring the enduring reality of the Ideas. What Coleridge glimpsed in this note, however, was the key insight that the artist, to show true imaginative power, must "imitate" not only the *image* which appears to the senses but the *process* by which that image was made. "The artist must imitate that which is within the thing, that which is active through form and figure . . . the *Natur-geist*, or spirit of nature" ("On Poesy or Art").[13] Imagination, that is, repeats an image not as a mirror does, or as a piece of wax repeats the image on the seal, but by repeating first of all the movements or natural forces which originally produced the image—the *Bildungstrieb*: "imitatio vel repetitio *Imaginis*—per motum? ergo, et motuum." Of course no human power can literally carry through the movements which created a real tree or a mountain. But the imagination may be able to imitate them, as a child acts out in little the things it sees older people doing. Coleridge's question, "Is there not a *link* between physical Imitation & Imagination?" refers perhaps to the seventh stanza of Wordsworth's "Intimations" Ode, in which a child is described putting on "A wedding or a festival, / A mourning or a funeral . . . As if his whole vocation / Were endless imitation." The child does not so much want to look like a bride or groom at a wedding, or a mourner at a funeral, but to "see what it feels like" to be those things. While the charade lasts, perhaps, he is what he pretends to be. Having learned this art of imitating-from-within as children, Coleridge suggests, those of us who are artists grow

12. Professor Coburn, in her note on this entry, points out that while for Blumenbach *Bildungstrieb* referred only to a kind of entelechy, Schiller in *Briefe über die ästhetische Erziehung des Menschen* and Herder in *Adrastea* used the term in the sense of "creative impulse" or "urge to form" (*CN* 3744n).

13. "On Poesy or Art," in *Biographia Literaria*, ed. J. Shawcross, (1907; reprint ed., London: Oxford University Press, 1965), 2: 259.

up to imitate, in imagination, the processes of the living world around us.

The essay "On Poesy or Art," possibly meant as part of the 1818 series of lectures on literature and first printed as such in *Literary Remains*, is the fullest example we have of Coleridge's version of the organicist argument. As might be expected, it draws heavily on Schelling (his 1807 "Academy Oration"), but it is not a mere translation. Coleridge imitated not Schelling's results merely, but the very processes of his thought. The essay defines "beauty" in a manner that concisely illustrates the marriage of mind to Nature, through the imitation of the *Bildungstrieb* by the mind of the artist:

> [Beauty] is, in the abstract, the unity of the manifold, the coalescence of the diverse; in the concrete, it is the union of the shapely (*formosum*) with the vital. In the dead organic it depends on regularity of form, the first and lowest species of which is the triangle with all its modifications, as in crystals, architecture, &c.; in the living organic it is not merely regularity of form, which would produce a sense of formality; neither is it subservient to any thing beside itself. It may be present in a disagreeable object, in which the proportion of the parts constitutes a whole; it does not arise from association, as the agreeable does, but sometimes lies in the rupture of association; it is not different to different individuals and nations, as has been said, nor is it connected with the ideas of the good, or the fit, or the useful. The sense of beauty is intuitive, and beauty itself is all that inspires pleasure without, and aloof from, and even contrarily to, interest.
>
> If the artist copies the mere nature, the *natura naturata*, what idle rivalry! . . . Believe me, you must master the essence, the *natura naturans*, which presupposes a bond between nature in the higher sense and the soul of man. (P. 257)

This has, certainly the appearance of being "most favourable, on the level of abstract justification, to the poet's art," but anyone who is not a pantheist will be tempted to ask whether there is any essential *distinction*, in this kind of scheme, between "nature in the higher sense" and "the soul of man." Coleridge's answer, or rather Schelling's, was that only humankind possessed "reflexion, freedom and choice," whereas in Nature thought and the product of thought were one. Humankind was at once the culmination of Nature, "the very focus of all the rays of intellect which are scattered throughout the images of nature," and a responsible, freely acting being ("On Poesy or Art," pp. 257–58). As W. K. Wimsatt lucidly expresses it:

There is at least one respect in which the physical organism, either growing plant or animal, is immeasurably surpassed by the human poetic consciousness. I mean, in its capacity for self-revision, rearrangement, mending. . . . there is no action of any physical organism that remotely approaches the power of the human mind to revise and recast *itself*, constantly to reaffirm or to cancel its own precedent action, in whole or in part. We confront here self-involution, a spiritual power.[14]

To a mind as thoroughly devoted to biblical values as Coleridge's, however, this attempt to preserve the spiritual nature of Imagination by making its capacity for self-revision the culminating development of the formative processes of Nature, an inexplicable evolutionary leap into the human, was bound to appear, in the long run, deeply suspect. Indeed both Greek religion, in the myth of Prometheus's theft of fire from heaven, and Hebrew religion, with its frequent examples of the supernatural kindling of fire on the sacrificial altar (Leviticus 9:24, Judges 6:21, 1 Kings 18:30–39, 2 Chronicles 7:1), seemed to say that poetic and prophetic power must be grounded in something not found in Nature. Though Nature might be viewed by both poet and philosopher as permeated by the creative energies of God, by the end of the second decade of the century it had become vitally important for Coleridge to keep clear the distinction between God as ground of all things and "creaturely spirit," *natura naturans*, or the manifestations of God's power in Nature.

One of Coleridge's marginalia in the so-called "Law" edition of Boehme's *Works* found in Boehme the exemplary instance of a confusion between creaturely spirit and "deific energies in Deity itself," an error that the pantheist, Coleridge felt, was particularly liable to fall into. (The note was dated by Coleridge "27 August, 1818.")

The Errors of this extraordinary Man fall under two heads. The first, easily separable, as a mere scum, by the thoughtful Reader, and which calls only for a forgiving Smile, is the occasional substitution of the Accidents of his own ~~a~~ peculiar acts of association (for instance, his exemplification of the language of Nature) for the laws and processes of the creaturely Spirit in universo. The second, componental and dissolved thro' the whole, which it requires a spiritual Chemistry, and the addition of a new ~~substance~~ ingredient to decombine and precipitate—the confusion of the creaturely spirit in the

14. W. K. Wimsatt, "Organic Form: Some Questions about a Metaphor," in David Thorburn and Geoffrey Hartman, eds., *Romanticism: Vistas, Instances, Continuities* (Ithaca: Cornell University Press, 1973), p. 22.

great moments of its renascence ανακοσμησέως) thro' the Breath and Word of Comforter and Restorer for ~~the~~ deific energies in Deity itself. . . . In the first instance his error is radically the same as that of Spinoza, and in both instances the same as that of Schelling and his followers. (*CM*, 1: 601–2)

As the flaws in Schelling's *Naturphilosophie* became clearer, Coleridge directed his attacks not only against Schelling's primary error, that of making Nature absolute, but also against the consequent mistake of elevating "Entelechies" (or the drive of each created thing towards self-perfection) into "hyperousian realizing powers." ("Hyperousian" is a Coleridgean neologism meaning "above being.") In the autumn of 1818, Coleridge formulated his objections to Schelling in this way (referring to Schelling's *Einleitung zu seinem Entwurf eines Systems der Naturphilosophie*):

In my letter to Mr Green [30 September 1818: see *CL*, 4: 873–6] I detect two fundamental errors of Schelling—1. The establishment of Polarity in the Absolute—and 2. the confusion of Ideas, with Theorems on onc~~c~~e side, and ‹with› Anticipations on the other, so as to make one and the same at once self-evident and yet dependent on empirical Proof.—But these and all his other errors, together with all his failures are referable to the one πρῶτσν ψευδος —the making *Nature* absolute. . . . Observe that Aristotle as soon as in opposition to Plato he made Nature absolute, ~~a~~ invented what Schelling has adopted—his Entelechies, or Imaginary *simple Actions*—to which all Nature would be reduced, if it were reducible to its primary constituents. Thus we have *impossible* realities, nay, worse, hyperousian realizing powers, that yet are impossible!! (*CN* 4449)

The idea that Imagination may be a psychic development of the tendency to individuation that pervades the natural world, expressing itself in entelechy or the perfection of functions in animals, in the sexual instinct ("generation"), and in our mental creative processes, may seem in some respects like a more subtle version of the doctrine put forward in the conversation poems and "The Destiny of Nations" that all of the appearances in Nature are a living alphabet that trains humankind up to the knowledge of God. Both ideas offer a rationale for poetry, as an interpreter and indeed a model of the universal creative process, as it works itself out through the partnership of the external and internal worlds. Such thinking, however, tended to confuse the distinction between Creator and creature; allowing too much power to an immanent deity, or to shadowy "hyperousian realizing powers," it banished the Christian God to a remote corner of the living universe, reducing Deity to an abstract, indifferent Intelligence. Poetic creation, too, was robbed of its element of divinity. In removing transcendence from the scene, *Naturphilosophie* also removed the "*Poet's Fire*" (Pope's phrase in the *Essay on Criticism:* line 100), that spark of the divine which was the essential impulse of the poetic genius, the flame kindled from above on the altar of the poet's humanity. Coleridge's "one Life," by contrast, is a Christian idea, in that it does not confuse or identify God with Nature but demonstrates that Nature, organized as it is according to laws that can be grasped by the human mind, must be grounded in something that is neither mere inchoate Substance nor a mere impersonal First Cause, but a transcendent Being.[15] A law implies a pre-existing author of that law, and one possessing a will by which the law is put into effect. Coleridge glossed the first verse of Genesis thus in a letter to Charles Tulk, a Swedenborgian friend:

> All that exists has a beginning—and God, whose essence is the *ground* of all things, is by his Will, thro' the *utterance* of his Will (= the Word, Λόγος) the Beginner of their *existence*; i.e. God *createth* all things. He not only *formeth* them, i.e. establisheth their relativity and correspondent relations, but he likewise *groundeth* them—*in* him they have their *Being, from* him they receive their *existence*. God is not merely the Cause of the Universe, for that would be atheism, in which the Mens or Νοῦς would be a part of the Universe, viz. the first Link of the Chain. (*CL*, 4: 770)

Quoting part of this letter, Owen Barfield points out that Coleridge's thought can be classified as "pantheistic" only if we ignore his frequently made distinction between "The Father God, as the Will underlying creation," and God the Son, who "is, or is potentially, one both with nature and with man."[16] Milton, in book 7 of *Paradise Lost*, expressed the distinction dramatically when he made the angel Raphael narrate to Adam and Eve the "great Expedition" of Jesus, the Word of God, to effect the creation of the universe.

To the claim that a pantheistic faith offered the poet a greater scope for sublime description, praise of the living soul uniting all Nature's forms, and exultant invocation of the *anima mundi*, Coleridge would

15. Douglas Brownlow Wilson, "Two Modes of Apprehending Nature: A Gloss on the Coleridgean Symbol," *PMLA* 87 (1972): 48.

16. Barfield, *What Coleridge Thought*, p. 149.

have answered that the Bible, founded on a faith that was as different as it could be from pantheism, exhibited a greater sense of the One Life, grounded in God's otherness, than even pantheism. Hebrew religion expressly forbade the attempt to give Godhead a visible, material form, and for this very reason the poetry of the Old Testament excelled all other literatures in "*Imagination*, or the *modifying*, and *co-adunating* Faculty" (*CL*, 2: 866), that human faculty which seized on the organic interrelatedness of matter, the life-principle which is not apparent to the senses, as evidence that matter is itself grounded in something that is *not* material.

It distorts Coleridge's theory of Imagination to treat of it solely in the context of "Romantic organicism," therefore. True, in writing *Biographia Literaria*, where the associationism of Hartley and Priestley emerged as the main antagonist of a true theory of Imagination, Coleridge saw that it was essential to establish a sound basis in *psychology* for the existence of this "*co-adunating* Faculty," and he found this basis, as McFarland has shown, in the psychological enquiries of Johann Nicolas Tetens. Tetens had argued that the mental power of representation (*Vorstellungskraft*) included, besides the power of perception (*Perceptionsvermögen*) and that of reproducing long-stored sensations at will (*Phantasie*), a third power, that of creating new images (*Dichtungsvermögen*). This power of spontaneous creation, creation *ex nihilo*, was essential, Tetens suggested, to the poetic genius, and it strongly resembles, of course, Coleridge's Secondary Imagination just as Tetens's *Perceptionsvermögen* resembles the Primary Imagination and his *Phantasie* recalls Coleridge's Fancy.[17] Coleridge's use of Tetens is significant, however, not as just another piece of ammunition for those who would see him as no more than a floundering plagiarist, but as demonstrating that he was determined to harmonize his experiences as a reader and author with the most recent advances in scientific thought. For this reason, he "could hardly fail to be attracted by the most scientific and soberly professional psychologist of the German enlightenment."[18] The apodictic manner Coleridge adopted in chapter 13 of *Biographia* conceals his desire not to falsify his mature

17. Thomas McFarland, "The Origin and Significance of Coleridge's Theory of Secondary Imagination," in Geoffrey Hartman, ed., *New Perspectives on Coleridge and Wordsworth*, English Institute Papers (New York: Columbia University Press, 1972), pp. 208–10.

18. McFarland, "Secondary Imagination," p. 216.

understanding of a complex subject. We should not be surprised that Coleridge was indebted to a scientist for an analysis of the imaginative power that he found manifested in the highest degree in the Bible; however much Coleridge's philosophical speculations ran ahead of his theology, or his scientific interests swerved away from his literary interests, his goal was always to bring these varied activities back into one cohesive whole.

Coleridge can, perhaps, be accused of confusing readers of *Biographia Literaria* by providing a Schellingian prolegomenon (chapter 12) to a theistic formulation (chapter 13). The Schellingian chapter, which in a passage transcribed from the *System des transzendentalen Idealismus* asserts roundly that all thought must begin either with the objective (Nature) or with the subjective (Self or Intelligence), seems so resoundingly conclusive that no further argument is possible. We are locked into an ultimately monistic *Weltanschauung*: a view of mind and Nature that treats each as being fully explicable in terms of the other. The examination of Nature leads us inexorably to perceive it as Intelligence, and reflection on Self or Intelligence proves to us that there must exist "things without us," the objective world, or Nature (*BL*, 1: 255–59). The attempt to impose on top of this monism, or to uncover concealed behind it, a theory of imagination that is indissolubly linked with the Judaeo-Christian idea that God is the ground of all things, and exists before all worlds, must be recognized as having misfired. The trichotomous logic used in the opening paragraphs of chapter 13 is as unfamiliar to most modern readers as it must have been to Colerige's contemporaries. Lacking the necessary theological and philosophical clues which would point us away from Schelling and towards Baxter and St. Augustine,[19] we tend to read the whole of chapter 13 as a development from chapter 12, announcing, therefore, a theory of Imagination that is essentially organic (or at least a development of organicism); whereas it is much more in the nature of a gloss.

To view Coleridge's doctrine of Imagination in its proper context, however, it is not necessary to dismiss the Schellingism of chapter 12 as a mere aberration or tactical error. If Coleridge, as McFarland puts it, "was badly off his philosophical form when he wrote the *Biographia*,"[20] it is still important to recognize, as McFarland does, what Coleridge owed to Schelling and to pantheism in general. In the

19. Barfield, *What Coleridge Thought*, pp. 179–93.
20. McFarland, *Pantheist Tradition*, p. 41.

1820s, long after his repudiation of "fundamental errors" in Schelling, he continued to affirm everything that a pantheist would wish to affirm of intelligible Nature and the striving for form, or *Bildungstrieb*. Where Coleridge differed from the pantheist position was in affirming also what the pantheist would deny, namely that the very possibility of knowledge, of "the coincidence of an object with a subject,"[21] the meeting of Nature and Self, must point to the prior existence of a being who is not comprehended *either* in Nature *or* in Intelligence. Schelling's primary error, from which all his other errors sprang, was to make Nature—intelligible Nature—absolute.[22] Nature may suggest to us the operation of a divine Intelligence, but it cannot in itself possess "will," for will can only be the attribute of a personal being. Lucretius and Spinoza nothwithstanding, humankind has believed from the earliest times that Nature owed its existence not merely to chance, nor yet to abstract, impersonal Intelligence, but to the specific creative *act* of a being possessing the attribute of will; to, therefore, a personal God. (As a later Notebook puts it, "the Personality of the Creator, and the Creative Act of the Divine Person were the two fundamental Articles of the primeval Faith.")[23]

The "Ten Theses" of *Biographia Literaria*, chapter 12, then, can be read as Coleridge's reaffirmation of the Schellingian doctrine that the first principle of knowledge must be an identity of a subject with an object; but with the important (if insufficiently clarified) addition that the very possibility of such an identity of subject and object depends upon the existence of a being or spirit—the I AM—who *acts*, in order to achieve self-consciousness or self-contemplation. The "principium commune essendi et cognoscendi" (or "common principle of being and of knowing") subsists, Coleridge states in his ninth thesis, "in a WILL, or primary ACT of self-duplication" (*BL*, 1: 281 and n2). This view of self-consciousness as constituted by an *act*, and Coleridge's "insistence," as Douglas Moffat puts it, "on the bond between self-consciousness and freedom, on the essential freedom of the self-conscious ACT,"[24] prepare the way for the definitions of primary and

21. *BL*, 1: 174; compare Schelling, *Werke*, 3: 339.

22. See James D. Boulger, *Coleridge as Religious Thinker* (New Haven: Yale University Press, 1961), pp. 109–11.

23. Quoted from Notebook 26, f. 42v, by Boulger, p. 167.

24. "Coleridge's Ten Theses: The Plotinian Alternative," *The Wordsworth Circle* 13 (1982): 29. Moffat argues that "For Coleridge, the I AM (Biblical though the term may

secondary Imagination in chapter 13, with their parallel emphasis on freedom—the human creature's freedom as well as the Creator's—as "a ground of philosophy" (*BL*, 1: 280).

If Imagination includes the power to grasp the "living principle" of Nature, it can not be a mere manifestation of that principle. Any competent actor, we assume, can understand the plot of the play he or she is acting in, and even suggest changes in the script, because the actor's mind remains independent of the plot even while—in another sense—participating in it. Coleridge's idea of the secondary, or poetic, Imagination is, therefore, that it *coexists* "with the conscious will." It does not supersede or override the will, nor is its operation dependent on involuntary movements of consciousness, states of dream or trance. The secondary Imagination, as an "echo" of the primary Imagination, which is identical with it "in the *kind* of its agency," derives not from the *anima mundi* or from the impersonal entelechies of Nature but from the distinctly volitional (and therefore personal) "act of creation in the infinite I AM" (*BL*, 1: 304). James Engell points out the similarity between Coleridge's phrase "co-existing with the conscious will" and Kant's term *willkührlich*, which Kant applied to the productive Imagination in his *Menschenkunde oder philosophische Anthropologie*. "By *willkührlich*," Engell observes, "Kant clearly means discretionary, aimed at some end, and not arbitrary or random."[25] A poet in the highest sense, for Kant as for Coleridge, is not a person helpless in the grip of some prophetic frenzy or disordered experience but rather one who can guide the mind's productive power towards the creation of a unified artefact.

It must be emphasized that, far from robbing Imagination of its human characteristics, in this definition Coleridge was rescuing the human character of Imagination from the very present threat of being

---

be), the 'spirit, self, and self-consciousness,' has [the] properties that Plotinus attributes to NOUS," and that "the self-conscious ACT . . . is the Plotinian 'contemplation' for all intents and purposes" (p. 29). I should prefer to say that in his choice of an indisputably biblical term Coleridge may be trying to harmonize both Schelling and Plotinus with his own essentially biblical idea of God, the self, and their relationship one to the other. As Leslie Brisman has it, "the 'primacy' of the primary imagination is the primacy of God" ("Coleridge and the Supernatural," *Studies in Romanticism* 21 [1982]: 127).

25. James Engell, *The Creative Imagination: Enlightenment to Romanticism* (Cambridge, Mass.: Harvard University Press, 1981), p. 136.

swallowed up by the voracious Absolute of pantheism, by denying that it was a merely "natural" function and linking it instead with the God who transcends Nature. Even if we wish to ignore or set aside Coleridge's religious thought and consider him purely as a literary theorist, we have to recognize that in the central statement of his best known theoretical work, he wished to guarantee the distinctively human character of Imagination and could do so only by grounding his definition on the biblical phrase that called back the Jewish prophets and chieftains to the acknowledgment of God's personëity and established Judaic religion as "the reference of an intelligent responsible Will Finite to an Absolute Will."[26] It is, as Geoffrey Hartman has said, ironic, given the clairvoyant nature of English Romanticism as a whole, that in the thirteenth chapter of *Biographia Literaria* Coleridge almost introduced a German-style philosophical criticism into England and that his failure to complete the attempt put the seal on a division between "European" and "Anglo-American" criticism that is even now proving difficult to heal.[27] It may be, however, that there was great strength in Coleridge's weakness. In rescuing his theory of Imagination from the philosophical absolutism of the early 1800s, he may have posted an effective warning against allowing any future absolutisms to encroach on the radical independence of Imagination from man-made systems. Lacking the stern single-mindedness of a Blake, he is nevertheless, in the last analysis, with Blake—and Milton—and against Schelling and Hegel.

What is clear, however, is that to grasp the full scale of Coleridge's idea of Imagination we must look, not at Schelling, but at Coleridge's patient and, in his time, adventurous attempts to understand how the Bible shows "*Imagination*, or the *modifying*, and *co-adunating* Faculty" working within Jewish tradition as an organ of faith, and at how these studies dealt with the difficult question of the "inspiration" of the Bible.

26. Quoted from "MS 'C' " by J. H. Muirhead, *Coleridge as Philosopher* (London: Allen and Unwin, 1930), p. 36.

27. Hartman, *Criticism in the Wilderness* p. 47.

III

Inspiration and Freedom: The "Letters on the Inspiration of the Scriptures"

ALL Coleridge's writing on the Bible, up to and including the "Letters on the Inspiration of the Scriptures," was directed towards the removal of various obstacles the Protestant churches had unwittingly placed between the individual reader and the human witness of Scripture. The main objects of his attack were literalism, the doctrine that the Scriptures do not err, and the more recent perversion of miracle-narratives into "proofs" or "evidences" of the truth of Christianity. First among English thinkers, says Herbert L. Stewart, Coleridge realized the importance of "that most pregnant distinction between saying that Scripture *is* the word of God and that Scripture *contains* the word of God."[1] To demand of Scripture what it could not—simply as words on the page—provide was the frequent error of Protestants, exemplified, Coleridge thought, by Chillingworth's view that "the whole Religion of Protestants not only is in the Bible, but is capable of being demonstrated from it, without assistance of Tradition, or the writings of the Fathers" (*CN* 3743).[2]

It is perhaps too much to claim that Coleridge also overturned by anticipation the radical Hegelian idealism of David Friedrich Strauss's *Das Leben Jesu*; but what is certain is that Coleridge saw very clearly the havoc that idealism of the Schellingian-Hegelian variety would wreak with the human witness of Scripture and made it one of his chief objects to vindicate, before it was too late, his perception that

1. Herbert L. Stewart, "The Place of Coleridge in English Theology," *Harvard Theological Review* 11 (1918): 21.

2. See the helpful discussion of Coleridge's views on the authority of church versus the authority of Scripture in Barth, *Coleridge and Christian Doctrine*, pp. 79–84.

the reader of the Bible is, first and foremost, a human being called into relationship with another human being, not a disembodied intellect addressed by another disembodied intellect.

Early acquaintance with the results of biblical criticism had already convinced Coleridge that any religion built on the straightforward belief that "Scripture *is* the word of God" must collapse as soon as it was exposed to the chill winds blowing from Germany. To appear in its true light as a "scheme of Redemption," Christianity must be based on more than the incessant repetition, even in a devout spirit, of biblical texts (*CN* 3803). In a note that may have been prompted by the occasion of his nephew's matriculation at Oxford, Coleridge wrote that the "great speculative difficulties" involved in the inspiration of the Scriptures "fade into nothing if taken as all religion ought to be practically—thus—if inspired, yet *for* you they are not unless the truth, they contain, enter your understanding & marry with your desires & impulses . . ." (*CN* 3440). From the ordinary Christian's point of view, then, the question of *which* words of the Bible were "inspired" was a question of "vital practical Religion," rather than of a priori demonstration (*CN* 4140).[3] In line with this belief, Coleridge even gave it as his view that instruction in Christian belief should normally *precede* the study of the Bible (*CW*, 5: 607).

In no sense, however, did his principle make the critical investigation of biblical texts illegitimate. Coleridge's own researches into the history and human expressiveness of the Old Testament show in a remarkable degree his capacity for what Herder called *Verstehen*: imaginative comprehension, the ability to enter into the spirit of the text and re-create the thought-world of the original author or authors. He held, for example, that the first two chapters of Genesis could hardly have been intended as a factual account of the making of the world and that to treat them as such was to demolish their value as human testimony by forcing them on to the Procrustean bed of biblical inerrancy. Genesis 1 and Genesis 2:1–4a were, he suggested (working from a hint of William Warburton), a Mosaic hymn, prefixed to the books of Moses by their compiler. Genesis 2:4b–25 was probably "an account of Man's Fall, & Creation translated from Hieroglyphic Column" (*CN* 4325). A second theory, jotted in his copy of Eichhorn's

3. Compare *CN* 3581; and see Stephen Prickett, *Romanticism and Religion: The Tradition of Coleridge and Wordsworth in the Victorian Church* (Cambridge: Cambridge University Press, 1976), p. 52.

Einleitung in das Alte Testament, was that Genesis 1 and 2:1–4a contained "the physical theory of the earth," while Genesis 2:4b–25 and 3 held "the moral or spiritual theory" of Man (*CN* 4325n). Both ideas involved the admission, or claim, that the mythopoeic faculty of the Hebrew people had a part in the composition of Genesis; that it must be received as a work of the human imagination, responding to the profound experience of God's presence in the world, not as a literal account of actual events. The desperate expedients to which literalism was forced in making sense of the Genesis narrative were exploded by Coleridge in a margin annotation to Fascicle 2 of Johann Jahn's *Appendix Hermeneuticae*:

> ως εμοιγε δοκεῖ it is all over with a literal Interpretation, when the Interpreter is forced to play the Interpolator—ex. gr. to choose to assume that Eve had selected the Forbidden Tree ~~for~~ as the shady Bower for her afternoon *Siesta*—fell asleep, and *dreamd* that she saw this, and heard that!! and then that all the aweful Catination of Words and Thoughts from v 11. to v 20. was suggested to Adam and Eve by a peal of Thunder acting on an alarmed conscience—No! if an *historical* interpretation be any way practicable, it must still be as *mythic History*. Adam and Eve must represent together with their Eden, the *first* Race of Mankind—and the primeval State. viz: the horticultural. . . .[4]

The use of miracle narratives as "proofs" or "evidences" of the Christian religion was a pernicious by-product of literalism, introduced by Grotius and particularly represented in England by the writings of William Paley. The obvious deficiencies of this method were seized on by Shelley, in an "Essay on Miracles and Christian Doctrine" (not known to Coleridge, but adopting a line of argument familiar to him from the sceptical tradition of Bayle and Voltaire): Paley's "proofs" of Christian religion involved a circular argument, first asserting that miracles are related in the Bible in order to authenticate the doctrines of Christianity, then claiming that the miracles are known to be true, because the doctrines they support are true.[5] Besides its logical weakness, however, the argument from miracles drew attention away from the *real* matter of the Old Testament nar-

4. Margin note on Johann Jahn, *Appendix Hermeneuticae* (Vienna, 1813–15), Fascicle 2, pp. 215–28; transcribed by James Dykes Campbell and unknown hand, Victoria University Library, Toronto, MS LT 44, fol. 4r.

5. Claude Brew, "A New Shelley Text: Essay on Miracles and Christian Doctrine," *Keats-Shelley Memorial Bulletin* 28 (1977): 24–25.

ratives, the progressive realization among the Hebrew nation that their God was a being who could not be represented in any visible form—"the excitement of the idea of their Creator as a spirit—of an *idea* which they were strictly forbidden to realize to themselves under any *image* . . ." (*Friend,* 1: 501). As Herder had pointed out, wonders and miracles were incidental, not essential, to the Hebrew prophets' vocation. They naturally used what came to hand, whether "miraculous" or not, as "signs," symbolic events, to fix the attention of their people on an important truth; but many other oriental nations could point to similar miracles: "we must interpret prophetick signs and wonders according to the usus loquendi of the East."[6] Coleridge was in agreement with Herder on this point: "the Jew would have contended," he wrote, "that nothing was more likely than that evil Spirits should enable some agent to work miracles," so that building a religion on the evidence of miracles was thoroughly un-Judaic and nowhere authorized in either the Old or the New Testament (*CN* 3897).[7] Hebrew religion, and the religion of Jesus, in all essential respects resisted the natural human desire for ocular proofs of God's agency. The description of visual forms, and attempts to give emblematic forms to the sacred—the prophet's vision of the sacred chariot and the cherubim in Ezekiel 10, for example—were developed comparatively late in Israel's history, as both Coleridge and Herder pointed out.

The aim, the method throughout was, in the first place, to awaken, to cultivate, and to mature the truly *human* in human nature, in and through itself, or as independently as possible of the notices derived from sense, and of the motives that had reference to the sensations; till the time should arrive when the senses themselves might be allowed to present symbols and attestations of truths, learnt previously from deeper and inner sources. Thus the first period of the education of our race was evidently assigned to the cultivation of humanity itself; or of that in man, which of all known embodied creatures he alone possesses, the pure reason, as designed to regulate the will. (*Friend,* 1: 500–501)

The distinctively biblical quality of Coleridge's idea of the Imagi-

6. *Spirit of Hebrew Poetry,* 2:59; *Werke,* 12:53.

7. See Barth, *Coleridge and Christian Doctrine,* pp. 38–39. Coleridge criticized the superstition and ignorance of the Gentile Fathers, and "the general Mania for portents & miracles among the early Christians": "Fly-catchers, No. II (1827)," transcribed in two unknown hands, with notes by Henry Nelson Coleridge and Ernest Hartley Coleridge, Victoria University Library, Toronto, MS BT 30 vol. 2, fol. 31r.

nation derives from this understanding of the Old Testament as true history: not, that is, as a mere sequence of events, but as the raising-up, cultivation, or education of Israel, as one of the parties to a Covenant which was to be fulfilled not in one lifetime, nor in many lifetimes, but only after countless generations. The children of Abraham "died in faith," said the writer of the Epistle to the Hebrews, "not having received the promises, but having seen them afar off, and were persuaded of them, and embraced them, and confessed that they were strangers and pilgrims on the earth" (Hebrews 11:13). The Jewish historian did not merely chronicle events; he traced in them the provident will of Israel's God, or, in other words, treated events as expressive of the divine purpose, the whole meaning of which was of course hidden from them, but which could be progressively understood through an unfolding system of signs or symbols. These symbols were not exactly identical with revealed truth but were those truths adapted for reception by the human mind. (Coleridge used the term "consubstantial" to describe the relationship of the symbols to the corresponding truths, having in mind no doubt the Nicene description of Jesus as "consubstantial" with the Father.)[8] The narratives of the Old Testament, therefore, were to Coleridge "the living *educts* of the Imagination; of that reconciling and mediatory power, which incorporating the Reason in Images of the Sense, and organizing (as it were) the flux of the Senses by the permanence and self-circling energies of the Reason, gives birth to a system of symbols, harmonious in themselves, and consubstantial with the truths, of which they are the *conductors*" (*LS*, p 29).

Whether or not this represents, as James Boulger has argued, a transitional stage in Coleridge's thinking, "the high-water mark of Coleridge's transcendentalism," we can agree that it differs considerably from those versions of Coleridgean Imagination that, focusing on the *Biographia*, would place it in the context of "Romantic organicism." This definition credits the Imagination with the power to grasp the processes of history, as well as those of *natura naturans*, and to infuse hope regarding the ultimate destination of humankind, in place of a spirit of satirical pessimism (*C&S*, p. 32). Boulger, however, finds the passage tainted with a monism that is alien to Coleridge's essential religious outlook and alleges that it gives too exalted a role to "the

8. J. Robert Barth, S.J., *The Symbolic Imagination: Coleridge and the Romantic Tradition* (Princeton, N.J.: Princeton University Press, 1977), p. 11.

myth-making powers of man," which was corrected in Coleridge's later work.[9] Yet another commentator, Paul de Man, accuses Coleridge of dualism, or what he calls "ontological bad faith," in that Coleridge would not permit the symbols to be a purely human product, but grounded them in the transcendent.[10] The truth surely is that Coleridge tried here to define the Imagination, the "mediatory power," as a power which was fully human and yet at the same time was the channel of God's communication to humankind. The symbols this Imagination created were the "*conductors*" of eternal truths (so presumably not identical with them) and yet were "consubstantial" with those truths.

This apparent conflict in logic can be solved only by pointing to Coleridge's now fundamentally Trinitarian beliefs as the unstated premise of the definition. Trinitarianism, after all, is in one sense a way of attempting to understand how it is that God can be both unchanging—an "Ipseity," in Coleridge's term—and yet present in history, an "Alterity," the Word which is fully realized and incarnate, according to St. John's Gospel, in the person of Christ. Imagination can be seen as a mediatory power in the same sense as that in which St. John sees Christ as mediator. The second person of the Trinity is more than just God's messenger. He is God made present to human apprehension in human form. Similarly, as Leslie Brisman has pointed out, Imagination is "the medium between the supernatural and natural faculties," between supernatural Reason and natural Understanding, and yet is also "entitled to be called itself supernatural."[11] Coleridge did not assert with Blake that "the divine body of the Saviour" *was* "the Human Imagination."[12] He did, however, establish a relationship between Imagination and Reason which was *analogous* to that between the Son (Alterity) and the Father (Ipseity): that of "separative projection," by which eternal truth was incarnate (or "incorporate") in the temporal and yet remained itself and unchanged ("the Imagination . . . *incorporating* the Reason in Images of the Sense").[13] The Imagination remained fully human, therefore, but was the means by which Reason made itself accessible to human apprehension; and "inspira-

9. Boulger, *Coleridge as Religious Thinker*, pp. 106, 110–11.

10. Paul de Man, "The Rhetoric of Temporality," in Charles S. Singleton, ed., *Intepretation: Theory and Practice* (Baltimore: Johns Hopkins Press, 1969), p. 194.

11. Brisman, "Coleridge and the Supernatural," p. 126, note 5.

12. David V. Erdman, ed., *The Notebook of William Blake: A Photographic and Typographic Facsimile* rev. ed. (n.p.: Readex Books, 1977), pp. N69–N70.

13. Barfield, *What Coleridge Thought*, p. 147.

tion" became in this formulation the intercourse or community between Reason and Imagination. (Brisman suggests a somewhat less rigid Trinitarian parallel, in that he prefers to identify Imagination with the third rather than with the second person of the Trinity, and continues: "Imagination, the Son and the Holy Ghost are sometimes apprehended as mediators, at other times taken to be at one with the higher term" [p. 126, n. 5]). In this way the Old Testament duality (or "binitarianism") of God and the Logos, or God and his first creation, Wisdom (which in some interpretations of Proverbs 8:22–23 is seen as the consort of God, sharing his throne and participating in the mystery of creation), prefigured the New Testament Holy Trinity of Father, Son, and Holy Spirit. The passage does not rule out inspiration of a different kind—direct revelation from God—but is mainly concerned to set out a "philosophical" view of the Old Testament narratives as containing the Word of God, in a form that prefigured and required the New Testament revelation of the Word become flesh.

It was in New Testament studies, however, that the need for a readjustment of the understanding of scriptural authority had become most acute in Coleridge's time, and it was just here, of course, that the findings of biblical criticism were most liable to be accused of impiety, for they tended to throw doubt on the credibility of the acts and utterances attributed to Jesus.

In an attempt to salvage the idea of inspiration as somehow guaranteeing the truth of the New Testament, theologians had argued that inspiration may have had a twofold nature. First, the "matter" that was to be recorded was communicated to the scriptural writers (the "inspiration of suggestion"); then, in order to prevent the scriptural writers from "material error," they were guided in their work by the Holy Spirit (the "inspiration of superintendency"). But, as Connop Thirlwall pointed out in his lucid and—for England—remarkably advanced introduction to his translation of Scheiermacher's *Critical Essay on the Gospel of St. Luke*, it was hardly possible to argue that the writers of Scripture were prevented from what he called "inadvertencies," quite apart from the difficulty of deciding a priori which passages showed the higher and which the lesser degree of inspiration.[14] Many inconsistencies between the four Gospels had been pointed out by Eichhorn, Schleiermacher, and others. In John's Gospel,

14. Thirlwall, introduction to Schleiermacher, *Critical Essay*, pp. xii–xvii.

Jesus declared himself to be the Messiah at the beginning of his ministry (John 1:35–41), while in the three synoptic Gospels, this centrally important claim was not made until much later, and even then was treated as a secret not to be publicly revealed (Mark 8:29–30). The Gospel of St. John placed Jesus' ministry chiefly in Jerusalem, the synoptics in Galilee. Only Mark mentioned a specific occasion on which the Twelve were ordained as Apostles (3:14); there was no such formal appointment of the Twelve in the other three Gospels. The accounts given by Matthew and John of the events following the crucifixion were so different that it was evident they could not *both* be based on eye-witness reports. There were many scarcely less significant differences between the three synoptic Gospels, especially between the descriptions of the circumstances of Jesus' birth in Matthew and in Luke. St. Luke has it that before the birth of Jesus, Mary and Joseph lived at Nazareth, in the province of Galilee (Luke 1:26, 2:39); Matthew took the province of Judaea to have been the normal place of Joseph's residence (Matthew 2:1, 2:22–23). Mary's three-months' stay at the house of her cousin Elizabeth after the Annunciation (Luke 1:56) was difficult to reconcile with Matthew 1:18–25, in which it was Joseph who was told of the divine origin of Mary's child, while there was no indication that Mary herself knew of it.[15]

Not every critic accepted the radical solution offered by Eichhorn in his *Einleitung in das Neue Testament* (1804). He argued that the synoptic Gospels, though assembled in something resembling their present form by A.D. 100, suffered a long period of obscurity and did not come into ecclesiastical use until after the end of the second century. This, of course, would put them well past the period during which the Apostles of Jesus could have written them or exercised personal editorial control over their contents. To account for the close similarities between certain sections of the three Gospels, particularly their record of the sayings of Jesus, Eichhorn suggested that an original Aramaic document existed, an *Ur-Evangelium*, in which a bare outline of Jesus' life and collections of his sayings were set down. (In the second edition of the *Einleitung* (1820), Eichhorn revised this original proposal and suggested no fewer than four Aramaic *Ur-Evangelia*, one of which supplied the materials for Matthew and part of Mark, another for Luke and part of Matthew, yet another for the remainder

15. The difficulties over Joseph's place of residence and Mary's visit to her cousin are pointed out by Schleiermacher: *Critical Essay*, pp. 45–46, 48.

of Mark, and a fourth for Mark and part of Luke.)[16] There was much disagreement with Eichhorn's hypotheses, yet he set the ground of critical debate for his generation. As Schleiermacher pointed out in the preface to his essay on Luke, it was now necessary to recognize the work of the Holy Spirit not only in those who were witnesses to the events of Jesus' life, but also in the person who collected, marshalled, and digested the various reports, and who may not have been (indeed was unlikely to have been) one of the Twelve.[17] To Schleiermacher, it seemed much more likely that several circumstantial memorials of Jesus— ἀπομνημόνεῦματα —were in circulation before the Gospels came to be written than that a single, brief narrative should have been drawn up.[18]

Schleiermacher's own method was to analyse the Gospel of St. Luke into sections, shorter narratives that showed some evidence of having had an independent existence before being incorporated into the Gospel itself. In Luke 2:1–20—the story of the shepherds—he saw a traditionary legend that was rescued from oblivion only after Jesus had become widely known as a prophet and healer.[19] Luke 4:31–44, 5:1–11, 5:12–16, and 5:17–26 (accounts of miracles), and Luke 5:27–39, 6:1–11, 6:12–7:10 (accounts of speeches), each appeared to have been collected by a different compiler.[20]

Yet this did not mean that the Gospels were deprived of a unifying principle. They were united, Schleiermacher argued, by "the spirit of Christianity recognizing its own work," that is to say, by the single *purpose* of the finished narrative rather than by its having had one and only one author.[21]

The results of the work of Eichhorn and Schleiermacher, Coleridge saw, would be in no sense detrimental to Christian faith and would even strengthen it, provided it was recognized that not every part of

16. See S. L. Greenslade, ed., *The Cambridge History of the Bible: The West from the Reformation to the Present Day* (Cambridge: Cambridge University Press, 1963), p. 273; Albert Schweitzer, *The Quest of the Historical Jesus: A Critical Study of its Progress from Reimarus to Wrede*, trans. W. Montgomery, 2nd ed. (London: A. and C. Black, 1922), p. 89; and Thirlwall, introduction to Schleiermacher, *Critical Essay*, pp. xlii–xliv, lxxxiii.

17. *Critical Essay*, p. v. Northrop Frye refers to this argument in general terms (*The Great Code*, p. 203) but does not, I think, give it the respect it deserves.

18. *Critical Essay*, p. 10.

19. *Critical Essay*, pp. 31–35.

20. *Critical Essay*, pp. 68–69.

21. *Critical Essay*, p. v.

the Gospel narratives could be treated, or was originally intended, as imparting "sober History." There was no threat to essential Christian doctrine in regarding such stories as those of the wonderful portents heralding Christ's birth, and of the Temptation in the Wilderness, as poetic or parabolic narratives, not meant to be interpreted literally. Apostolic teaching—the teaching of St. Paul and St. John—was confined to the sayings, parables, miracles, and sufferings of Jesus. Coleridge was quite prepared to accept the substance of Eichhorn's hypothesis that the four canonical Gospels were preceded by some kind of *Ur-Evangelium*. The preaching of the Apostles might well have been taken down by interpreters or amanuenses, and there was scriptural precedent (in Jeremiah 36:18) for a prophet authorizing the noting down of his words by an amanuensis. Only an extremely rigid adherent of the doctrine of verbal inspiration would deny that the resulting written records had an authority equal to anything the prophet had written himself.[22]

The positive good that such a new understanding might do would be immense, for it would immediately make obsolete the old supposition that the task of establishing Christianity was left to the Apostles alone. It would turn the attention of Protestants away from their superstitious veneration for the letter of the New Testament and instil more awareness of the spirit that animated the whole of the early church. As long as Protestants clung to the idea of verbal inspiration as the only guarantee of the Bible's authority, however, such a change would remain a forlorn hope.

> Alas! the narrow view of Christianity kept up mainly by the mistaken notion of *Inspiration*, and *inspired* writings i.e writings dictated by a supernatural Informant, as if the 12 Apostles had the whole work of establishing Christianity. . . . In this respect even the Romish Faith in Christ ever present in the Church, as a living power having authority according to the occasions and circumstances has great advantages over the Protestant scheme as too generally taught.[23]

If it could be accepted, without damage to Christian belief, that the synoptic Gospels were redactions of several earlier narratives, there was still room for debate about the manner in which the evangelical

22. See "Fly-catchers, No. III," Victoria University Library, Toronto, MS BT 30 vol. 3, fols. 9–13; and MS BT 30 vol. 2, fol. 7r.

23. Victoria University Library MS BT 30 vol. 6, fol. 2r. Compare *CW*, 5: 605–6.

materials were brought together. What was the unifying principle? Schleiermacher seemed to go too far towards treating St. Luke's Gospel as a mere anthology of anecdotes. The collecting of historical and biographical information about Jesus for its own sake was not the aim: rather, the aim had always been the propagation and vindication of the claim that Jesus was Messiah. In a margin note written in Thirlwall's translation of Schleiermacher, Coleridge argued:

> If I am right (and I am persuaded, that I am) in my premise, that the first Discourses of the Apostles, whether held in the ordinary Synagogues or the Assemblages of Jews & Jewish Converts consisted mainly in the collation of Passages from the Old Testament which the Jewish Church had before the Birth of Christ agreed to interpret of the Messiah, with the gradual addition of other passages in which the Apostles themselves discovered ~~a~~ ‹this› prophetic Bearing ~~on Christ~~—the collation of these with the Acts and incidents of the Life of Christ, each with each, yet so that all converged and found a focal fulfiment in Jesus, Schleiermacher's theory of a multitude of detached unconnected Narratives must appear alike improbable and unnecessary.[24]

Schleiermacher committed a far more serious error, however, when he hinted that the evangelists themselves may have been incapable of distinguishing between what was fact and what fiction and that Luke and Matthew both personally sanctioned the incorporation into their Gospels of purely fictive passages. Though far short of the thoroughgoing mythological speculations of a Strauss, this suggestion aroused Coleridge's indignation:

> These Imaginations of Schleiermacher poison the very sources of the Christian Religion. While he represents the Eye-witnesses, the chosen Apostles & Preachers of the Faith, the only competent Recorders of the Actions and Doctrines of Christ, as men capable of blending Facts & Fictions, without leaving any clue to the Labyrinth. I dare affirm, that it is impossible—. One or the other of three cases must be supposed. Either all is fiction; or all is fact; or the former is not apostolic.[25]

Coleridge the exegete and Coleridge and literary critic were here at one. Later mythological accretions around a core of factual narrative were one thing, but the detection of a *blend* of fact and fiction in the

24. Margin note in Schleiermacher, *Critical Essay*, in British Library, London, shelfmark C. 126.h.9, pp. cxvi–cxvii.

25. Margin note in *Critical Essay*, pp. 52–53.

original narratives supposedly written by the Apostles themselves, or at least taken down from the Apostles' own lips, was quite another. Coleridge was again insisting on the recognition of a human experience that remained to be uncovered beneath the accretions of later times. He insisted that the human integrity of the Gospel's originators be respected and firmly held that part of this human integrity must have been the wit to discriminate between events at which they themselves were present and events—possibly fictitious ones—narrated by others. Though Coleridge went a long way with the mythological school of biblical criticism, recognizing with them that—as he remarked of his own Ancient Mariner—"every human being who . . . has at any time believed himself under supernatural agency" takes the phenomena excited by the experience to be "real" (*BL*, 2: 6), he resisted the final plunge into the Straussian world where every statement made by the evangelists may potentially, till it is proved otherwise, possess "some admixture of the mythical."[26] To argue that Luke adopted "hearsays" and treated them in exactly the same way as events he himself had witnessed—that he would pick up any invention, no matter how fantastic, and throw it into the narrative to impress the gullible—contradicted Coleridge's sense of the human reality of the third evangelist.[27] It was for just this reason Coleridge was convinced that the "Christopaedia," the story of Jesus' miraculous conception, birth, and childhood in Luke 1 and 2, must have been a later unapostolic interpolation.

Those who demanded as a test of Christian belief the unquestioning acceptance of such passages as having equal authority, on the level of factual accuracy, with all other parts of the Bible, were as guilty of ignoring this human reality as the extremest sceptic. Coleridge's position was equidistant from that of the sceptics, rejecting all of the Bible because parts of it were evidently mythical, and from that of the bibliolaters, who would accept every statement in the Bible, from the first words of Genesis to the last of Revelation, as equally true and possessing the same kind of truth.

Coleridge's position might seem to some, who were neither nec-

26. David Friedrich Strauss, *The Life of Jesus, Critically Examined*, trans. from the 4th German ed. [by George Eliot], 3 vols. (London: Chapman, Brothers, 1846), 1: ix–x. (Strauss's German original speaks of his intention to take each part of the Gospel narrative "alles in ihr kritisch darauf angesehen, ob es nicht Mythisches an sich habe": *Dans Leben Jesu, Kritisch Bearbeitet*, 2 vols. (Tübingen: C. F. Osiander, 1840), 1: iv.)

27. Margin note on Schleiermacher, *Critical Essay*, pp. 66–67.

essarily sceptics nor bibliolaters, to take away all authority whatsoever from the Bible and introduce a dangerously subjective element into Christian apologetics. By admitting that the Bible was not unequivocally, literally true, had he not given up the only ground for asserting the truth of the Christian religion itself?

The basis of Coleridge's answer to this charge can be found in the note written for the benefit of a possibly imaginary nephew, in which Coleridge suggested that as far as practical religion was concerned, the question was not whether or in what sense the Bible as a whole was inspired, but whether the truth contained in this or that passage could "enter your understanding & marry with your desires & impulses" (*CN* 3440). Any passage of which this could be said was "inspired" for the reader, in the only sense really relevant to ordinary Christian faith. Its language would come to the reader not as a "supernatural" language but in the highest sense as human language, speaking of experiences which any human being is capable of sharing. With Paul—speaking to the people of Lystra, who wanted to sacrifice bulls to Barnabas and himself as to the incarnate forms of Zeus and Hermes—it says "We also are men, of like nature with you" (Acts 14:15). If this is subjectivity, it is so only in the sense in which every human statement is subjectivity, or belongs to the human world rather than to the supposedly objective world of phenomena.

A margin note that Coleridge wrote in the anonymous 1817 work *Eternal Punishment Proved to Be Not Suffering, but Privation* makes a similar point: "Every Book worthy of being read at all must be read in and by the same Spirit, as that by which it was written. Who does not do this, reads a Sun Dial by moonshine."[28] In the two works which were to be the *summa* of his theological and philosophical endeavours, the "Opus Magnum" and the "Opus Maximum," Coleridge stressed that Scripture in itself was not and could not be the all-sufficient *ground* of Christian belief. It was the main beam of the building, but not its foundation.[29] That foundation was to be looked for in Reason, ex-

28. Margin note in *Eternal Punishment Proved to Be Not Suffering, but Privation* (London: J. Hatchard, 1817), in British Library, London, shelfmark C.126.g.3, p. xi. Quoted in Edward Kessler, *Coleridge's Metaphors of Being* (Princeton, N.J.: Princeton University Press, 1979), p. 10.

29. "Opus Magnum," Victoria University Library, Toronto, S MS 28, first notebook, fol. 11. (Note: This manuscript consists of three parts: a notebook made by folding six sheets together, not sewn, the first page headed "A"; an "account book," sewn and with a cardboard cover, the first page headed "10"; and a notebook of three gatherings, originally sewn and glued but now split, the first page headed "18." My designation of

perienced first in the individual mind as the awakening of conscience, or the knowledge of a responsible individual will. Will, or "the *power* of *originating* a *state*," was not to be confused with instinct nor seen as an aggregate of several attributes, but set apart as *ens simplicissimum*, something that has to be experienced rather than explained.[30] This first experience of Reason was supported and confirmed by reflection on our own capacities and on the organization exhibited by the world around us. Religion, considered subjectively, was therefore "an energy operating in the individual soul."[31]

This approach, Coleridge held, was the only possible one given the demonstrable "chasms" and "uncertainties" of historical, or "outward," testimony.[32] Proofs of the "authenticity" of the Scriptures—their historical provenance, as established by the researches of scholars—could demonstrate no more than the mere chronology of the doctrines contained in them. If Christians were to avoid the *petitio principii* of basing the authenticity of the Scriptures on the truth of the doctrines they contained, and the truth of those doctrines on the authenticity of the Scriptures, they had to give, in the first instance, "proofs or presumptions at least of the circumstances and characters of the Writers drawn from other sources than the Writings themselves."[33] The conformity of Christian doctrine, as represented in the New Testament, to the universal human experience of Reason was proof presumptive of the Scripture writers' veracity. Scripture was thus finally authenticated by, and drew its authority from,

> the absence of self-contradiction and of whatsoever contradicts the self-evidence of *Reason* ~~and~~ or the imperative Laws "written in the *Heart*" of Man, as the main contra-distinguishing mark of our Humanity; and vice versâ, the excellent fitness of the Credenda to those excellent ends, the *Idea* of which, inherent in the Reason, is brought into consciousness and bears witness to

---

the six unsewn sheets as "first notebook" is for convenience only, and reflects a judgment that the material in these pages is introductory in character. The text of the "first notebook" does not seem to be continuous with that of the "account book," although that of the "account book" *is* apparently continuous with that of the three-gathering notebook.)

30. "Opus Maximum," Victoria University Library, Toronto, S MS 19, vol. 1 (Say MS 3), fols. 23–26.

31. Victoria University Library S MS 29, vol. 2 (Say MS 2), fol. 132v.

32. Victoria University Library S MS 29, vol. 1 (Say MS 3), fol. 21.

33. "Opus Magnum," first notebook, fol. 6v.

the co-incidence ~~of the doctrines~~ ‹and correspondency› of the doctrines, in the moment ~~that the Conscience~~, ‹~~awakened from without~~› ~~prescribes their realization~~ that, the latter having been once intelligibly announced, the Conscience, awakened from without or from within, prescribes their realization as the Maxim (= regula *Maxima*) or uppermost Rule of [illegible word deleted] ‹will› and [illegible word deleted] Deed.[34]

Coleridge was here speaking of the New Testament only, but he believed that the same principle could by extension apply to the whole Bible, establishing its essential unity (despite the different circumstances surrounding the composition of its many parts) through its "correspondence to the prescript of the pure reason."[35] These are Kantian terms, and Coleridge had evidently learned from Kant's *Die Religion innerhalb der Grenzen der blossen Vernuft* that the unity of the canon—in particular, the claim that the New Testament fulfilled the promises set forth in the Old—could not be saved without an appeal to something that was extrinsic to the actual documents collectively referred to as Scripture.[36]

Of the works published in Coleridge's lifetime, only *Aids to Reflection* offered even a partial explanation of these views, and that work, because of its unorthodox interpretation of the meaning of Atonement, was criticized as heretical, even by some who were otherwise sympathetic to Coleridge.[37] The "Letters" were not published until 1840, when they appeared under the apologetic title *Confessions of an Inquiring Spirit*, and were therefore read, like much else that Coleridge wrote, in isolation, detached from the context in his mature system of thought which was their origin and their justification. Except for J. H. Green, Coleridge's constant companion and amanuensis in his later years, those who read the "Letters" in manuscript—Sterling, Hare, Thomas Arnold—could hardly have been fully aware of their place in the larger scheme of his thought. It was not surprising, there-

34. "Opus Magnum," first notebook, fol. 7v. Coleridge's mature religious views are discussed more fully by Boulger, *Coleridge as Religious Thinker*, pp. 115ff.

35. "Opus Maximum," vol. 2, fol. 23v.

36. See Frei, *Eclipse of Biblical Narrative*, pp. 263–64.

37. Noah Porter, "Coleridge and his American Disciples," *Bibliotheca Sacra* 4 (1847): 117–71, though generally approving of Coleridge's work and influence, criticizes Coleridge's "metaphysical" notion that the spiritual in humankind is identical with the free will and the Reason, citing as an example Coleridge's heterodox interpretation of the meaning of Atonement (*CW*, 1: 309–18; and Porter, pp. 146–49).

fore, that the "Letters" were vilified as containing little more than German infidelity. The *English Review* saw the issue in stark terms:

> The inspiration of Scripture, as the Word of God, is, happily, still firmly believed by the whole Christian world. . . . All Christendom are on one side of the question; while on the other are the Rationalists, and Mystics and Philosophers of Germany, and their followers here and there, in America and England, who are, all of them, in insurrection against the hereditary belief of their own Churches and Communions.
>
> This country has, however, not been exempt from the contagion of infidel doctrines on this vital point.[38]

Even a modern critic as sympathetic to Coleridge as Elinor Shaffer comes close to accusing him of duplicity, of wanting to mine the foundations of Christian belief in order to reinforce the ramparts: "No one had been more successful than Coleridge as an apologist who adopted a wide range of the critics' damaging findings while appearing to fend them off; the *Confessions of an Inquiring Spirit* is a masterpiece of the genre."[39]

The book was not meant, however, to stand alone. It was intended as one of a series of six "Disquisitions," described in a letter of 23 May 1825 to J. A. Hessey (of Taylor and Hessey, the publishers of *Aids*). Coleridge's fanciful title for the series was "The grey-headed Passenger: or Conversations on Ship-board during a voyage to the Mediterranean, supplemental of the AIDS TO Reflection by S. T. Coleridge" (*CL*, 5: 464). The imaginary companion, to whom the disquisitions were to have been addressed, was to have been a young clergyman of "fine intellect" and "generous feelings," who was nevertheless an unreflective adherent of Paley's watered-down and unphilosophical Christianity. The "Letters" would thus form part of a systematic introduction to a new, "philosophical" Christianity that should be "agreeable to the Reason, Moral Being, and all the contra-distinguishing Attributes of Humanity" (*CL*, 5: 465)—in other words, a faith founded on the principle that the Scriptures *contained* the Word of God rather than on the no longer tenable assumption that they *were* the Word of God.

Negatively, the "Letters" were undoubtedly what Herbert L. Stewart

38. Anon., "*Confessions of an Enquiring [sic] Spirit* . . . by Samuel Taylor Coleridge . . ." *The English Review* 12 (June–December 1849), 248–49.

39. Elinor Shaffer, "*Kubla Khan" and The Fall of Jerusalem*, p. 197.

called them: a protest, though an ineffectual one, against literalism and "bibliolatry." As Stewart points out, however, England was hardly ready to listen to such a protest in 1825—or even in 1840. Thirlwall's preface to his translation of Schleiermacher was almost the first competent attempt in English to examine critically the doctrine of verbal inspiration.[40] The great mass of the public continued in virtual ignorance of the whole question until the publication in 1860 of *Essays and Reviews*, which created a storm in the English churches that might well have been avoided if Coleridge's approach had at least been discussed and propagated more widely.[41] Fear of anything that bore the taint of German thought was partly to blame: not until George Eliot began translating Strauss and Feuerbach, in the late 1840s and early 1850s, did the substance of "new" German biblical criticism become at all familiar to the ordinary educated English reader.[42] Yet Coleridge's "Letters" should not be treated merely as an attempt to render German insights palatable to English minds. Where German authors often seemed to make the construction of a philosophical system their primary aim, Coleridge, as the *Athenaeum* quietly pointed out, was much more immediately concerned to affect the way his readers lived, their moral, religious, aesthetic, and political selves, as well as their intellects.[43]

Positively, then, and most simply summarized, the aim of the "Letters" was to show "the place of man's humanity" in scriptural witness.[44] Despite the attacks of the *English Review* and other upholders of orthodoxy, such an aim was not, in Coleridge's view, equivalent to attacking the "authority" of the Scriptures or denying that they offered a record of God's communications with humankind. To understand how certain human beings had tried to give expression, in human language, to the Word of God within them, how their words had been

40. Stewart, "Place of Coleridge in English Theology," pp. 9–10.

41. The extent to which Coleridge's arguments in the "Letters on the Inspiration of the Scriptures" are repeated by J. C. Hare and Thomas Arnold, and later in the century by Benjamin Jowett and Charles Gore, is pointed out by Maurianne Schifreen Adams, "Coleridge and the Victorians: Studies in the Interpretation of Poetry, Scripture, and Myth," Ph.D. diss., Indiana University, 1967, p. 26.

42. See Rosemary Ashton, *The German Idea: Four English Writers and the Reception of German Thought 1800–1860* (Cambridge: Cambridge University Press, 1980), p. 24.

43. Anon., "Coleridge and the Germans. A Dialogue," *Athenaeum*, no. 101 (30 September 1829), p. 613. Adams suggests F. D. Maurice and John Sterling as likely authors of this dialogue: "Coleridge and the Victorians," p. 300.

44. Barth, *Coleridge and Christian Doctrine*, p. 84.

recorded and transmitted to later generations, and how the resulting documents were credited in both the Jewish and the Christian churches with a power that was of divine rather than of human origin—this was no denial of the divinity of Scripture, but rather a new way of affirming its divine power. To claim more, to claim that "all that exists in the sacred volume . . . was—not alone inspired by, that is, composed by men under the actuating influence of, the Holy Spirit, but likewise—dictated by an Infallible Intelligence" (*CW*, 5: 582), was to confer on Scripture an authority nowhere claimed by the Scripture writers themselves and, worse, to "petrify" the living blood of Scripture, to turn it into "a colossal Memnon's head, a hollow passage for a voice" (*CW* 5: 591).

As J. Robert Barth points out, the essence of Coleridge's position for the theologian is in the distinction he draws between inspiration and revelation. Inerrancy can be predicated only of those parts of Scripture that are revealed, as well as inspired: that is, those parts that the author refers to "a direct communication from God" (*CW*, 5: 589).[45] To extrapolate from this to the more general claim that *every word* of Scripture is revealed, or that the Bible is in every part inerrant, is to turn aside from the spirit of the sacred text in a vain attempt to rescue the letter. The claim that Shakespeare was a genius cannot be refuted by quoting a lame line or two from *Henry VI*, part 1. No more can the claim that the Bible contains the Word of God be refuted by pointing to verses 6–20 of Psalm 109 or to historical inaccuracies in chapters 1–6 of the Book of Daniel. David's cruelty to the people of Rabbah (2 Samuel 12:31) does not negate the Christian admonition to do good to them that hate us (Matthew 5:44). To hold that the "letters and articulate sounds" by which the Word of God is "communicated to our human apprehensions" must themselves be divinely communicated (revealed) is "superstitious and unscriptural" (*CW*, 5: 585). "Every sentence found in a canonical Book, rightly interpreted, contains the *dictum* of an infallible Mind;—but what the right interpretation is,—or whether the very words now extant are corrupt or genuine—must be determined by the industry and understanding of fallible, and alas! more or less prejudiced theologians" (*CW*, 5: 602).

The "Letters" opened up, however, an important insight even for those readers who were not concerned with the theological difficulties

45. Barth, *Coleridge and Christian Doctrine*, p. 60.

inherent in the doctrine of scriptural infallibility. This was that the Bible offered an unparalleled series of testimonies from the human spirit *in extremis*: Deborah blessing the defenders of Israel against their oppressors, and cursing the cowards; Job answering in a passionate outburst the hollow truisms of his comforters; John swept up in a vision of the destruction and glory that was to come at the fall of Jerusalem. Without the recognition that their utterances were human expressions arising from deep inner conviction, and not the mechanically dictated words of a "superhuman . . . Ventriloquist," all this would be lost (*CW*, 5: 593). Such an insight, radical enough in Coleridge's day, is now virtually a commonplace of the pulpit and the classroom and hardly needs defending to a modern reader of Coleridge. What is more difficult for a modern reader to accept is the more conservative side of Coleridge's argument: that all utterances that are "referred by the sacred Penman to a direct communication from God," and all those noted down by an amanuensis which a prophet is recorded as having claimed were the Word of God, received directly from a "superhuman Intelligence," must be received as constituting God's revealed Word in the fullest sense (*CW*, 5: 589). Herder's denial of the possibility of direct communication from God to humankind, D. F. Strauss's unequivocal assertion that claims of direct inspiration from God were themselves part of the prevailing *mythos* of biblical times[46]—these are surely much more credible, much more in line with the thought of a post-mythological age, than Coleridge's careful distinction, which appears to us as little more than a timid concession to orthodoxy.

The charge of timidity is an easy one to make, and Coleridge in many respects can be said to have invited it. Before we accept as proven the charge that a disillusioned John Sterling hurled against his mentor, however, let us see what if anything Coleridge might have gained by his "concession"—for it certainly did not save his credit with most orthodox believers in the nineteenth century.

In his marginalia on Schleiermacher, as we have seen, Coleridge insisted that the fictitious or poetic parts of St. Luke's Gospel *must* be unapostolic, because to ascribe them to Luke himself was tantamount to attacking the human integrity of the evangelist, insinuating that he saw no reason to discriminate between deeds of Jesus witnessed by

46. Herder, *Spirit of Hebrew Poetry*, 2:59; *Werke*, 12:53; Strauss, *Life of Jesus*, 1:25; *Das Leben Jesu*, 1:28.

himself and invented tales narrated to him by others. Coleridge in effect drew a line here, beyond which he would not pass in his long journey down the road of the higher criticism. The Gospel of St. Luke, pared of all mythic and poetic accretions—of everything a later age would refer to as *Aberglaube*–was a testimony to one man's experience of Jesus. If that human reality were dissolved into a congeries of traditionary tales, fables, and wishful thinking, the essential function of that Gospel would be destroyed. The reader of that Gospel would no longer be a human being called into relationship with another human being; in place of the human author there would be only a vague somewhat, a cultural milieu, the mythopoeic faculty of a given community at a given point in history.

Just as pantheism and its offshoot, Romantic organicism, threatened to extinguish the human reality of the imaginative power, driving Coleridge to a desperate and apparently inconsistent attempt to guarantee it by grounding it in the transcendent reality of God, so the higher criticism, having first pointed out the human, historical elements in the received texts of Scripture, now seemed about to dissolve it once more, by replacing the human with another dangerous abstraction: a "cultural milieu," a "tendency to mythologize." Worse, even such a sensitive critic and devout Christian as Schleiermacher seemed unaware that by picturing Luke as an entirely passive tool of the myth-making tendency, he was robbing the evangelist of the only guarantee of his integrity, his possession of "an intelligent responsible Will Finite."[47]

The same conviction informed Coleridge's apparent concession in the "Letters." To deny that a prophet could truly claim to have spoken the directly revealed Word of God was to make that prophet less than a fully responsible human being and consign him to the all-smothering power of his "milieu," the prevailing myths of his time. If the nineteenth-century critic could claim to be free of mythology, to have passed into an era where people were motivated not by passively accepted myths but by the freely adopted prescripts of the Reason, how could such a critic deny the same full humanity to the prophets of the Old Testament and the Apostles of the New? And how else could their freedom, their responsibility be guaranteed but by grounding it in transcendence?

Paul de Man, pointing out that the Romantics' tendency to relegate

47. Quoted (from "MS 'C' ") by Muirhead, *Coleridge as Philosopher*, p. 36.

allegory to a position inferior to that of symbol has concealed the fact that for the Romantics *both* figures designated a "transcendental source," has expressed his regret at this "act of ontological bad faith." The problem was related, as he shows, to the problem of providing a stable centre for the self. Wordsworth inclined to "borrow" this needed stability from Nature; Coleridge "borrowed" it from God.[48] Both solutions de Man finds "regressive," a charge that, like the charge of timidity, is easily made; but perhaps we should beware of making it until we are more certain that there is a better answer than Coleridge's to the problem raised by Kant—how to preserve the idea of human freedom. Coleridge followed Schelling until he found that Schelling's system appeared to threaten human freedom at its very core; he followed the higher critics until their conclusions threatened to obliterate his sense of a corresponding free human acknowledgment of the divine in Scripture. Neither Nature or myth could be allowed such dominance over humankind as that. To Wordsworth, Nature was ultimately something that must be overcome; and similarly, Coleridge used myth to assert his freedom from myth, just as Blake had. What may finally be the most important fact about the "Letters" is not that Coleridge adopted the findings of higher criticism while appearing to fend them off, but that, as in the thirteenth chaper of *Biographia Literaria*, he affirmed, in opposition to the evident trend among biblical critics, that human beings are and always have been free to pass beyond their myths and to participate in the eternal act of creation. As a modern theologian, Hans Küng, tellingly puts it, "we misunderstand God if we think we have to protect our freedom from him."[49]

48. De Man, "Rhetoric of Temporality," pp. 177, 181–82, 194.

49. Küng, *On Being a Christian*, p. 312.

IV

The Broad Church, F. D. Maurice, and Coleridge's "Letters on the Inspiration of the Scriptures"

WHEN Coleridge died in 1834 the "Letters on the Inspiration of the Scriptures" were still unpublished, and they remained so until 1840, when Henry Nelson Coleridge brought out his edition of the work. This was the edition which gave the "Letters" their present, rather apologetic name, *Confessions of an Inquiring Spirit*, and in doing so sanctioned the aura of illicit speculation that remained with the work for the rest of the nineteenth century. To the small but noteworthy group of thinkers who read the "Letters" in manuscript they were known simply as "Letters on Inspiration."

The reticence with which even Coleridgeans treated this rather cautious little work was, in part, a defensive measure. The Established Church, except for the more outward-looking party that centred on J. C. Hare, Thomas Arnold, Connop Thirlwall, and others,[1] undoubtedly feared the ecclesiastical instability that would follow (it was felt) from any erosion of the "authority" of the Bible; and it regarded with equal distrust attempts to ground Christian belief on anything other than the literal truth of the Bible—for example, on its "innate reasonableness" or its correspondence with the essential needs and capacities of humankind. The question of biblical "fallibility" acquired even more significance as the Tractarian movement gathered strength. Once historicist criticism had cast doubt on the

1. On the origins of the term "Broad Church" see Owen Chadwick, *The Victorian Church*, 2 vols. (London: Adam and Charles Black, 1966), 1: 544. See also Charles Richard Sanders, *Coleridge and the Broad Church Movement* (Durham, N.C.: Duke University Press, 1942). My judgment that F. D. Maurice is best treated separately from the Broad Church movement (which in any case was never an organized, homogeneous group) is reflected in the title of this chapter.

possibility of a unitary meaning for the Bible, it could be argued that scriptural meaning was once more a matter for private judgment, and—as the Tractarians pointed out—this might be thought to rob any Protestant church of its central principle of cohesion. How could any definite teaching arise from the clash of a multitude of private judgments? As Newman said: "We must determine whether on the one hand Christianity is still to represent to us a definite teaching from above, or whether on the other its utterances have been from time to time so strangely at variance, that we are necessarily thrown back on our own judgment individually to determine, what the revelation of God is, or rather if in fact there is, or has been, any revelation at all."[2] For many Anglican churchmen, therefore, to abandon the doctrine of plenary inspiration was to capitulate to the "Romanizing" tendencies of the Tractarians.

Even before Tractarianism was perceived as a distinct threat to a protestant Established Church, however, Coleridge's "Letters on the Inspiration of the Scriptures," mild as they were, were tainted by the memory of Coleridge's youthful dalliance with various forms of heterodoxy—Necessitarianism, Unitarianism, Spinozism, and his own "Pantisocracy." James Martineau, in an essay first published in 1856, admitted that there was no "Cambridge Theology" in the sense in which there did exist an "Oxford Theology": one could appropriately speak of a theology "formed by Cambridge men," however, and he singled out J. C. Hare and F. D. Maurice as the foremost evangelists of the Coleridgean-Platonic "gospel."[3] But it is instructive, in this connection, to look at the series of letters that passed between Hare and William Whewell, shortly after Coleridge's death. Acting, apparetly, on a suggestion made by John Sterling, Hare proposed setting up a Coleridge Prize at Cambridge University. The prize would be awarded for an essay on the philosophy of Christianity. Hare mentions that he agreed to Sterling's plan from two motives: the wish to see Coleridge's name publicly associated with Christian faith and the wish

2. John Henry Newman, *An Essay on the Development of Christian Doctrine*, 2nd ed. (1878; reprint ed., London: Longmans, Green and Co., 1920), p. 9.

3. James Martineau, *Essays, Reviews and Addresses*, 4 vols. (London and New York: Longmans, Green and Co., 1890–91), 1 (1890): 224. Charles Merivale, a student at Cambridge in the 1830s, reported that "Coleridge and Wordsworth were our principal divinities, and Hare and Thirlwall were regarded as their prophets" (quoted in David Newsome, *Two Classes of Men: Platonism and English Romantic Thought* [London: John Murray, 1974], p. 78).

to show that philosophy and Christianity need not be antagonistic to each other. Whewell was sceptical at first; but persevering in his original objective, Hare drew up a formal proposal which, Whewell cautiously agreed, represented "a more feasible scheme than as [he] had conceived it."[4] A few months later, however, Whewell had to inform Hare that there was no hope of the scheme's being realized: "The V[ice]. C[hancellor]. informs me that the answer to your application to them is that they are not disposed favourably towards such a proposal: and I have both from him and from our Master that the objection is not to any accidental and extraneous part of the scheme, but to the name of Coleridge."[5] Whewell suggests that this antipathy to Coleridge's very name was a result of the "vagaries" of his earlier life, meaning, presumably, his somewhat inglorious career as an undergraduate. It is hard not to conclude, however, that this was partly a peg on which to hang several varieties of distrust—distrust of unorthodox religious views, of German philosophy, and perhaps of metaphysical speculation in general. Yet Christopher Wordsworth (the Master of Trinity College), and the Vice-Chancellor of the University, George Archdall, cannot have been entirely unaware that the Anglican Church, and religious belief in general, were approaching a state of crisis. Even the gradualist views implied by William Whewell's cautious attitude towards Coleridge's "philosophical Christianity" had little attraction for Thomas Arnold, who was well aware at this time that the position of the Established Church seemed weaker almost by the day. Arnold wrote of a "moral crisis" confronting England and a widespread sense of impending change, and in many of his letters suggested that to his eyes England in the 1830s resembled France in the revolutionary period.[6] He wrote to a correspondent in 1832:

4. Trinity College, Cambridge, Add. MS a 215, fol. 36r. Hare's scheme is discussed by G. F. McFarland, "Julius Charles Hare: Coleridge, De Quincey, and German Literature," *Bulletin of the John Rylands Library* 47 (1964–65): 188, and by N. Merrill Distad, *Guessing at Truth: The Life of Julius Charles Hare* (Shepherdstown, W.Va.: The Patmos Press, 1979), pp. 154–55. On religious conservatism in Cambridge during this era see D. A. Winstanley, *Early Victorian Cambridge* (Cambridge: Cambridge University Press, 1955), p. 88, and Martha McMackin Garland, *Cambridge before Darwin: The Idea of a Liberal Education, 1800–1860* (Cambridge: Cambridge University Press, 1980), pp. 15–17, 70–77.

5. Trinity College, Cambridge, Add. MS a 215, fol. 39r.

6. See Arthur Penrhyn Stanley, *The Life and Correspondence of Thomas Arnold, D.D.*, 2 vols. (London: B. Fellowes, 1844), 1: 272, 303.

Phrases which did well enough formerly, now only excite a sneer; it does not do to talk to the operatives about our "pure and apostolical church," and "our glorious constitution," they have no respect for either; but one must take higher ground, and show that our object is not to preserve particular institutions, so much as to uphold eternal principles, which are in great danger of falling into disrepute, because of the vices of the institutions which profess to exemplify them. The Church, as it now stands, no human power can save; my fear is, that, if we do not mind, we shall come to the American fashion, and have no provision made for the teaching Christianity at all.[7]

Aware that they could no longer appeal unequivocally to the Bible as the sole, sufficient defining term of Protestant belief, yet seeing that a "philosophical Christianity" would be considered by churchmen and lay people alike as either heterodox or vapid, young intellectuals like Hare, Arnold, and Sterling expected from Coleridge's "Letters" not merely the last words of a wise and well-read man, but the seeds of a renewed system of belief, and above all a new way of reading the Bible that would not bear the taint of German "infidelity." The "Letters" were, as Sterling well knew, cautious and muted by comparison with what Coleridge felt himself permitted to write in his private notebooks or voice in conversations with his friends. Yet they might provide at least a beginning, some clue which would lead them out of the sterile controversies of the eighteenth-century church. As Frederic Henry Hedge remarked of the Broad Church itself, the "Letters" were both progressive and conservative, "careful of all essential sanctities, careful also of the rights of the mind, of the interests of science, and the 'liberty of prophesying'."[8] Arnold even saw the publication of the "Letters" as an aid towards the rescuing of Christianity from bigotry, the establishment of a new and more exalted faith, above the divisions of sectarian argument. He wrote to Mr. Justice Coleridge on 24 January 1835:

Have you seen your Uncle's "Letters on Inspiration," which I believe are to be published? They are well fitted to break ground in the approaches to that momentous question which involves in it so great a shock to existing notions; the greatest probably, that has ever been given since the discovery of the falsehood of the doctrine of the Pope's infallibility. Yet it must come, and will

7. Stanley, *Life and Correspondence of Arnold*, 1: 319.

8. Frederic Henry Hedge, introduction to Frederick Temple et al., eds., *Essays and Reviews*, 3rd American ed. (New York: Henry Holt and Co., 1874), p. xiii.

end, in spite of the fears and clamours of the weak and bigoted, in the higher exalting and more sure establishing of Christian truth.[9]

John Abraham Heraud, one of Coleridge's most devout and uncritical followers, wrote even more melodramatically in the peroration to his *Philosophical Estimate* (1831) of those ministers of religion and of law who "misunderstanding the symbols of that religion which they pretend to teach, and not at all inquiring into their meaning, . . . continually resist the exercise of reason in matters of faith, and, extinguishing their own, present to their trembling worshippers the sign instead of the thing signified, which is of the essence of idolatry."[10]

Against the literalism and idolatrous blindness of such as these, Coleridge's "Letters" were to be a major weapon. For all their alleged heterodoxy, the tone of the "Letters" was nothing if not reverent, and the spirit of "compromise and reserve" which Coleridge had exercised and which later gave Sterling grounds for bitter criticism of the "Letters" was considered by Arnold to be a strong argument in favour of using them as an advance guard to penetrate the bibliolaters' camp. Indeed, even Hare's extremely pious sister-in-law Maria praised Coleridge's stance:

There are some letters on the inspiration of Scripture which Mr. Sterling lent me, showing strongly the mischief done to many minds by insisting on the *verbal* inspiration of the historical Scriptures, and making a distinction I never saw before between the revealing word that spoke in the law and by the prophets, from the *assisting Spirit* that kept the other sacred writers from all essential error in their narratives; but with all this there is mingled such a deep spiritual feeling of the *depth* of God's word, such beautiful application of it, and sense of its life and spirit, as only one could have who had drunk deep of the well of living water.[11]

Still, the doctrine of verbal inspiration was considered by many to

9. Stanley, *Life and Correspondence of Arnold*, 1: 396. J. C. Hare had made a copy of the "Letters" for Arnold. See McFarland, "Julius Charles Hare," p. 189, and Adams, "Coleridge and the Victorians," pp. 57–58. On the treatment of Coleridge's unpublished work by the Coleridge family, see Coburn, *Experience Into Thought*, pp. 6–8.

10. John Abraham Heraud, *A Philosophical Estimate of the Controversy respecting the Divine Humanity* (London: James Fraser, 1831), p.39.

11. Augustus J. C. Hare, *Memorials of a Quiet Life*, 12th ed., 2 vols. (London: Daldy, Isbister and Co., 1875), 2: 93–94.

be a central part of the structure of Anglican orthodoxy: Arnold in 1827 had compared it to the Roman Catholics' belief in the infallibility of their Church.[12] Even such a theological progressive as J. C. Hare shrank from the idea of a public crusade to overthrow it. When a reviewer challenged Hare to declare himself openly for or against verbal inspiration, Hare circumspectly replied that the reviewer had failed to understand how those dissatisfied with the accepted view might nevertheless "hesitate to bring forward what they feel to be immature and imperfect, nor how they should shrink from the shock it would be to many pious persons, if they were led to doubt the correctness of their notions concerning the plenary inspiration of every word in the Bible."[13] Such a response to a direct challenge seems excessively cautious today, yet there were good reasons why Hare should have been unwilling openly and unequivocally to attack the doctrine of plenary inspiration. First, the precise nature of the Bible's authority had to be debated and redefined. Stephen Prickett has remarked that a significant part of Broad Church thinking about Scripture was that "the Bible is impoverished if it is held to be literally inspired, because such a concentration on the individual words denies the life and unity of the whole."[14] While perfectly true in itself, this statement leaves aside a central concern of Hare's, which was to re-establish the "unity" of the whole Bible on a new and better basis. If plenary inspiration could no longer be appealed to as a kind of guarantee of the unitary meaning of the Bible, some other principle must be substituted, or the scriptural text would dissolve into a mere collection of stories. In Germany, as Hare knew, there were many competing schools of thought on the matter of the "unity" of the scriptural canon. In England, therefore, where the very idea of progressive revelation was quite unfamiliar to the majority of believers, to take away plenary inspiration without at the same time substituting some other principle of biblical interpretation could only be seen as a recipe for Voltairean infidelity. The important task at hand was to educate the public in the "developmental" reading of the Bible, showing that each biblical text speaks according to the beliefs and customs of its time yet still contributes some essential element to the developing

12. Stanley, *Life and Correspondence of Arnold*, 1: 81.

13. Julius Charles Hare, *Thou Shalt Not Bear False Witness Against Thy Neighbour: A Letter to the Editor of the English Review* (London: John W. Parker, 1849), p. 26.

14. Prickett, *Romanticism and Religion*, p. 46.

pattern (Coleridge's "system of symbols") which was the basis from which Christianity emerged. Revelation, that is to say, takes place over historical time.

Hare's attack on bibliolatry in his 1840 sermon *The Mission of the Comforter* was therefore a careful one, and while giving Coleridge the credit that was his due (in the preface to the second edition) he was careful to emphasize the limitations imposed on Coleridge's studies by the fact that his starting-point was "the meagre rationalism of Eichhorn and Bertholdt."[15] Hare stressed the more modern developmentalist argument in treating the unitary nature of the biblical narrative. (Hare was well acquainted with more recent German authorities: indeed it was through Hare that Connop Thirlwall, in 1822, had first become familiar with Schleiermacher's work on the Gospel of St. Luke.)[16] Scripture narrates events that occurred over a wide span of historical time: but from the standpoint of faith, Hare argued, all coheres into one progressive pattern. "Truth in Scripture," he wrote, "is set before us livingly, by examples, by the utterance of principles, in the germ, not by the enunciation of a formal dogmatical system."[17] But once even this concession is made—that the Bible contains principles only "in the germ"—some element of interpretive variability enters the picture, and the stance of the reader towards the text becomes a matter of great, of overwhelming, importance. The function of the apologist for Christian belief changes significantly: whereas before the apologist could expound the sacred text from a position that presupposed the "dogmatical system" and derive such authority as he or she needed more or less directly from the text itself, now he or she must be as much of an educator as a preacher and make the audience aware of some point of reference outside the text (for example, their consciousness of their need for a Saviour) by virtue of which the text becomes meaningful.

From Hare's point of view, of course, it was quite wrong to interpret this change merely as a weakening of spiritual authority. He saw that a false and superstitious veneration of the mere words of a text—and Hare went so far as to demonstrate how misleading some of the

15. Julius Charles Hare, *The Mission of the Comforter: From the Second London Revised Edition* (Boston: Gould and Lincoln, 1854), p. xvi.

16. See J. J. Stewart Perowne, D.D., and Louis Stokes, eds., *Letters Literary and Theological by . . .Connop Thirlwall* (London: Richard Bentley and Son, 1881), p. 74, and Distad, *Guessing at Truth*, pp. 85, 87.

17. *Mission of the Comforter*, p. 248.

translations in the King James Bible were—could now be replaced by a devout reverence for the Word, spiritually understood and received. F. D. Maurice, defending Hare against the charge that he had covertly introduced German scepticism and infidelity into his teaching, wrote that literalism in reading Scripture was not the same thing as reverence for the Word: "All in Germany have been shaken who mistook letters for life; or, to put the thing in another form, who did not believe in a Word of God, but only believed in the evidence that vindicates the authority of certain documents."[18]

With this change in the function of the Christian apologist, however, some form of historical understanding became an essential part of any Broad Churchman's intellectual equipment. F. D. Maurice's *The Kingdom of Christ*, for example, aimed at showing Quakers that the inner light they cherished was only to be found historically realized within the Church of England. Maurice in this way tried to give full recognition to the validity of Quaker tenets but could plead at the same time that they needed to be completed by being realized within a visible, historical Church (*KofC*, 2: 12–15).

The rise in importance of historical thinking among the Broad Church writers is best demonstrated, however, by Thomas Arnold's decision to devote himself to the study of ancient history rather than of sacred scripture. Arnold, contemplating what Price later referred to as "the unripeness of England for a free and unfettered discussion of scriptural Exegesis," decided that he would serve his country better by devoting his time to the study of the history of Rome. Nevertheless, what he did write on biblical interpretation was of great significance. Arnold, Price wrote,

> approached the human side of the Bible in the same real historical spirit, with the same methods, rules, and principles, as he did Thucydides. He recognized in the writers of the Scriptures the use of a human instrument—language; and this he would ascertain and fix, as in any other authors, by the same philological rules. Further too, the Bible presents an assemblage of historical events, it announces an historical religion; and the historical element Arnold judged of historically by the established rules of history. . . .[19]

18. [John Frederick Denison Maurice,] introduction to Julius Charles Hare, *Charges to the Clergy of the Archdeaconry of Lewes* (Cambridge: Macmillan, 1856), p. lvii.

19. B. Price to A. P. Stanley, in Stanley, *Life and Correspondence of Arnold*, 1: 216. On the importance of philology and of historical imagination for the Broad Church see Robert [Otto] Preyer, *Bentham, Coleridge, and the Science of History* (Bochum-Langendreer: Verlag Heinrich Pöppinghaus OHG, 1958), pp. 35–36, and Owen Chad-

Arnold exercised great caution in his own use of scriptural texts and severely criticized those preachers who responded to popular discontent merely by urging—with appeals to scriptural authority—the duty of obedience to worldly powers. Why, he asked, do they not read those parts of the Bible which are "addressed to persons circumstanced most like ourselves"—that is, to those faced with mass poverty and political oppression?[20] For Arnold, clearly, reading the Bible took place not in a spiritual and moral limbo but in a firmly historical, practical, and even political context. The virtue he emphasized in commenting on the study of Scripture was not Hare's ποῦ στῶ, the point of reference provided by a prior leap of faith, but rather historical imagination, the ability to grasp the linguistic and cultural context of each biblical narrative.

Indeed, Arnold expressly advised a young ordinand, T. F. Ellis, to read Scripture not in the light of dogmatic theology but rather with philological and antiquarian works at his elbow.[21] Naturally he assumed that Ellis and those like him would find plenty of correspondences between the situations historically encountered by the Israelites and those faced by Arnold's contemporaries in England. The Old Testament narratives would declare their relevance to the modern Christian provided he or she were equipped with sufficient historical insight. What was more, only Jewish history culminated in the incarnation of a Saviour: and this essential corollary of Old Testament study would be, to Arnold, an impregnable defence against the possible charge that he wished to place Old Testament narratives on the same secular level as Thucydides or Herodotus. For a similar reason, Arnold valued the liturgy of his Church far above its Articles, because liturgy placed the words of the Bible in the kind of context in which they were meant to be understood, whereas the Thirty-Nine Articles expressed truth abstractly. Overemphasizing dogma, he felt, could lead to the American evil: "each man quarrelling with his neighbour for a word."[22]

Arnold's advice to Ellis should not be misinterpreted as saying that the Bible should be read solely for its history, however. In the important *Two Sermons on the Interpretation of Prophecy*, Arnold distinguished be-

---

wick, *From Bossuet to Newman: The Idea of Doctrinal Development* (Cambridge: Cambridge University Press, 1957), p. 85.

20. Stanley, *Life and Correspondence of Arnold*, 1: 283–84, 308.

21. Stanley, *Life and Correspondence of Arnold*, 1: 393.

22. Stanley, *Life and Correspondence of Arnold*, 1: 363.

tween prophecy and history, warning against the popular misconception that a prophecy could be somehow proved wrong if it were not realized in subsequent history. The Jews were, at best, but imperfect representatives of God's cause: human nature itself is imperfect and cannot achieve the perfection envisioned in prophecy, except through Christ. This human limitation affected also the nature of inspired utterance. "The prophet expresses in words certain truths conveyed to his mind; but his mind does not fully embrace them, nor can it; for how can man fully comprehend the mind of God?"[23] The full meaning of prophetic utterance is never present to the mind of the prophet: it remains to be explicated, progressively, through the working-out of subsequent human experience, and in the light of faith. So, in interpreting Judges 5:24, Christians are not asked in the first instance to decide whether these words of Deborah and Barak are inspired; still less, to take the action for which they praise Jael, her murder of Sisera, as a literal model for Christian conduct; they are asked to emulate the "zeal" of the Jewish heroine in their Christian life.[24] Salvation lay not in reverencing the inspired words of Scripture but in applying their spirit to the reform of the believer's own life. As Arnold wrote to W. W. Hull (some years before he read Coleridge's "Letters on the Inspiration of the Scriptures"), the Bible is a guide to conduct only as far as it is addressed to persons whose circumstances resemble our own.[25]

Though prophecy remained, then, in some sense separate from history, in shifting the focus away from dogma and towards historical experience and "conduct" Arnold undoubtedly sanctioned the tendency among his contemporaries to see Biblereading as participation in a historical process rather than as an act having intrinsic and unconditioned spiritual value.[26] In this climate of opinion, it obviously becomes a matter of great importance to establish the history of the Jewish nation on sound scholarly principles. Arnold wrote in these very terms to Baron Bunsen in 1835: "what Wolf and Niebuhr have done for Greece and Rome seems sadly wanted for Judaea."[27] Yet

23. Thomas Arnold, *Two Sermons on the Interpretation of Prophecy* (Oxford: J. H. Parker, 1839), p. 51.

24. Thomas Arnold, *Sermons Chiefly on the Interpretation of Scripture* (London: B. Fellowes, 1845), p. 84.

25. Stanley, *Life and Correspondence of Arnold,* 1: 308.

26. See David J. DeLaura, *Hebrew and Hellene in Victorian England* (Austin and London: University of Texas Press, 1969), p. 8.

27. Stanley, *Life and Correspondence of Arnold,* 1: 406.

Arnold himself had rejected the opportunity to carry on this vital work. Not surprisingly, Sterling, while praising Arnold's clear view of the moral and political evils that beset England, criticized him for narrowing his thought down to a point where it became ineffectual (*E&T*, 1: xxx). Both Sterling and Maurice found the Broad Church position unsatisfactory; but for very different reasons.

It seemed to Frederick Denison Maurice that the liberal, or Broad Church, party wished to preserve the revelation contained in Scripture by diluting and weakening it beyond recognition. "They include all kinds of opinions," he wrote. "But what message have they for the people who do not live upon opinions or care for opinons?"[28] In Maurice's writing, as in Schleiermacher's *Der christliche Glaube* and Coleridge's *Aids to Reflection*, the individual's awareness of an inner need for faith was the starting-point of all religion—preceding even the reading of Scripture. If Arnold's strength was his realization that the Established Church must reform, and reform quickly, if it was to meet the unprecedented demands of a revolutionary new age, and Hare's was his dialectical skill and far-sighted understanding of historical developments, then Maurice's was his conviction that nothing could replace the original tenets of Christian faith and that they would reveal new depths of meaning as they encountered the challenge of the new age. He made no claim to acquaintance with German biblical criticism. Despite his defence of Hare, cited above, he regarded German notions in general as poor food for English stomachs. His religion, like that of the American scholar James Marsh, was rooted in personal experience and not in a merely intellectual assent to certain doctrines; indeed he wrote (in the dedication to the 1842 edition of *The Kingdom of Christ*) that Coleridge's *Aids to Reflection* had delivered him "from a number of philosophical phrases and generalizations, which I believe attach themselves to the truths of the Creed."[29] His

28. Frederick Maurice, ed., *The Life of Frederick Denison Maurice Chiefly Told in His Own Letters*, 4th ed., 2 vols. (London: Macmillan and Co., 1885), 1: 184.

29. [John] Frederick Denison Maurice, *The Kingdom of Christ: or, Hints to a Quaker*, 2nd ed., 2 vols. (London: J. G. F. and J. Rivington, 1842), 1: xv. Compare Maurice, *Life of Maurice*, 1: 511: "In revising my 'Modern Moral Philosophy', which is to be published separately, I can now see how much I lost of simplicity in the study of great living books like the Scriptures, from being addicted to formulas, which my understanding, educated by a much higher one [Coleridge's], supplied." Maurice felt that Coleridge's mind was too addicted to "formulas"—except in *Aids to Reflection*, which for this reason he valued above Coleridge's other works.

strong sense of the human participation in the divine order—he asserted for example that "human relationships are not artificial types of something divine, but are actually the means, and the only means through which man ascends to any knowledge of the divine" (*KofC*, 3: 288)—made it natural for him to stress the human agency by which the Scriptures were communicated to believers, without fearing that this in any way impugned their authority. Like Coleridge, Maurice responded strongly to the scriptural evidence of the divine and the human coming together in a single act or enterprise. Along with this strong belief in the biblical assertions that the divine and the human had, historically, come together went an equally strong belief in the perpetual reality of such coming-together, including its continuation into the present moment. As James Martineau succinctly put it, "States of humanity which we are apt to represent as successive, and to string together as passages of an historical process, [Maurice] treats as always co-existent in all men."[30] It was Maurice's great gift to see in every creed, no matter how remote from his own on a superficial view, and in every human being, an expression of some aspect of God's plan for the world. A "heresy" such as pantheism was not, for Maurice, to be condemned and ignored; nor yet "tolerated" in a flaccid live-and-let-live manner; but answered—that is, shown to be merely the pale imitation or forerunner of a truth much more fully expressed in Christianity.[31] Maurice's maxim was that "you can only combat any prevalent error by seeking for the divine principle of which it is the counterfeit."[32]

Maurice's major work in the field of apologetics, *The Kingdom of Christ*, was not therefore a counterblast against heresies but an attempt to persuade those outside the Church—specifically, Quakers—that only within "Church Christianity" could their spiritual needs be fully satisfied. So far from condemning Quaker principles as un-Christian, he asserted that they were "at the foundation of" Christian institutions (*KofC*, 1: 8). His intense feeling of the closeness of the divine realm to the human, and his respect for spiritual leaders (such as Fox and Barclay) with viewpoints very different from his own, suffuse the work

30. Martineau, *Essays, Reviews and Addresses*, 1: 262.

31. This attitude to other beliefs was the starting point of Maurice's important 1845–46 Boyle Lectures, published as *The Religions of the World and Their Relations to Christianity* (London: John W. Parker, 1847).

32. [John] Frederick Denison Maurice, *What is Revelation? A Series of Sermons on the Epiphany* (Cambridge and London: Macmillan, 1859), p. 44.

with an earnestness that is very different from the loud polemics of some of his contemporaries. He claimed in fact to take Quaker doctrine more seriously than did the Quakers themselves. Yet at the same time, Maurice was concerned to justify the Anglican position, to show the reason for the Anglican way of doing things. On the relationship between the Bible and the creeds used in Anglican liturgy, for example, Maurice was careful not to appear to concede ground to the Tractarians (whom he characteristically referred to as "antiquarian theologians") by saying that the early Church—whose work the creeds were—had superseded Scripture as the Church's chief source of doctrine. He argued instead that a creed was required, not to *replace*, but to *complement* the Bible, to witness to the truth contained in it. Just as the vegetable kingdom is an essential, life-giving part of the world we inhabit, though no one would confuse a vegetable with a human being, so the creeds are a result of the Bible without being in any sense a replacement for it (*KofC*, 2: 27).

In Maurice's adaptation of the developmental argument, even pagan thinkers such as Cicero are shown to have experienced the same conflict between evil and good, darkness and light, as the Jews; but the Jews were given "a brighter and better hope as to its solution" (*KofC*, 1: 23–24). Among all the peoples of antiquity only the Jewish nation became aware, through the divine "education" granted to it, of the human being's need for a Mediator between humankind and God.

> How shall each man feel himself to be a sinner, and yet feel that the body to which he belongs is a pure and holy body? The Jewish mind, educated by its divine law, is itself taught to answer the question; the feeling is awakened in it, of the necessity of a Mediator between it and God . . . ; the yearning in the hearts of men before the coming of Christ was not for a light, since that they had already, but for that to which the light pointed—for a personal manifestation; for some one who should bind men together in one commonwealth, by binding them first to God,—one who should appear as the Head of the race,—to establish a communion between the race and its Father, and by doing that, should bind the members of the race to each other. (*KofC*, 1: 40, 43)

This is the heart of Maurice's theology, as of his Christian socialism: the conviction that "man wants not a *system* but a *polity*" (*KofC*, 3: 331). Convinced, like Coleridge, that no theoretical model of the human community could replace that of the family, he was repelled by the

St. Simonian arguments for setting aside the claims of kinship. His teaching was fundamentally opposed, also, to the transcendentalists' brand of individualism and "Self-Reliance," which arguably owed something to the Quaker doctrine of the Inner Light. Only by entering into the conditions of humanity, and *renouncing* individuality, could a person satisfy the soul's craving for knowledge of a Divine Being. As under the Old Covenant, so under the New, such communion was promised not to each individual but to humankind in community. "Nothing is more characteristic of Maurice," writes a modern historian of the Christian socialist movement, "than the energy with which he combated individualism."[33]

From this standpoint, Maurice could treat much of the debate about the inspiration of Scripture as a technical one, having little immediate bearing on the lives of believers. He explained to his readers that "the object of the Scriptures, and not the manner in which they were delivered, is the point with which we are most directly concerned" (*KofC*, 2: 62). It is perhaps strange, as Maurianne S. Adams has observed, that the 1842 dedication to *The Kingdom of Christ* should have omitted any mention of the "Letters," while *Aids to Reflection, Biographia Literaria, The Friend*, and *Lay Sermons* were warmly praised.[34] Yet if—as Maurice believed—inspiration in the sense of communication with God was possible for the contemporary Christian, through Christ's Church, then it was impossible not to believe that the biblical writers were granted that degree of inspiration which was necessary to achieve its object. What mattered most to Maurice was the clear and coherent purpose revealed in *all* Scripture: not the minute assessment of the precise degree of inspiration vouchsafed to this or that writer. Scripture, Maurice affirmed in an attack on the fundamentalist viewpoint, "is not merely a collection *of texts*, but the exhibition of a grand and coherent scheme, by which God has trained man to the knowledge of his true position, and of Himself" (*KofC*, 1: 49–50).

Similarly, he argued that the desire to know conclusively which books of the Bible were canonical and which were apocryphal arose from a misguided wish to read Scripture as a Koran-like, oracular, entirely supernatural work, neglecting the human character which was essential to it (*KofC*, 2: 29). Accusing the fundamentalists, or

33. Torben Christensen, *Origin and History of Christian Socialism* 1848–54, Acta Theologica Danica, 3 (Aarhus: Universitetsforlaget i Aarhus, 1962), p. 24.

34. Adams, "Coleridge and the Victorians," p. 77.

"biblicists," as he called them, of putting the worship of a book in place of the worship of God, he also impugned the rationalists for making an idol out of our mechanical, judgment-forming powers (powers of the Understanding merely, as Coleridge would have phrased it) (*KofC*, 2: 69). Maurice was opposed, therefore, not to critical study of the Bible as such but only to such criticism as was carried out in a negative and self-sufficient rationalistic spirit. To the question whether we should read the Bible in the same manner as we read Thucydides and Æschylus, Maurice's answer was: "I agree with those authors who say, (none have said it so much as the Germans), that a student who does not humble himself to his author, who does not sit at his feet, who does not wish to learn of him, is good for nothing"(*KofC*, 2: 67).

To Maurice's biblicist readers, such a statement would undoubtedly have seemed to concede far too much ground to the "infidel rationalism" he pretended to oppose. It is important to realize, however, that for Maurice the Bible itself was not the beginning of religion. Like Coleridge, Maurice held that the first basis for all religious belief must be the sense already existing within the individual of religion's "desirableness," although Coleridge stressed more the individual's ability to profit from self-knowledge, while Maurice emphasized the dangers of individualism and the individual's need to enter into community with the universal Church. (Maurice liked to emphasize the lack of exclusiveness practised by the Church of England as opposed to the Roman Catholic and Dissenting churches: his defence of the priesthood, however, was somewhat at odds with this claim of catholicity, as his Dissenting critics did not hesitate to point out.)[35] This sense of religion's desirableness provided the reader of Scripture with the necessary "pre-understanding" without which interpretation was impos-

35. One reviewer used the phrase "priestly arrogance": *Eclectic Review*, ser. 4, 7 (January–June 1840): 153. See also *Eclectic Review*, ser. 5, 2 (July–December 1851): 260–61. A typical comment is the following, from a Unitarian journal: "We greatly prefer therefore when he speaks of Christianity as he receives it immediately from Christ, and of the direct aspects of God and Religion to his own spirit, than when he attempts to make the Church of England the adequate exponent and representative of this his Christianity" ("Maurice: *The Church a Family*," *Prospective Review*, 7 [1851]: 26). John Coulson pertinently contrasts Maurice with Newman: "Maurice is with Coleridge—content to stand within received opinions and institutions, and to respond to the truth they safeguard. Newman moves closer to Bentham by asking of what we accept why it is true, and how we become certain of its truth" (*Newman and the Common Tradition*, p. 81).

sible. Both Maurice and Coleridge agreed that the Bible was not meant to provide a set of opinions or theories about God, nor yet so-called evidences of the truth of Christian doctrine, but an answer to the truth-seeking individual in the form of an account of God's presence in and to successive generations of Jewish men and women. In Maurice's words—which summarize well the essential purport of Coleridge's "Letters"—"the book is most recognized as divine, when it is most felt to be human; the acknowledgment of its being delivered by real men, is at the same time the acknowledgment of its origin from God" (*KofC*, 2: 8). Luther himself, Maurice argued in opposition to Newman, saw the Bible first and foremost as a history, as a book "for men."[36]

Maurice's gift of being able to see in diverse forms of religious belief besides that of his own Church sincere and valuable testimony to the universal sense of the divine, and his willingness to acknowledge that even in "pagan" thinkers the apprehension of the divine is present, not in illusory form, but as a feeling actually called forth by God, earned him the ungrudging admiration of such questioners of orthodoxy as John Sterling.[37] Yet Sterling held also that it was too late to continue reaffirming the doctrines of orthodox Christianity as if they had remained essentially untouched by the progress of biblical criticism; as if the scheme of salvation set forth in the Bible could be completely isolated from the texts in which that scheme was exhibited. Sterling felt that there was considerable pathos in Maurice's noble and, within its limits, learned reaffirmation of Christian doctrine. Like Hare, Maurice had insisted on the principle of interpreting history from a standpoint. In addressing himself to the Quakers in *The Kingdom of Christ*, for instance, Maurice judged himself entitled to take "higher" ground and—on the assumption that it was the Quakers who were blundering about in mists of their own creating, while he compassionately observed their struggles from above—to interpret the Quakers' position and their "difficulties" for them. Given the arguments he wished to use, of course, Maurice could scarcely have done anything else; but Dissenters felt entitled to retort upon Maurice that the Church of England had not always shown itself so understanding

36. [John] Frederick Denison Maurice, *The Epistle to the Hebrews*; *Being the Substance of Three Lectures* (London: J. W. Parker, 1846), p. vii.

37. Maurice's stance is reflected in all his writings, but see especially *Religions of the World*, pp. 255–56; *Theological Essays*, 2nd ed. (1853; reprint ed., London: James Clarke and Co., 1957), p. 21; and *What is Revelation?*, p. 6.

towards those who took a different approach towards Christian truth and that it was quite possible for an honest man to disagree with Maurice's chosen standpoint within the Anglican Church and interpret church history in quite a different light.

Sterling, however, in his private remarks upon Maurice's book, went further.

> Every day the state of thought in England seems madder and madder, and every day the number of minds who seek for truth earnestly comes out on one more violently. Maurice has just published the second edition of his *Kingdom of Christ*. It reads to me like Tauler or T. à Kempis alive in the tomb, hearing the movements of the world, and striving (vainly) to make his devout orthodoxy rhyme with this new world. Yet for nobleness of feeling and dialectic force the Church of England has had for generations nought like it. As an answer to the Germans it is quite impotent.[38]

What qualified Sterling to dismiss so bluntly the work of the best theologian the Church of England had produced for generations? To answer that question we must look at the rapid development Sterling's views underwent during his brief adult life, and in doing so clarify the problems, literary as well as theological, that beset the nineteenth-century believer for whom the plenary inspiration of the Bible was no longer a tenable doctrine. Sterling saw the problem of the inspiration of the Bible as the overwhelming question for the Church in the nineteenth century. To others, especially Hare and Maurice, this preoccupation of Sterling's betrayed the university-bred intellectual and the outsider who (despite his brief spell as curate at Herstmonceux, where his friend Hare was Rector) lacked sufficient firsthand knowledge of the role the Church was called on to play in the social crisis of the time.

Maurice, though a subtle reasoner in his own sphere, disliked being seen as a thinker or an intellectual. He wished to be thought of as a practical man, and for him the overriding need of the time was for a living Church of Christ which would "bind men together in one commonwealth, by binding them first to God." In Maurice's perspective, the debate about the infallibility and inspired character of Scripture was an important one, certainly, but one that should not be separated from the larger question of how the true commonwealth

38. William Coningham, ed., *Sterling's Letters to Coningham*, 3rd ed. (London and Bath: Simpkin, Marshall and Co., R. E. Peach, c. 1872), p. 28.

might be built. Maurice anticipated the modern trend in biblical interpretation towards viewing the Bible as a book that speaks to, and speaks for, a particular community, the Church. In that respect perhaps he "answered the Germans" more fully than Sterling could recognize. Yet we cannot dismiss Sterling's criticisms out of hand. He is a good representative of a class, the Victorian "honest doubter"; at the same time, he stands apart from other doubters in his initially quite close relationship with leaders of the Broad Church movement, in his breadth of reading, and in his capacity for original insights. He read Coleridge's "Letters" in manuscript, copying them for his own use, yet he became, ultimately, dissatisfied with the "progressive-conservative" position they outlined.

Basil Willey, in an influential essay on Coleridge in his *Nineteenth-Century Studies*, has made a very large claim for the "Letters": "Coleridge's literary and spiritual insight placed him upon a point of vantage from which he could overlook the nineteenth century in front of him, and reply in advance to all that the *Zeitgeist* would thereafter bring forward. The standpoint of the *Letters* transcends the level of the later Science-and-Religion controversies, none of which need have arisen had his ground been firmly occupied from the beginning."[39] Willey's claim has some substance, but the *Zeitgeist* brought more than just a debate between religious fundamentalism and scientific enquiry into the origins of the human race. It also brought the beginnings of a far-reaching change in our understanding of the nature of language. Significance, instead of being a quality inherent in things themselves (as it was for Aquinas, for instance), comes to be seen as something bestowed on things by our naming of them. The aim of thought is no longer to mediate an absolute Truth fully or partially apprehended by our finite minds, but to be (in Sterling's phrase) "properly *constructive*." This development, which Sterling glimpsed through his reading in Hegel and in David Friedrich Strauss, would make even the modified view of inspiration advanced by Coleridge difficult or impossible to hold. The meaning of inspired utterance cannot be considered as having been guaranteed by a transcendent order; and the concept of inspiration itself becomes (as for Strauss) part of the mythic underpinning of the Bible, and, in the language of the twentieth century, itself a primary candidate for demythologization.

39. Basil Willey, *Nineteenth-Century Studies* (Harmondsworth: Penguin Books, 1964), p. 48.

V

John Sterling and the Universal Sense of the Divine

DESPITE HIS ASSOCIATION with J. C. Hare, and the fact that Hare was his first biographer, John Sterling demands to be treated separately from the group generally associated with the term "Broad Church," because Sterling's knowledge of biblical criticism increasingly led him towards disillusionment with what he saw as the parochial and irrelevant squabbles of the Victorian Church. He was an intelligent and trenchant critic of the churches, and especially of their refusal to treat German Higher Criticism as anything more than a malevolent attempt to subvert true faith. To Sterling, an eager student of Coleridge and Schleiermacher, such obstinacy appeared a wilful rejection of a much-needed opportunity to bring imaginative verve and spiritual growth back into religious life in England. In a small way, Sterling was one of the group of apologists for a new understanding of spirituality who, as Basil Willey phrases it, "faced obloquy and condemnation" to cure the nineteenth century of its misapprehension that every statement in the Bible must be received as literal truth.[1]

Sterling's career is of interest in another respect, too: the Hellene in him never entirely conquered the Hebrew, so he stands as a fascinating instance of one man's attempt to resolve the contradictions which governed so much of later Victorian writing. He was perhaps too much the child of Romanticism, and of sensibility, to be mentioned in the same breath with Matthew Arnold; yet in his perception of a prophetic impulse or "sense of divinity" in both the Greek and the Hebrew traditions, he can be said to have glimpsed a way of finding

1. Willey, *Nineteenth-Century Studies*, pp. 47–48.

common ground between the two forms of spirituality that is in some respects more attractive than Arnold's more cautious Hellenism.

The argument of this chapter is that if we remove J. C. Hare's memoir and Carlyle's *Life* from their privileged positions as rival but somehow definitive explanations of the meaning of Sterling's life, and recognize that Sterling himself had something to say, we shall at least see the extent to which Sterling tried to make honest, informed choices from among the intellectual paths open to him. Until we treat him as an independent (if minor) thinker, rather than as a mere register of other peoples' influences, we shall never understand the ways in which he both resembled and differed from other "honest doubters" often cited as typical of Victorian religious difficulties; nor why in the end he had to turn to Emerson and Carlyle as the spokesmen of a revolution in spiritual awareness that the churches, so far, had refused to countenance. After the crucial winter of 1836–37, I shall contend, Sterling broke through, not to an anti-religious aestheticism, but to a latitudinarian creed which emphasized the spiritual faculty in all human beings, not just Christians, and recognized the Bible as vivid human testimony to the sense of the divine within us. Before this liberating perception could be more widely received, however, Sterling recognized that the shibboleth of biblical infallibility had to be overthrown.

Previous critical commentary, in treating Sterling far more as an instructive case than as a thinker in his own right, has muffled Sterling's own voice, which, if not nearly as commanding as Carlyle's or Emerson's, is distinctive and sometimes original. Sterling's personal qualities were such that those who knew him could call his character, without embarrassment, beautiful, and his powers of mind were equally admired. J. S. Mill's testimony was warm: no one, he told Sterling, possessed more of the qualities than he, Mill, lacked, than Sterling did. Hare, in his private correspondence, testified to Sterling's simplicity, gentleness, and frankness. Both Thomas and Jane Welsh Carlyle repeatedly assured Sterling of their high regard for him. Yet, in their published biographies of Sterling, Hare and Carlyle were both driven to use what they knew of him to make what were essentially propaganda points. In Hare's memoir what chiefly emerges is the danger that lies in unauthorized speculation and the pursuit of intellectual problems in isolation from a purposeful, practical Christian life; in Carlyle's biography, the irreparable damage that can be done to susceptible minds by the attempt to revive exhausted theological dogma. Sheer jealousy also played its part in creating the distortions that even now make the true significance of Sterling's intellectual career almost inaccessible to us: Carlyle was prompted to write his *Life of Sterling* in part at least by his resentment at the favourable treatment given to Coleridge in Hare's memoir.[2] Few of Sterling's friends outside the church, and none within it, were capable of understanding *why*, let alone *how*, Sterling's literary and theological interests were interwoven, and as a result Sterling has generally been relegated to a footnote in the history of nineteenth-century unbelief. J. A. Stoughton's verdict is representative of the view taken by orthodox churchmen: "He affords a striking example of that state of religious speculation which was setting in before 1830. . . . After a college life at Cambridge of great promise, and a transient, hopeful ministry at Hurstmonceaux [sic], where he assisted his friend Hare, he devoted himself to other than clerical pursuits, lost his hold upon the gospel, got surrounded by thick fogs of doubt, and passed away in early manhood, to the sorrow of his friends."[3] The very fact that such a comment could still be made towards the end of the nineteenth century shows how immense was the opposition to the school of thought Sterling represented, and how little attention some churchmen had paid to Benjamin Jowett's warning: "The Christian religion is in a false position when all the tendencies of knowledge are opposed to it. Such a position . . .

2. For Mill, see Edward Alexander, *Matthew Arnold and John Stuart Mill* (New York and London: Columbia University Press and Routledge and Kegan Paul, 1965), p. 49. The words "simplicity," "gentleness," and "frankness" are used by Hare in a letter of 1 June 1834 to William Whewell: Trinity College, Cambridge, Add. MS a 206, fol. 162. For the Carlyles' opinion, see Alexander Carlyle, ed., *New Letters of Thomas Carlyle*, 2 vols. (London and New York: John Lane, The Bodley Head, 1904), letters 1, 3, 9, etc. For the "propaganda points," see especially John Sterling, *Essays and Tales . . . Collected and Edited, with a Memoir of His Life, By Julius Charles Hare*, 2 vols. (London: John W. Parker, 1848), 1: cxxxv, and Carlyle's *Life of John Sterling*, centenary edition of Carlyle's *Works*, 30 vols. (London: Chapman and Hall, c. 1895), 11: 96. The reluctance with which Hare embarked on the task of publishing Sterling's works is stressed by Distad, *Guessing at Truth*, pp. 174, 176. On Carlyle's attitude to Coleridge's influence, see William Blackburn, "Carlyle and the Composition of *The Life of John Sterling*," *Studies in Philology* 44 (1947): 672–87, and Charles Richard Sanders, "The Background of Carlyle's Portrait of Coleridge in *The Life of John Sterling*," *Bulletin of the John Rylands University Library of Manchester* 55 (1972–73): 443.

3. J. Stoughton, *Religion in England from 1800 to 1850: A History*, 2 vols. (London: Hodder and Stoughton, 1884), 1: 170.

can only end in the withdrawal of the educated classes from the influences of religion."[4]

A more sympathetic sketch of Sterling is given by Hallam Tennyson, in his memoir of Alfred Tennyson, showing Sterling as a radical and ardent Shelleyan in his youth, filled with a desire to overthrow existing institutions, but in later life favouring a more reformist approach through education and political gradualism.[5] The only major study of Sterling to be published this century, Anne Kimball Tuell's *John Sterling: A Representative Victorian*, provides valuable corrections to both Hare's account and Carlyle's, by showing how Hare virtually ignored all the beneficial aspects of Sterling's continuing friendship with the Carlyles, while Carlyle consistently underemphasized Sterling's real engagement with theological issues, which continued long after he ceased to describe himself as the "Reverend" John Sterling. Tuell's account still, however, interprets Sterling's life as exhibiting a conflict between theology and literature, or Christianity and aestheticism, both of them dichotomies which receive no sanction from Sterling himself.[6]

To Owen Chadwick, Sterling exemplifies the confusions that beset unorthodox religious thought in the Victorian period, rather than any consistent attempt to resolve the difficulties of nineteenth-century faith: "He was a man of fervid romantic enthusiasms, passionate now for Coleridge, now for radical democracy, now for Maurice, now for Carlyle."[7] Chadwick treats Sterling's reading of David Friedrich Strauss's *Das Leben Jesu* as an act of no interest in itself, being merely a final, irrevocable step into infidelity, and he completely ignores Sterling's criticism of the Established Church.

The best clue to the meaning of Sterling's career is contained in a defence of Sterling against the misrepresentations of both his biographers published in the *Prospective Review* eight years after Sterling's death. The article was anonymous, but its author is known to have been Francis Newman, brother of John Henry Newman. Francis

4. Benjamin Jowett, "On the Interpretation of Scripture," in Frederick Temple et al., eds., *Essays and Reviews* (London: John W. Parker, 1860), p. 374.

5. [Hallam Tennyson,] *Alfred Lord Tennyson: A Memoir* (London: Macmillan, 1906), pp. 59–60.

6. Anne Kimball Tuell, *John Sterling: A Representative Victorian* (New York: Macmillan, for the Sophie Hart Fund of Wellesley College, 1941), pp. 199–201.

7. Chadwick, *Victorian Church*, 1: 539. Even Peter Allen, in his sensitive study of the Apostles, comments rather patronisingly on Sterling's "emotional instability": *The Cambridge Apostles: The Early Years* (Cambridge: Cambridge University Press, 1978), p. 91.

Newman became friends with Sterling during the last years of the latter's life. He had, as Sterling told Carlyle, "run through many phases of orthodoxy & dissent & seems now on the verge of latitudinarianism—which is the Creed that I profess."[8] In Sterling, Francis Newman saw an unusual and estimable religious sensibility but felt that his friend had allowed greater men, such as Carlyle, to overshadow him. Writing to the American essayist and biographer Moncure Conway on 16 October 1869, Newman told him that Sterling's great fault was that he was always too easily dazzled by those he took to be men of genius, and in particular that Sterling "did not hold himself up firm enough towards Carlyle." In the *Prospective Review* article, however, Newman emphasized those rare qualities of Sterling's that he felt Carlyle had not portrayed adequately in the *Life*. He alleged that Sterling possessed until the end a truly religious sense of wonder, which Coleridge bequeathed to him, but could not remain within the Church, because his intellect rebelled against "Biblical Infallibility."[9]

Francis Newman's judgment is borne out by the fact that in Sterling's correspondence, criticism of the Church almost always occurs in close proximity with discussion of biblical infallibility. The contending parties in the great Victorian religious controversies—the Tractarians, the Evangelicals, the Dissenters, the Broad Church party—all seemed to him to be culpably ignorant of the real question that faced the Church. What was the point of arguing about vestments, the Thirty-Nine Articles, or even the lack of a scriptural basis for infant baptism, if large portions of the Gospel narratives now had to be treated as historically untrustworthy (stories of Jesus's nativity and childhood), legendary (the raising of Lazarus), or compilations from numerous traditionary sources? Writing in 1840 to a young friend who had taken up a post in Sweden, George Webbe Dasent, Sterling said:

> Of English matters I have little or nothing to tell you. That wretched Oxford squabble chatters and yelps on with some increase of animation and absurdity. *Stupidity run mad* is still the motto for both parties. . . . Reasonable men who know that there is a spirit of Christianity which is something more than either

8. John Sterling to Carlyle, 15 August 1839: National Library of Scotland MS 1766, fol. 70v.

9. Donald F. Winslow, "Francis W. Newman's Assessment of John Sterling: Two Letters," *English Language Notes* 11 (1974): 282; [Francis W. Newman,] "John Sterling," *Prospective Review* 8 (1852): 5.

the letter of the Bible or the tenets of one—and especially one very ignorant age such as that of the Early Fathers—must leave these people to fight their own way completely out of, or more deeply into, there [sic] own beloved confusions.[10]

Without regarding himself as having relinquished Christianity, Sterling felt that he had to abandon, even in his overtly Christian writings, the traditional theological vocabulary, which was too closely entwined with a mode of reading the Bible that was no longer defensible. Compromise and reserve had done nothing but harm to the theological endeavours of Coleridge, who could otherwise have made a valuable beginning in weaning the British public away from bibliolatry (*E&T*, 1: cxlii). Even the German critic Neander had fallen prey to a spirit of sectarianism as he tried to adapt traditional theological language to new forms of belief.[11] To Carlyle, Sterling wrote in October 1836:

I hope it is not from diminished Faith or Zeal but I confess I have lately felt more freedom & expansion of mind in the attempt at poetic creation than in any other mental exercize—& I have been trying to clothe in shape & language the Ideas & Feelings which Xianity presupposes or declares without using the terms of Theology. But I am if possible more deeply impressed than ever with the sense of the want of Science & of evangelical strength in England or at least in as much of my own country as I have known.[12]

As Sterling knew Carlyle to be hostile both to the use of poetry as a medium, and to the propagation of the "exhausted" dogmas of Christian theology, Sterling is here somewhat on the defensive, finding it necessary to remind Carlyle how profoundly he disagrees with the views of orthodox churchmen. Towards the end of his life, however, Sterling grew if anything still more critical of the obstinate refusal of churchmen and the universities to tolerate open debate on the subject of biblical infallibility. Their reluctance, as Sterling pointed out to another correspondent, William Coningham, had a political side to it. Like G. H. Lewes, Sterling suspected the Church of putting political interests before the love of truth: "Few things have lately struck me

10. John R. Dasent, ed., *Letters from John Sterling to George Webbe Dasent 1838–1844* (Edinburgh: privately printed 1914), pp. 19–20.

11. Coningham, *Sterling's Letters to Coningham*, p. 23.

12. John Sterling to Carlyle, 1 October 1836: National Library of Scotland MS 1766, fols. 38v–39r.

as more remarkable, than the connexion of causes—the interest of the rich in the Established Church, and that of the clergy in extirpating inquiry, which have as yet, completely excluded from this country all knowledge of controversies, that have really revolutionized the thought of all the rest of Europe."[13] To the same correspondent, a few weeks later, Sterling wrote that he expected the Tractarian dispute to lead to no sudden changes in the constitution of the Established Church. "All parties at the Universities and among the clergy are quite resolved to take no liberties that will eject them from their present comfortable position."[14]

The intellectual journey which led Sterling to criticize so sharply the church into which he had been ordained began in 1827, the year in which he met Coleridge. At Cambridge, Sterling had admired and been influenced by J. C. Hare, Connop Thirlwall, and William Whewell, the three Cambridge men who were most knowledgeable about the progress of biblical criticism in Germany. Even Thirlwall admitted, however, that the deplorable lack of a philosophical spirit in English intellectual life could not simply be filled by the wholesale importation of "German" thought: there was a need for some independent and original English thinker to restore philosophy and theology to their proper role in the English mind.[15] At first, it seemed to Sterling that Coleridge might be this much-needed original thinker. As Sterling told Hare in 1836, his education, in the fullest sense, was owing to Coleridge. From Coleridge, undoubtedly, he derived the view that "the suitableness of the Christian scheme to the higher and better demands of the conscience, and the sanctified reason," not miracles and other external evidences, must be the ground of belief. Like Coleridge in *Aids to Reflection*, Sterling treated Christian belief as a matter of personal knowledge, not logical or other proofs. Though

13. *Letters to Coningham*, pp. 18–19. G. H. Lewes deplored the decline of religion into a mere "profession" in a margin note to his copy of Coleridge's *The Friend* (1837), now in Dr. Williams's Library: see Ashton, *The German Idea*, p. 108.

14. *Letters to Coningham*, p. 20. Writing to Emerson on 28 December 1841, Sterling mentions two great enemies of a more enlightened view of Scripture: ecclesiastical dogmatism, and the "mechanical pedantry of our Monastic Colleges at Oxford and Cambridge": Edward Waldo Emerson, ed., *A Correspondence between John Sterling and Ralph Waldo Emerson* (Boston and New York: Houghton, Mifflin, 1897), p. 47.

15. See Thirlwall's letter to Baron Bunsen, 20 January 1823: Perowne and Stokes, *Letters Literary and Theological*, pp. 65–66.

F. D. Maurice made the fuller public acknowledgement of his debt to Coleridge, Maurice had never summoned the courage actually to meet his great mentor, so for a time Sterling even acted as a kind of mediator between the two men.[16]

In May 1828, the day after his second meeting with Coleridge, Sterling wrote to a clerical friend, James Dunn, that Coleridge had promised to show him some manuscript letters: "They relate to the true meaning of the inspiration of the Scriptures. He says that the first chapter of Genesis is a much later, & more valuable account of the Creation than that which begins at the fourth verse of the 2nd chapter. The latter he says seems to be a description taken from some very ancient γλυφαι."[17] The Reverend Dunn evidently objected that Coleridge was an unreliable guide in such matters, for later (in 1834, during his curacy at Herstmonceux) we find Sterling eagerly defending Coleridge against the charge of heterodoxy: "I think you greatly undervalue my dear & ever honored friend & master Coleridge as a theologian. But perhaps we cannot discuss the matter on fair grounds for I am familiar with his M.S.S. & Conversations which exhibit a far higher degree of Spiritual ~~writing~~ ‹life› than almost anything in his published works."[18] According to Hare, Sterling read the "Letters on the Inspiration of the Scriptures" with delight and made a transcript of them for his own use (*E&T*, 1: cxxix).

It was expected after Coleridge's death, in 1834, that Sterling would publish an edition of the "Letters" together with the essay on the Book of Genesis and an essay on the Creed. Richard Chenevix Trench indeed said that he rather *feared* than *awaited* such an edition.[19] This collection never appeared; J. H. Green had hoped that Sterling and F. D. Maurice would edit Coleridge's theological papers, but they seem never to have begun the work. By the time H. N. Coleridge published the "Letters," in 1840, Sterling had become convinced that their usefulness was severely hampered if not nullified by Coleridge's fear of giving offence to the pious.[20]

16. See *E&T*, 1: xlv–xlvi; *Letters to Coningham*, p. 11; and (on Sterling's role as mediator) Charles Richard Sanders, "Maurice as a Commentator on Coleridge," *PMLA* 53 (1938): 234. (This essay is reprinted as part of *Coleridge and the Broad Church Movement*: pp. 185–200.)

17. National Library of Scotland MS 1765, fols. 95v–96r.

18. National Library of Scotland MS 1766, fol. 28r.

19. Tuell, p. 251.

20. Tuell, p. 264, and see also *E&T*, 1: cxlii.

In March 1836, after being forced by ill health to give up his curacy at Herstmonceux, Sterling planned to write a series of "Discourses on Revelation," one group of which would discuss inspiration, miracles, and prophecy. He was increasingly sceptical, however, about the veracity of the Old Testament narratives of miracles; as he wrote to Hare,

> I will own to you that, the more I go into the Old Testament, the more ground I find for hesitating about the great physical miracles. . . . But I am far from giving the thing up; for it is impossible to overlook the continuity of the faith in a revealed Monotheism among the Jews from Abraham to Christ, or to doubt that scientific enquiry and inward experience bring out more and more the reality and exclusiveness of His claims as the Son of God, and the Redeemer of mankind. (*E&T,* 1: lxi)

The biblical critic who most perfectly combined "scientific enquiry" with "inward experience" at this period was probably Schleiermacher, and it is not surprising to find Sterling, a few months after having written this letter to Hare, enthusiastically praising Schleiermacher's "energy" and "acuteness."[21] Although the letter to Hare referred only to Tholuck—whose *Die Lehre von der Sünde und vom Versöhner* Sterling had translated—and Olshausen, these critics were soon to be displaced in Sterling's estimation by Schleiermacher.

Like Schleiermacher, Sterling emphasized above all the "Jewish colouring" of the Gospels, the fact that in the first instance they were meant not as self-sufficient narratives but as illustrations of the early Christian preachers' claims about Jesus. Schleiermacher's great sensitivity to the inherent logic of narrative forms enabled him to see that such episodes as the Journey of the Magi in Matthew, and the two (differing) accounts of the Temptation in the Wilderness in Matthew and Luke, were not originally parts of one chronological, sequential narrative, but separate narratives in their own right, devised in order to illustrate certain doctrines that the early Christians needed to clarify as their sect grew. Yet though Schleiermacher's reasoning obliged him to classify certain portions of the Gospels as poetic rather than historical—that is, as enhancing their claims for Jesus' divine nature through the insertion of a variety of parabolic, mythic, typological, and devotional materials into the written record of real events that were actually witnessed—it is important to realize that Schleiermacher carried out this task, not in a spirit of rationalistic

21. Tuell, pp. 287–89.

reductionism, but with a high degree of imaginative and spiritual sympathy with the aims of the early church. It was precisely this essential relationship between the synoptic Gospels and the Old Testament that was obscured by the literalists.

The early evangelists had to show that the whole of Jewish history led up to, and required, the coming of the Messiah and that Jesus was that Messiah. So far from its being a mark of dishonesty in them to add poetic episodes to the record of historical events, it was but further proof of their complete conviction that Jesus was the Redeemer promised by the Hebrew prophets. The Gospels were, that is to say, what was demanded by the conditions of their time (and not by eighteenth- or nineteenth-century expectations of historical veracity).

As Sterling pointed out, this not only accounted for the Jewishness of the synoptic Gospels but was its main justification. Had it not been for the Jewish faith, as it developed historically, "the Gospel would have dropt from the clouds like a meteoric stone, instead of rising into view as the purest portion of a vein co-eval with the creation, and of which everything else is but, as it were, the ore or dross" (*E&T*, 1: lxiii). The view that Christ's life on earth took place at a time when both the Hebrew and the Gentile worlds had reached a crisis, and that Christianity was in some sense prepared for by the whole course of previous history, pagan as well as Jewish, was one on which Hare and Sterling could have agreed, without any great straining of either's conscience: indeed, such a developmental argument was a characteristic tool of Broad Church apologetics. (It was Maurice, though, who chiefly challenged this aspect of Broad Church thought from his Platonic standpoint, viewing the successive stages of human "progress" as being *simultaneously* present in all humankind.)[22]

Sterling's immersion in biblical studies had had another effect, however, not quite so reassuring to Hare. In November 1836, Sterling wrote that he no longer wished to publish his work on the Old Testament, as he now found the earlier portions of the Old Testament "too uncertain" to justify professing a faith in them which he could not entertain. In the same letter, he admitted that he could not find

22. A fact pointed out by James Martineau, "Personal Influences on Present Theology," in *Essays, Reviews and Addresses*, 1: 262. (This essay first appeared in the *National Review* 3 (1856): 449–94.) On "development" as a key concept in the work of Hare and Sterling, see Anthony John Harding, "Development and Symbol in the Thought of S. T. Coleridge, J. C. Hare and John Sterling," *Studies in Romanticism* 18 (1979): 29–48.

in Scripture any evidence that Christ or the Apostles sanctioned the setting up of a priestly rule in the Church (*E&T*, 1: xcv–xcviii).

The winter of 1836–37, spent at Floirac, near Bordeaux, saw a further change in Sterling's relationship with the Church, though this should not be taken to imply that he was entirely abandoning theological questions for aesthetic ones.[23] It was certainly true that Sterling's convictions, after the beginning of 1837, increasingly led him beyond the boundary tacitly laid down by his friends in the Church. The essay on Carlyle, published in the *Westminster Review* in 1839, which opened with an outright attack on the shallowness of religious life in England, was undoubtedly a conclusive sign for some that Sterling was completely under the influence of the pagan prophet and had abandoned the Christian camp, although it was often Coleridge rather than Carlyle who was blamed for Sterling's apostasy.[24] Yet Sterling's writings, in this last period of his life, show rather that he was perfectly capable of forming his own judgments on the literature and theology of his nation and that—though Carlyle indeed encouraged him in his reading of German literature, especially of Goethe—his preference for the Germans was in every significant sense a view reached independently of his mentor. Both the Carlyle essay and the later "Characteristics of German Genius" (published in the July 1842 issue of the *Foreign Quarterly Review*) show Sterling beginning to formulate, not an aesthetic as opposed to a theological creed, but a new, more radical theology. What James Martineau noted in Coleridge and Newman as well as in Carlyle—their sense of "the perennial Indwelling of God in Man and in the Universe"[25]—was carried yet further by Sterling and gained additional support from his readings in German literature and biblical criticism. "Existence is itself divine," Sterling wrote in his essay on Carlyle, "and awakens in him who contemplates, a sense of divinity, such as men of old were fain to call prophetic" (*E&T*, 1: 258); and yet this sense was not confined to the chosen prophets of

23. As is suggested by Tuell, p. 290, though she feels that the real crisis was not reached until 1839–1840.

24. See for instance the review of *E&T* (with some works by Baron Bunsen, Augustus Neander, J. C. Hare, and others), written by the Oxford Tractarian William Palmer in the *English Review* 10 (June–December 1848): 399–444 (running title: "On Tendencies towards the Subversion of Faith"); for attribution, see Chadwick, *Victorian Church,* 1: 541. See also the review of *Aids* and other works in the *Eclectic Review*, ser. 5, 1 (January–June 1851): 1–22, especially p. 10.

25. James Martineau, "Personal Influences on Present Theology," *Essays*, 1: 280.

Israel, nor yet to that wider body now calling themselves Christians, but is the heritage of all humankind, even though Christianity (and this is where Sterling begins to diverge from Carlyle) is the highest realization of this truth that has yet come about.

> The gospel, the good tidings of Jesus of Nazareth, not merely have now come to be taken for granted by the many, but are recognised by whosoever is of purest purpose and most comprehensive thought among civilized men, as, on grounds of intelligible reason, of experienced accordance with our deepest cravings, and of unquestionable results in history and in the hearts of men, the most effective word of truth ever communicated to this earth. The countless dreams which have been spun around it, the frauds practised in its name, the carnal battles waged for its spiritual watchwords, the bewildering varieties of schemes, sects, heresies, speculations, laws, rites, customs, crimes, and miseries, which have been joined to it, and have seemed to spring from it, are all but so many proofs of the far-spreading roots which it has struck into the world, and which have twisted themselves among all the fibres that fill the whole soil of human life, and have modified the growth of all its products. The plough, the hammer, and the loom, the Roman laws, the arts of Greece, including among them the alphabet which Greece imported, are not more inextricably bound up with all civilized existence, than the influences, avowed or disguised, of the message published by the Hebrew fishermen. The full and clear power of Christianity rises indeed so far above the heads of any but the fewest, that to most it seems cloudlike amid the clouds. But it works unseen and under many names; and it has victories prepared for it beyond the splendour of its prophetic symbols, tinged as these are with the colours of one period and country; while its spirit will inevitably spread to all, and diffuse itself through every instant of future time. (*E&T*, 1: 261–62)

This passage would have offended most English Christians of Sterling's time—not only because it makes explicit reference to the *Aberglaube* that had accumulated around the authentic Gospel of Jesus ("countless dreams which have been spun around it"), but more especially because it avoids claiming that Christianity has superseded and replaced all other systems of belief. It seems to suggest, indeed, that Christianity will have a wider and wider influence in the world, but only by shedding most of the Hebraic imagery and terminology with which it is suffused ("it has victories prepared for it beyond the splendour of its prophetic symbols, tinged as these are with the colours of one period and country. . ."). This is of a piece with Sterling's announcement, in a letter of 1 October 1836 to Carlyle, of his intention to "clothe in shape & language the Ideas & Feelings which Xianity presupposes or declares without using the terms of Theology." Unlike Carlyle, Sterling believed that the enterprise of theology was worth continuing and that the Christian dispensation was not at an end but at the threshold of a more glorious and much less exclusive era. To the great majority of English believers, however, a Christianity mingled with other forms of belief—even if in a dominant position—was no longer Christianity. In Germany, Sterling argued, there was a freer recognition, at least among intellectuals, of the inevitability of such a process.

It was from this high ground that Sterling turned round to criticize, though sympathetically, his friend. Carlyle in fact recognized the justice of Sterling's criticisms in the *Westminster Review* article, though refusing to give ground—"you are right, and yet I myself am perfectly right too, and know not well how I could find terms to express myself in, less liable to contradiction."[26] Carlyle, Sterling pointed out, was much less generously open to the ideas and beliefs of previous ages than to their great men and famous deeds; he emphasized the spirit in which a belief is held, at the expense of the "quality and amount of truth" contained within it. What has sometimes, misleadingly, been called Sterling's idealism was really an intense awareness of the independent power of ideas, considered apart from their particular expressions through the accidental circumstances of one person's mind and experience: in this respect he was much closer to Coleridge, and to Shelley, than to Carlyle. Carlyle's abhorrence of the abstract had misled him, Sterling felt:

> It is no unfruitful and minute, but a spacious and teeming field of thought, which spreads before us when we begin to inquire, not so much what manner of man was Heraclitus, or Plato, Athanasius, or Luther, or Leibnitz,—as what was the doctrine that each of them taught; what view did it unfold of Nature, Man, and God; how was it linked with what had gone before, and what followed it; and how did the truth of the one mind become moulded by the thoughts of generations, before it passed into the reason of the following sage; and how changed by him did it again go forth to create and burn within the bosoms of its next inheritors? (*E&T*, 1: 281–82)

26. Alexander Carlyle, ed., *Letters of Thomas Carlyle to John Stuart Mill, John Sterling and Robert Browning* (London: T. Fisher Unwin, 1923), p. 224 (letter no. 86: 29 September 1839).

In a related criticism in the same essay, Sterling questioned Carlyle's condemnation of all introspection and interior reflection as a constant "rehearsing the same paltry drama before the same beggarly audience." There is, Sterling admitted, a form of self-examination which is narcissistic and sterile; but this is to be distinguished from that more philosophical form of introspection which goes to produce knowledge—"introspection of a man's being . . . so far as it is the exemplar, and the only one that he can primarily study, of the being of all other men." So far from being analogous to parading ourselves before a cracked looking-glass, such self-interpretation—"when the self is regarded as a product of higher forces"—is the only means by which the sense of our own individuated existence can be connected with our apprehension of the world around us (*E&T*, 1: 326–27). Sterling even gave a prophetic warning of what would be the consequence if Carlyle's precepts were followed to the letter: if the consciousness of humankind were not *more* widely awakened than heretofore, he stressed, the race would inevitably sink back into barbarism. Glancing at the Coleridge of *Aids to Reflection*, whose spirit indeed presided over much of this essay, Sterling continued: "it may be observed, that, of the men who have arisen to public view as thinkers in England during the last twenty years, the one of the most fervid, sincere, far-reaching genius, is also one of the keenest and deepest self-consciousness" (*E&T*, 1: 349).

Self-consciousness could lead, admittedly, to a state of Hamlet-like indecision. But in the wholesale rejection of Coleridgean dreaminess in favour of a Carlylean love of decisiveness, action, and leadership, there was a danger of losing touch with the first principles which Coleridge had tried to keep before his public. Men and women confronting the rapid changes of nineteenth-century England had to become *more* reflective not less so. Coleridge's *Aids* had at least marked out one route by which self-consciousness could bring the reader to a mature, active faith, based on the inescapable realities of Will and Conscience, not to a torpid Romantic narcissism. Sterling's American friends, Emerson and Alcott, saw nothing wrong with such a positive use of self-consciousness.

As the basis of a *philosophical system*, self-consciousness or "self-interpretation" was the original doctrine of F. W. J. von Schelling in the *System des transzendentalen Idealismus*, as Sterling well knew (here again, Sterling was open to an aspect of German thought that was to all intents and purposes ignored by Carlyle). It is Schelling that Sterling appears to have in mind when he mentions the understanding of one's self as "a product of higher forces." The introspected mind, as understood by Schelling, manifests the *unconscious* activity of Nature together with the *conscious* exercise of Will, and this conjunction of conscious with unconscious activity constitutes (for Schelling) the first principle of all knowledge, the only guarantee, in fact, that knowledge of any kind is possible. It is this strand in German idealism that led Sterling to link self-interpretation with our apprehension of the world around us, as he does in the essay on Carlyle. To seek knowledge both of one's own nature and of the nature of the universe were not to Sterling futile or incompatible aims. Rather, they were the essential human activity, the only activity by which humankind is entirely differentiated from the objective world which produced us.

This point was not merely a philosopher's quibble: it had a direct moral application, for Sterling was extremely critical of Carlyle's evasive and half-explicit exoneration of the French revolutionaries from responsibility for the massacres of September 1792. Carlyle, Sterling argued, had allowed his imaginative grasp of the revolutionists' impulses to cloud his moral judgment as to the criminality of the act itself. To defend the massacre as essentially an act of war was inadmissible, for though a battle might have left as many dead, there was a deeply signifcant difference in "the souls, the purposes of the men who do the deed" (*E&T*, 1: 369–70).

This Coleridgean—or Schellingian—emphasis on subjectivity, on *Innigkeit*, could not be reinforced by Sterling's reading in German literature, especially the sermons and biblical criticism of the much-admired F. D. E. Schleiermacher. Though Sterling eventually came to esteem Goethe's work highly, it is evident that his admiration for Schleiermacher was a stronger force and that he continued to find Goethe lacking in true feeling, even though respecting his mastery of form and his lyrical gift. Sterling's last published essay, "Characteristics of German Genius," a far-reaching survey of German literature which used Sarah Austin's *Fragments from German Prose Writers* merely as a starting-point, weighed such qualities as homeliness, affectionateness, mysticism, reflection, knowledge, and culture in an attempt to decide which was the distinctive characteristic of the Germans and finally pronounced that the underlying feature—and the *fons et origo* of all the others—was "Earnestness of heart" (*E&T*, 1: 409).

That Schleiermacher in particular represented this quality, and that his earnestness was not unconnected with his achievement as a biblical critic, is evident from Sterling's enthusiastic comment on Schleiermacher's "Discourse at the Grave of his Son": "It is in a great degree the want of faith, hope, and love, that makes people write on religion in a style suitable for bills of lading and kings' speeches; and it was partly the fulness of these in the Prophets that gave them their visionary and symbolic style" (*E&T*, 1: lxiv). In the same winter of 1836–37 Sterling wrote to the Reverend Dunn:

> It has lately been to me a source of great advantage & enjoyment to find so much of the deepest & simplest Devotion in a Dialectician as commanding & wonderful as Plato though writing Sermons not Dialogues less excursive. I mean the German Schleiermacher. . . . There is I suspect greatly too much thought in him for any but a very small number of English readers & moreover some of his opinions especially about the Infallibility of the writers of Scripture would bring down much abuse on a Translator.[27]

The reason for Sterling's feeling of frustration here is not far to seek. Schleiermacher had made great gains in the direction of a new mode of biblical criticism that would be less militantly rationalistic than Eichhorn's, more compatible with the essentials of Christian faith. He had done so by arguing that instead of recognizing only the putative "authors" of the Gospels as inspired, we should see the work of the Spirit also in those who witnessed and originally reported the events and speeches recorded in Scripture. Schleiermacher found no evidence that any of the Apostles had spontaneously decided to make written records of the life of Jesus; but he deduced, from the nature of the evangelists' narratives, that those who were converted to the new faith without having known Jesus in person wished to have some particulars of their Saviour's life on earth. From detached stories—some legendary, some based on actual events—the three synoptic Gospels were eventually compiled.

That Schleiermacher found himself forced to reject as unhistorical considerable portions of the synoptic Gospels did not, of course, diminish his worth as a critic in Sterling's eyes. Indeed, Schleiermacher's writings seemed to him to be pervaded by a reverence towards the spirit of primitive Christianity that was rare or non-existent in England,

27. Letter of 21 December 1836: National Library of Scotland MS 1766, fols. 40v–41r.

where it was usually just the literal meaning of the text that was reverenced.

I have emphasized the fiducial rather than the purely critical aspect of Schleiermacher's work partly in order to avoid imposing a false teleology on Sterling's ventures into higher criticism. Sterling's reading of Strauss was not the *result* of his reading of Schleiermacher. Schleiermacher did not point towards Strauss, any more than Coleridge did. Indeed Schleiermacher, while accepting the premise of the mythological school that a writer is always the product of the age he lives in, explicitly condemned that school for failing to understand the "power of Christianity to create new concepts and forms of expression."[28] The key to understanding the Gospels, for him, was not the generalized mythic consciousness of the entire Near Eastern population in the first two centuries of the common era, but rather the Christian Church of that time: a body called into existence by an experience of the divine which could *not* be responded to within the mythological paradigms that lay to hand.[29] Strauss, by contrast, allowed this Christian community no exemptions from his rule of mythological interpretation—indeed, he found the New Testament to be even more clearly mythic than the Old. Strauss insisted, however, that his work was constructive as well as destructive, because the clearing away of the mythological shell would enable a purified core of philosophical truth to be accepted by all humankind. It was this universalist, idealist aspect of his argument that chiefly appealed to the vehemently anti-sectarian Sterling. As Sterling recognized, however, Strauss was unlikely to get a fair hearing in England.

> We see at this instant an Oxford professor of unquestioned piety nearly worried to death for controverting or supporting (we forget which) St. Thomas Aquinas. A German may proclaim his agreement with Plato, Spinoza, or Shaftsbury, and his disregard of all the Fathers and all the Reformers; and in all probability, if he shows sincerity and genius in doing so, he will gain an increased salary, the cross of an order, and a larger body of pupils. It is not very difficult to perceive which plan is the more likely to make profound philosophical inquirers. (*E&T*, 1: 403)

28. Schleiermacher, "*The Hermeneutics*," p. 5.

29. See Schleiermacher's *Der christliche Glaube*, 2nd (rev.) ed., 2 vols. (Berlin: G. Reimer, 1830–31), 2: 103, 320.

Sterling's reading of *Das Leben Jesu* in 1839 was, to his ecclesiastical friends, the ultimate impiety. To Hare, Strauss was a "dexterous advocate," employed in merely picking holes in the New Testament in order to overthrow those truths which were the "lodestars of our moral nature" (*E&T*), 1: cxxxiv). But Sterling saw *Das Leben Jesu* simply as criticism—presenting a case which needed an answer. What was valuable in Strauss might be accepted; what was not, rejected. As he wrote to Emerson in 1842, "Thought is leaking into this country—even Strauss sells."[30] It had long been Sterling's view that the shibboleths of plenary inspiration and biblical inerrancy must be torn down and that it did not especially matter whether the work of destruction was done by a believer or a non-believer (*E&T*, 1: cvi). It was now meaningless for a thinking Christian to claim simply that he or she "believed the Bible." What was proved by works such as Strauss's, as Sterling told his young friend William Coningham in 1840, was that the claims of Christian faith must rest on its "suitableness . . . to the higher and better demands of the conscience, and the sanctified reason." Warning Coningham that he was plunging into deep and treacherous waters, Sterling stated his view that there were errors of both fact and opinion in the Bible: "Reduce this Scriptural fallibility within limits however narrow, yet our theology must be something else than belief in the whole Bible; and the creeds and traditions of the early church are quite as open to criticism, and as clearly marked by defect and error as the volume of either Testament."[31] Sterling did not publish any detailed examination of Strauss's *Das Leben Jesu*, so we cannot know with any certainty how Sterling might have defended or criticized Strauss, and perhaps have assisted George Eliot as interpreter of Strauss to the British public, had he lived longer. As we know, however, that Sterling read Strauss long before the appearance of George Eliot's translation in 1846, and that his initial reaction was on the whole favourable, if guarded, our account of Sterling's role as apologist for the Higher Criticism would be incomplete if it did not contain some account of Strauss's aims.

The researches of eighteenth-century historians such as Heyne and Jones had shown that it was impossible to treat pagan myths as containing nothing but falsehood and imposture while at the same time

30. Edward Waldo Emerson, ed., *Correspondence between Sterling and Emerson*, pp. 59–60.

31. *Letters to Coningham*, p. 11.

claiming supernatural sanction for the (often very similar) narratives of the Old Testament. Either Reimarus was right, and Moses was nothing more than a trickster using Egyptian magic to practise on the susceptibilities of his exiled race; or the rationalists of the eighteenth century had failed to understand the particular type of truth which all myth, Gentile as well as Hebrew, embodied. Heyne established the principle "All the history, and subsequently all the philosophy, of ancient peoples emerges from their myths."[32] In the hands of Gabler and Schelling, this became a tool for the unlocking of ancient history, and with Eichhorn its application to biblical narratives began. At first only the story of the Fall was considered mythic; but later, other parts of the Old Testament were treated from the mythological point of view. Schleiermacher's analysis of the evangelists' accounts of the Nativity had begun to demonstrate that the New Testament also contained an admixture of mythic narrative.

Here, however, a theological difficulty became apparent. If we assume the biblical writers to have been divinely inspired, "It certainly does appear improbable . . . that God should have admitted the substitution of mythical for actual representations of facts and ideas." Why make divine truth doubly inaccessible by concealing it in a tapestry of mythic narratives? To obviate this difficulty, Strauss was perfectly prepared to adapt to his own purposes the idea of the inspiration of Scripture itself: "A nearer examination of the scriptures shows that this very notion of inspiration, far from being any hindrance to the mythical interpretation, is itself of mythical origin."[33] Mythic narratives were created and evolved by the genius of a whole community or race of people, not by a single individual: and *as it became necessary to explain the origins of a particular myth, the community naturally evolved a supporting myth of divine inspiration.* Unlike the allegorical interpreter, therefore, who merely selects from a narrative whatever thought he or she considers worthy to be attributed to God and calls that the true meaning of the narrative, the mythical interpreter uses as guide the conformity of an idea or thought to the spirit and thought-forms of the people and age which produced the narrative. Claims of divine inspiration were themselves part of the thought-forms of biblical ages. Not only the Old Testament narratives, but also those of the New Testament, show evidence of their mythic origins. Indeed, the New Testament is

32. Quoted Strauss, *Das Leben Jesu,* 1: 27.
33. Strauss, *Life of Jesus,* 1: 25; *Das Leben Jesu,* 1: 28.

in a sense *more* essentially mythic than the Old, for it is centered on a being actually begotten by the Divine Spirit, who lives, suffers, and dies on earth. There is no such character in the Old Testament.[34]

Strauss discerned two kinds of mythic narrative in the New Testament: the "Evangelical mythus," which arose not from a factual occurrence in the life of Jesus but from an idea, doctrine, or devotional practice current among his first followers, and the "Pure mythus," which originated in their messianic expectations or in the impression left on their minds by Jesus' character and actions. The narrative of the Journey of the Magi, the angels' appearance to the shepherds, the meeting of Jesus and the woman of Samaria (John 4:7–30), and the rending of the veil of the temple at Jesus' death (Matthew 27:51, Mark 15:38, Luke 23:45) might be cited as examples of the former kind of myth; the expelling of demons into a herd of swine (Matthew 8:28–34, Mark 5:2–16, Luke 8:27–36), Jesus' manifestations of himself to his followers between his Resurrection and Ascension, and even the Resurrection itself, as examples of the latter kind.[35]

Sterling's statement to Coningham that Christian faith must now rest mainly on "an assertion of the suitableness of the Christian scheme to the higher and better demands of the conscience, and the sanctified reason" indicated not a wholehearted acceptance of all Strauss's arguments but a willingness to study and sift what Strauss had to say, without fearing that practical Christianity would thereby be endangered. Even if everything Strauss claimed for his mythological reading of Scripture were true, Sterling said, what would be left would be not a mere intellectual theory but "a practical morality and religion fitted to all mankind."[36]

This emphasis on the practicality and universality of a post-Straussian Christianity was consonant with the important "Concluding Dissertation" of *Das Leben Jesu*, in which Strauss, admitting that his critical inquiry had apparently annihilated Christian belief in all its essentials, claimed that the critic nevertheless has a positive and not merely a destructive role: "In proportion as he is distinguished from the naturalistic theologian, and the free-thinker,—in proportion as his criticism is conceived in the spirit of the nineteenth century,—he is

34. *Life of Jesus*, 1: 48, 69; *Das Leben Jesu*, 1: 55, 78–79.

35. *Life of Jesus*, 1: 200–269; 2: 48–49; 3: 281–83; 2: 244–68; 3: 358–74; *Das Leben Jesu*, 1: 226–306, 544–46; 2: 536–37, 10–47, 623–40.

36. *Letters to Coningham*, pp. 11–12.

filled with veneration for every religion, and especially for the substance of the sublimest of all religions, the Christian, which he perceives to be identical with the deepest philosophical truth; and hence, . . . he will feel urged to place that identity in a just light."[37]

Having given sympathetic but (in the end) negative evaluations of Schleiermacher's proposition that "the ideal man was historically manifested in the person of Christ" and of Kant's "symbolic" and hence unhistorical Christ-figure,[38] Strauss proceeded to outline the Hegelian position, this being the one that he intended to use as foil to his own. According to Hegel, the spiritual nature of God cannot be conceived of in separation from the spiritual nature of humanity. As a finite being, humankind lacks truth; but as infinite being, God lacks reality: "The infinite spirit is real only when it discloses itself in finite spirits; as the finite spirit is true only when it merges itself in the infinite."[39] Spirit really exists, therefore, neither in God alone nor in humanity alone, but in the interchange between finite and infinite. When the human race has reached the point in its history where it rejects the purely natural state of existence as corrupt, and the state of total submission to revealed law as miserable, then it is ready to experience in one individual's life the revelation of the God-man. "Man being once mature enough to receive as his religion the truth that God is man, and man of a divine race; it necessarily follows, since religion is the form in which the truth presents itself to the popular mind, that this truth must appear, in a guise intelligible to all, as a fact obvious to the senses: in other words, there must appear a human individual who is recognized as the visible God."[40]

As Strauss points out, the Hegelian argument effectively inverts the old relationship between the evangelical history and orthodox belief: instead of grounding belief on the veracity of evangelical history, Hegel's case is that because Christian belief in the existence of a God-man is true, therefore the accounts of the historical Jesus must be fundamentally true. "Proved to be an idea of the reason, the unity of the divine and human nature must also have an historical existence."[41]

Strauss, however, seizes on a difficulty in the Hegelian position.

37. *Life of Jesus*, 3: 397; *Das Leben Jesu*, 2: 664.
38. *Life of Jesus*, 3: 417–25, 437; *Das Leben Jesu*, 2: 687–95, 709.
39. *Life of Jesus*, 3: 433; *Das Leben Jesu*, 2: 705.
40. *Life of Jesus*, 3: 434; *Das Leben Jesu*, 2: 705.
41. *Life of Jesus*, 3: 436; *Das Leben Jesu*, 2: 707.

There is a considerable difference between imagining a divine power constantly at work in the history of the world and conceiving a single man endowed with the power to perform miracles, rise from the dead, and ascend to heaven. The philosophical notion that the suppression of natural existence is the resurrection of spirit cannot, in itself, "prove" that one man was actually raised from the dead. And why, Strauss asks, must we conceive that the perfect unity of the human and the divine was achieved once and once only? The idea, Strauss argues, is not exhausted by the production of one single exemplar: "it loves to distribute its riches among a multiplicity of exemplars which reciprocally complete each other. . . . And . . . is not the idea of the unity of the divine and human natures a real one in a far higher sense, when I regard the whole race of mankind as its realization, than when I single out one man as such a realization? is not an incarnation of God from eternity, a truer one than an incarnation limited to a particular point of time?"[42]

This speculative Christology, or radicalization of Hegel, was too thorough a rending of the veil of the temple for even Sterling to accept without qualms. We have seen, of course, how severely Strauss's conclusions were condemned by the Broad Church. Strauss himself recognized that any adherent of his "speculative theology" must be in an anomalous and unstable position if choosing to remain within the Church and yet could not leave the Church without seeming to set a bad example for others. A philosophical distillation of Christian truth had been preserved, the Christology of the Ebionites, which was accessible to all, but at the cost of removing the historical Jesus from the focal point of Christian thought. The popular imagination would continue to centre on the historical Jesus; so the task of the speculative theologian would be to make possible a transition from orthodox Christianity, based on acceptance of the literal truth of the Gospel narratives, to a new Christianity, in which the spiritual truth of the Gospels rather than their historical veracity would be emphasized.

In the popular mind, however, Strauss's subtle reasoning was soon displaced by the gaudier mixure of scepticism and piety offered by Rénan.[43] The new base from which radical Christian thought must now work had now been established in Strauss's "Concluding

42. *Life of Jesus*, 3: 437; *Das Leben Jesu*, 2: 709.
43. See Shaffer, "*Kubla Khan*" *and The Fall of Jerusalem*, pp. 191, 193.

Dissertation," however, and that base was the idea of perpetual incarnation: "is not an incarnation of God from eternity, a truer one than an incarnation limited to a particular point of time? . . . Humanity is the union of the two natures—God become man, the infinite manifesting itself in the finite, and the finite spirit remembering its infinitude. . . ."[44]

That Sterling understood, and broadly sympathized with, Strauss's proclamation of the divinely human, his radical claim that the Apostles and Evangelists were inspired by nothing that was not also part of the fully spiritual nature of each human being, is shown by the concluding paragraphs of Sterling's essay "Characteristics of German Genius." After accusing English and French philosophy of having tried to diminish humankind by explaining away the divine in it as something "small and frivolous," Sterling praises the Germans for their sense that

> there is a godlike within us, that feels itself akin to the gods; and if we are told that both the godlike and the gods are dreams, we can but answer that so to dream is better than to wake and find ourselves nothing.
>
> . . . What is all that is held most holy,—what all the godlike men whom religious tradition canonizes and glorifies,—but forms of a divine idea, ever to be kept before us and approached, though in each individual most imperfectly realized? And when in other words we speak of the Worth of Man, which philosophy explains, history displays in action, and poetry sings of and makes visible to the soul, we but declare that there is a greatness of human nature which rebukes the littleness of each, and yet is the common blessing and support of us all. (*E&T*, 1: 420–21)

It was the sad truth, however, that in England no poet had yet arisen who could "sing" and "make visible" that divine greatness of human nature. Sterling himself was certainly not such a poet, good as his best work undoubtedly was. Hints in Sterling's writings, and more particularly his "Hymn of a Hermit" (published in *Blackwood's* in March 1844), suggest that the poet who came closest to embodying this ideal for Sterling had been Shelley. But Shelley had been prevented, by his very English inability to grasp the philosophical and historical bases of Christian belief, from proceeding beyond an Enlightenment scepticism about the claim of Christianity to represent the sublimest truth about the human condition and had therefore wasted his genius in nothing more than "mad revolt . . . against nature and necessity, no

44. *Life of Jesus*, 3: 438; *Das Leben Jesu*, 2: 709.

less than laws and men" (*E&T*, 1: 393).[45] What was desperately needed, Sterling had come to feel, was undoubtedly a Christian Shelley. We might guess that the Robert Browning in whom (as Mrs. Orr expressed it) "the Evangelical Christian was allied . . . to the subjective philosophic idealist" would have impressed Sterling as the closest approximation the age could offer to his conception of the religious poet of the future.[46]

In America, the picture was a good deal brighter. Sterling's correspondence with Emerson is imbued with an optimism that is quite lacking in his correspondence with Coningham, Dasent, Dunn, Hare, or even Carlyle. Where the English climate appeared implacably hostile to the radical notion of divinity outlined by Strauss, Americans such as Emerson, Margaret Fuller, Bronson Alcott, and Henry David Thoreau were already making claims for the divinity and creative power of the human spirit that were remarkably similar to Strauss's radical Hegelianism. Americans had no Established Church to quash debate about the infallibility of Scripture: and the transcendentalists, while they abhorred the narrowness of Puritanism in some of its stricter forms, also owed to the Puritan tradition a strong regard for spiritual things that was not very different from the "earnestness of heart" that Sterling had discovered for himself in Schleiermacher. In his dislike of sectarian religion, and his strong sense of the "godlike within us," Sterling was closer to Emerson than to any of his contemporaries in England, even though the closest he ever came to Concord was St. Vincent, in the West Indies.

Sterling's own intellectual journey carried him farther than many less gifted thinkers travel in sixty or seventy years. He was certainly much more than the "representative Victorian" of Anne Kimball Tuell's title: his illness made him to a great extent an outsider, a looker-on in Victorian England's internecine quarrels who could at times see

45. According to Hallam Tennyson, the morality of Shelley's poetry was discussed by the Apostles (*Alfred Lord Tennyson*, p. 37), and there are frequent expressions of interest in Shelley in Sterling's correspondence. See for instance *E&T*, 1: lxxvii, and the letter of 30 May 1837 to Jane Welsh Carlyle in which Sterling says that he has considered writing an article on Shelley for the *London Review* (since it had amalgamated with the *Westminster Review* in 1835 and become the *London and Westminster Review*, Sterling's title for it was a year or more out of date): National Library of Scotland MS 1766, fol. 46v. See also Allen, *Cambridge Apostles*, pp. 50–51.

46. Alexandra Sutherland Orr, "The Religious Opinions of Robert Browning," *The Contemporary Review* 60 (July–December 1891): 887.

the larger issues more clearly than could those who were immediately engaged in the conflict. For this reason, it is pointless to speculate about what Sterling might have achieved had he been blessed with good health and a more normal life. Margaret Fuller's journal contains perhaps the most honest and sympathetic of all contemporary verdicts on Sterling's life: "The news was very sad: Sterling did so earnestly wish to do a man's work, and had done so small a portion of his own."[47]

47. Quoted in Ralph Waldo Emerson, William Henry Channing, and James Freeman Clarke, *Memoirs of Margaret Fuller Ossoli*, 2 vols. (Boston: Roberts Brothers, 1881), 2: 137.

VI

The Divinity in Man: Transcendentalism as Organized Innocence

INSPIRATION enjoyed a high place on the agenda of the New England Transcendentalists, embracing as it did two of their most persistent concerns: the human mind in its relations with God and Spirit, and the need for future poets of the young nation to "make it new," to escape from the servile imitation of European models. The feeling that new or at least rediscoverable sources of inspiration were needed for a new kind of literature gave the Transcendentalists' debates an urgency virtually unknown in England.

The topic announced for discussion at a meeting of the Hedge Club, or Symposium Club, in May 1840, at Emerson's house, fully illustrates this sense of urgency: "The Inspiration of the Prophet and Bard, the Nature of Poetry and the Causes of the Sterility of the Poetic Inspiration in our own Age and Country."[1] As Lawrence Buell has amply shown, in its desire to encourage and justify a native American literature that would be distinctive, original, and independent of European models, Transcendentalism elevated the idea of inspiration into an absolute prerequisite for literary art. "All Transcendentalist attempts to describe how art is to be created, and the impact which

1. See Ethel Seybold, *Thoreau: The Quest and the Classics* (New Haven: Yale University Press, 1951), p. 34. The name "Transcendentalists" was a sobriquet applied to the group by others, not a name adopted or approved by the members of the club themselves. The original name "Symposium Club" suggested the free interchange of ideas without any one participant taking a dominant part in discussion, but as Hedge was the most faithful attender at their meetings many Transcendentalists later referred to the club familiarly as "Hedge's Club" or "The Hedge Club." See George Willis Cooke, *An Historical and Biographical Introduction to Accompany "The Dial,"* 2 vols. (New York: Russell and Russell, 1961), 1: 54.

it should make upon its audience, begin and end with the idea of inspiration."[2]

Emerson recorded and analysed the visitations of his own inspiration, and in the process he made it sound, as Buell says, "a very natural thing, as natural as breathing, but also mysterious and involuntary," indeed something that one can experience in ordinary life without having to be a poet or a prophet.[3] Transcendentalism, in this as in other matters, did not preach the elevation of recalcitrant humanity to a superhuman, angelic plane, but was rather concerned to uncover the sources of prophecy and poetry in common human experience. Ultimately, for Emerson, these sources reached back to omnipresent Spirit, to Being, or to God. It was characteristic of Emerson's beliefs, however, that he should emphasize the omnipresence, the democratic universality of Spirit, rather than its identity with the God of the Bible. Nevertheless, Emerson was also deeply concerned with the liberation of ancient literatures, Oriental and Greek as well as Hebrew, from their imprisonment in the dead letter and a parallel and concomitant liberation of the living artist from the crippling belief that divine inspiration had somehow run out with the last words of the Bible. As Buell points out, it should never have been an occasion for surprise that the Transcendentalists, ostensibly enemies of institutional Christianity, and virulently attacked by orthodox apologists, adopted a "biblical" terminology in describing the creative process.[4]

What has not been perceived, even by Buell, is the extent to which Christian believers, especially Schleiermacher in Germany, Coleridge in England, and Marsh, Hedge, and Ripley in America, had already seen what vital renewal of faith might flow from the collapse of the old literalistic view of the Bible. The Puritan heritage—with its emphasis on the effectual power of divine grace—joined with a new spirit in the interpretation of the Bible to create a milieu in which the Transcendentalist understanding of inspiration could take shape. Even after resigning his position as a Unitarian minister in 1832, Emerson attacked, not Christ's teachings nor the spirit of the Hebrew Scriptures, but the attempt by the Christian churches to institutionalize the Bible and erect needlessly complex theologies around and over it. "I

2. Lawrence Buell, *Literary Transcendentalism: Style and Vision in the American Renaissance* (Ithaca, N.Y.: Cornell University Press, 1973), p. 55.

3. Buell, *Literary Transcendentalism*, p. 63.

4. Buell, *Literary Transcendentalism*, p. 58.

look for the hour when that supreme Beauty which ravished the souls of those eastern men, and chiefly of those Hebrews, and through their lips spoke oracles to all time, shall speak in the West also. The Hebrew and Greek Scriptures contain immortal sentences, that have been bread of life to millions. But they have no epical integrity; are fragmentary; are not shown in their order to the intellect" (*DSA*, p. 148).

We worship, Emerson wrote in his journal, a *past* revelation of God. "The new inspiration is always rejected" (*JMN*, 7: 543). There was no question, however, that (as far as Emerson was concerned) the new inspiration flowed from the same source as that of the Old Testament prophets, Jesus, and the Apostles. Emerson proposed no "new" source of inspiration, although the manner in which he spoke of the ancient source was not calculated to reassure more conservative thinkers. Emerson had lost, or had voluntarily relinquished, the older Puritans' strong sense of the transcendent: but his apprehension of the immanence of God, and especially of God's presence in the individual soul, was intense and was proclaimed with deep conviction.[5] In Emerson's early orations, particularly the "Divinity School Address" and "The American Scholar," it sometimes seems his main mission to urge his audience to claim for themselves the same divine inspiration as was given to the Old Testament prophets. When all Americans have the courage to walk on their own feet and speak their own minds, Emerson says in the peroration to "The American Scholar," "a nation of men will for the first time exist, because each believes himself inspired by the Divine Soul which also inspires all men" (*AmS*, p. 115).

Such trumpet-calls are an integral part of the symphony of Transcendentalist enthusiasms, however, and emerge from two decades of debate about the relation of scriptural inspiration to the mind of the believer. Admittedly, none of the inner circle of the Hedge Club had been acquainted at first hand with German biblical criticism, except for Hedge himself, who had studied at Göttingen and Schulpforta from the summer of 1818 to the end of 1821.[6] Their interest in questions of inspiration sprang primarily from a desire to channel

5. See Stephen E. Whicher, *Freedom and Fate: An Inner Life of Ralph Waldo Emerson* (Philadelphia: University of Pennsylvania Press, 1953), p. 23.

6. See Frederic Henry Hedge's letter of 1877 to Caroline H. Dall, quoted in Cooke, *Historical Introduction*, 2: 72–73; and Orie William Long, *Frederic Henry Hedge: A Cosmopolitan Scholar* (Portland, Me.: The Southworth-Anthoensen Press, 1940), pp. 3–7.

into American vessels the traditional and ancient wellsprings of creative power. Yet liberal Boston Unitarians in the 1820s, like the Bristol Unitarians with whom Coleridge associated in the 1790s, were open to German influences to a greater degree than any other Christian group in the English-speaking world: and most Transcendentalists were more or less closely associated with the Unitarian Church during at least the first part of their intellectual careers. (All the original members of the Hedge Club except Alcott were Unitarian ministers, though not all were active in 1836 when the club first came together.)[7]

In the early years of the century, the notion that every word of the Bible was equally and fully inspired had been overturned for many Unitarians by Joseph Stevens Buckminster. The immediate result had been an impoverishment of Unitarian preaching, since Unitarian ministers merely relegated the Bible to "a storehouse of analogies and illustrations" for their moralistic exhortations, instead of using them as straightforward evidences of the truth of Christian doctrine.[8] The realization that the Bible might actually be read with a livelier interest, and a livelier faith, now that its role as the literal repository of "God's Word" and source of evidences was ending, did not emerge on the American scene until the 1820s, after Edward Everett, George Ticknor, George Bancroft, and Frederic Henry Hedge, all of whom had studied in Germany, returned home with news of more recent developments in the higher criticism. Though Harvard did not at first take kindly to German methods of biblical exegesis, there were other methods of spreading the new gospel than through the lecture-hall. In 1823 Bancroft, in partnership with Joseph Cogswell, opened a school at Northampton, Massachusetts, where Schleiermacher's approach to the Bible was taught in conjunction with the educational philosophy of Pestalozzi. Bancroft had spent two years in Berlin and had met Schleiermacher, who quickly emerged as something of a

7. See Ralph Waldo Emerson, *Journals and Miscellaneous Notebooks*, ed. William H. Gilman et al. (Cambridge, Mass,: The Belknap Press of Harvard University Press, 1960—), 5: 194 and editor's footnote.

8. Accounts of Buckminster's study of German biblical criticism, and his influence on the Unitarian church, are given in Harold Clarke Goddard, *Studies in New England Transcendentalism* (1908; reprint ed., New York: Hillary House Publishers, 1960), p. 27, and Henry A. Pochmann, *German Culture in America: Philosophical and Literary Influences 1600–1900* (Madison, Wis.: University of Wisconsin Press, 1957), pp. 55–62. See also Buell, *Literary Transcendentalism*, pp. 108–9.

favourite among those attuned to German thought. (On 14 December 1834 Emerson recorded in his journal, "Hedge read me good things out of Schleiermacher" [*JMN*, 4: 360].)[9]

Readers of the Boston *Christian Examiner*, an influential organ of the Unitarian Church, were familiarized with the names and leading ideas of Herder, Schleiermacher, De Wette, and Strauss during the 1820s and 1830s.[10] In 1833, the *Christian Examiner* published a moderately favourable account of Coleridge's thought by Hedge. This, Hedge later felt, represented something close to official Unitarian approval of the trends Coleridge represented, though he had not, of course, discussed the "Letters" (still in manuscript at this time), and in fact expressed some doubts as to Coleridge's qualifications as a biblical scholar.[11] The same journal welcomed a translation by James Marsh of Herder's *Vom Geist der Ebräischen Poesie* and printed in its May 1835 issue a long and enthusiastic "Life of Herder" by George Ripley.[12]

Ripley formulated what we may take to be a fair encapsulation of the more progressive Unitarian view of biblical inspiration in a review of James Martineau's *The Rationale of Religious Enquiry* (1836). Ripley took issue with Martineau's attempt to cast doubt on the inspiration of the Apostles: they *did* experience divine inspiration, Ripley argued, even though this did not make their utterances infallible. Their inspiration was similar in kind to that received by Jesus himself. Such peculiar inspiration must, however, submit to be judged by the universal reason of humankind (and here he shows himself willing to defend a rather advanced definition of "reason"):

In this way and in no other, can it be distinguished from the fancies of enthusiasm, or the reveries of superstition. Every thing which claims to be of an immediate divine origin in history, must be brought to the test of that which is admitted to be of immediate divine origin in the facts of conscious-

9. Schleiermacher's importance is recognized by Octavius Brooks Frothingham, one of the first historians of the Transcendentalist movement: see his *Transcendentalism in New England: A History* (New York: Harper and Brothers, 1959), pp. 50–51. (The work was first published in 1876.)

10. See Pochmann, *German Culture in America*, p. 110.

11. [Frederic Henry Hedge,] "Coleridge's Literary Character" (review of *BL* [1817], *PW* [1829], *Aids* [1829] and *Friend* [1831]), *The Christian Examiner* 14 (March 1833): 108–29, especially p. 128. For attribution, see Cooke, 2: 72.

12. See *The Christian Examiner* 18 (1835): 167–221. For the attribution to Ripley, see Pochmann, *German Culture in America*, p. 110.

ness. The natural inspiration which is possessed by all must sit in judgment on the supernatural inspiration which is imparted to an elect few.[13]

Andrews Norton, a conservative Unitarian thinker, strongly reprimanded Ripley for his advanced views, even though Ripley's position was itself conservative in comparison to Martineau's.[14] Nevertheless, the fact that such a review could be published at all shows that free enquiry into biblical inspiration was possible within the Unitarian Church.

James Marsh, though Calvinist rather than Unitarian in his religious affiliation, had been early exposed to the findings of German biblical criticism through his association with Moses Stuart, professor of sacred literature at Andover seminary in New Hampshire. Stuart had accumulated a large library of German biblical scholarship in an attempt to correct what he saw as the superficiality of much theological instruction in America, and it was as a result of Stuart's encouragement that Marsh began his study of German literature.[15] Marsh was in no sense a Germanophile: even more than Hedge, he remained, despite doctrinal differences, firmly rooted in the religious traditions of New England. He warned his students at the University of Vermont against the "extravagances" of German criticism or of Andover (that is, Stuartian) exegesis, and in his essay "Ancient and Modern Poetry," published in the *North American Review* in 1822, he pointed out the dangers of turning religion into poetry—surely a thrust at the Higher Criticism.[16] Like Coleridge, however, Marsh abhorred "bibliolatry."[17] He fully agreed with Stuart that the American churches could not remain for long insulated from European advances in biblical criticism, and he sought to establish a sounder basis for Christian faith than that provided by the uneasy alliance of biblical fundamentalism and Lockean epistemology. In doing so, he had to admit that knowledge of one's own spiritual being, in a Kantian and (even more) a

13. "G. R. " [George Ripley], "*The Rationale of Religious Enquiry*. By James Martineau. London, 1836," *The Christian Examiner* 21 (November 1836): 247.

14. See Goddard, *Studies in New England Transcendentalism*, p. 33.

15. See Anthony John Harding, "James Marsh as Editor of Coleridge," in Crawford, *Reading Coleridge*, p. 226, and Pochmann, *German Culture in America*, p. 129.

16. [James Marsh,] "*Intorno all'ingiustizia di alcuni guidizii letterarii Italiani*," p. 131. See also Harding, "James Marsh as Editor of Coleridge," p. 234.

17. See John Dewey, "James Marsh and American Philosophy," *Journal of the History of Ideas* 2 (1941): 134.

Coleridgean sense, was a more important knowledge than that to be gained by scrutinizing the Bible for evidences of Christianity. Indeed, with considerable zeal Marsh propagated this radical new doctrine both through his teaching, which had a wide influence, and his writings, including the important "Preliminary Essay" in his edition of Coleridge's *Aids to Reflection* (*CW*, 1: 67–109). Marsh did not condone neglect of the Scriptures, of course: they were still to play a central role in the Christian life. "By awakening us to a deeper consciousness of spiritual reality," he said in a lecture, "they may at the same time bring us to a knowledge of God & of their own divine character—as light is its own evidence."[18] This strikes a modern reader as very distant from Emerson's radical trumpet-calls, and one modern commentator, Lewis S. Feuer, places James Marsh firmly in what he calls the "right wing" of Transcendentalism.[19] Yet to define the function of Scripture as that of "awakening us to a deeper consciousness of spiritual reality"—rather than that of proving the existence of God by irrefutable outward evidences—was in fact a radical break with older notions of biblical authority, and a significant step towards Emersonian and Thoreauvian individualism. To Marsh, American democracy owed its origins, not to Locke and the traditions of eighteenth-century empiricism, but to the Bible and "the great ultimate principles of human reason, which it announces."[20] Rationalists the Puritan Fathers were not, and yet they had found in the Bible a sublime vision of a community in which all could hear the Word of God for themselves, unobstructed by the intervention of a priesthood and speaking directly to the conscience of the individual.

Where Marsh departed most profoundly from the thought of such men as Jonathan Edwards was in his proclamation of the Will as constituting "the spiritual" in humankind. (Here, too, he is not as distant from Emerson as a modern reader might assume, for Emerson—despite the fatalism that breaks through in many of his later writings—was driven in *Nature* to admit that the natural world

18. James Marsh Collection, Guy W. Bailey Memorial Library, University of Vermont, Folder 3.2, S.8, fol. 1.3

19. Lewis S. Feuer, "James Marsh and the Conservative Transcendentalist Philosophy: A Political Interpretation," *The New England Quarterly* 31 (1958):5.

20. James Marsh, *An Address delivered in Burlington, upon the inauguration of the Author to the office of President of the University of Vermont, Nov. 28, 1826* (Burlington, Vt.: E. and T. Mills, 1826), p. 13.

remains incomplete and imperfect until the human will is present [*N*, p. 25].) For Marsh, Coleridge's most vital contribution to theology was undoubtedly his emphasis, in *Aids to Reflection*, on the division between nature and spirit: the fundamental practical importance of the Pauline distinction between the "natural man" and "the mind of Christ" (1 Corinthians 2:14, 16). This much, at least, emerges clearly from Marsh's "Preliminary Essay." Coleridge's forthright statement that "if there be aught spiritual in man, the will must be such" (*CW*, 1: 192) seemed likely to prove a bulwark against the inroads of Spinozism, Schellingism, and all other varieties of pantheistic belief. It is worth pointing out that W. G. T. Shedd, the American editor of the first collected edition of Coleridge's works, described Coleridge in the introduction to that edition as "the foremost and ablest English *opponent* of pantheism" (*CW*, 1: 16; my italics).

In combating the spectre of pantheism through his adoption of a Kantian-Coleridgean doctrine of the will, Marsh left himself open to attack by more conservative Calvinists, especially for his unorthodox interpretation of the meaning of "Atonement."[21] Despite these attacks, however, Marsh's edition of *Aids* and his propagation of Coleridgean principles through his lectures at the University of Vermont had an immense impact not only on New England but, through his students, on many other regions of the emergent nation.[22] The younger generation of enquiring minds in America began to see Coleridge as a lonely upholder of spiritual values in an England sunk in scepticism and materialism. To George Barrell Cheever, the obloquy suffered by Coleridge in his own country was "the appropriate testimony of an age of littleness and superficiality, towards one, who towered in

21. See Harding, "James Marsh as Editor of Coleridge," pp. 243–44; on Marsh's misreading of Kant, see Pochmann, *German Culture in America*, pp. 137–38; on his "subjective" interpretation of Atonement, see Marjorie Hope Nicolson, "James Marsh and the Vermont Transcendentalists," *The Philosophical Review* 34 (1925): 37, and John J. Duffy, ed., *Coleridge's American Disciples: The Selected Correspondence of James Marsh* (Amherst: University of Massachusetts Press, 1973), p. 20.

22. The scope of Marsh's influence is attested by the anonymous reviewer of Victor Cousin's *Fragmens Philosophiques* (Paris, 1828) and other works (running title: "Cousin's Philosophy"), *American Quarterly Review* 10 (September–December 1831): 305. See also Nicolson, "James Marsh and the Vermont Transcendentalists," p. 49, and Peter C. Carafiol, "James Marsh's American *Aids to Reflection*: Influence through Ambiguity," *New England Quarterly*, 49 (1976): 27–28.

such grandeur beyond the measure of all his contemporaries."[23] More temperately, Emerson wrote in his journal: "In England ethics & philosophy have died out. How solitary is Coleridge & how conspicuous, not so much from his force as from his solitude," and: "How much died with Coleridge" (*JMN*, 7: 431, 468).

It would be quite false to suggest that Emerson derived his idea of "the divinity in man" straight from Coleridge. According to his own statement in the essay "Circles," Emerson was "an endless seeker," taking whatever illumination offered itself to him, from whatever quarter it might come, prizing nothing but as it struck an answering chord in his own mind. Emerson's journals do show that in 1834, during a period of renewed interest in Coleridge, he adopted and frequently referred to Coleridge's famous distinctions between Imagination and Fancy, Genius and Talent, and Reason and Understanding. In addition, an important philosophical basis for the idea of "divinity in man" was established in 1831 when, reading the 1818 edition of *The Friend*, Emerson came across the claim that by introspection a human individual is able to discover that the ground of reality is independent of himself, yet is at the same time "a modification of his own being," so that each person possesses an inner guarantee of the existence of a permanent reality, a "ground common to the world and to man" (*Friend*, 1: 509, 508).[24]

Coleridge gave Transcendentalism a method of enquiry, however, rather than a specific philosophical system. This method was (in Marsh's phrase) to "turn the mind continually back upon . . . the inherent grounds of truth and error in its own being" (*CW*, 1: 68). It was for Marsh a reawakening of the inner, subjective life, which traditionally had been part of the Puritan heritage of America. Margaret Fuller learned from Coleridge the need to "re-educate" herself, and though an admirer of Carlyle, she found the Scottish prophet myopic, in comparison with Coleridge, where the mind's own powers and struc-

23. [George Barrell Cheever,] "Coleridge. The Friend: a Series of Essays . . . 1818," *North American Review* 40 (January–April 1835): 299. For attribution, see Richard and Josephine Haven and Maurianne Adams, *Samuel Taylor Coleridge: An Annotated Bibliography of Criticism and Scholarship*, vol. 1: 1793–1899 (Boston: G. K. Hall and Co., 1976), item 631.

24. See Frank T. Thompson, "Emerson's Indebtedness to Coleridge," *Studies in Philology* 23 (1926): 60.

tures were concerned. Alcott, dedicated to the education of young minds, was himself indebted to Coleridge for intellectual education rather than for any particular dogma.[25]

Nevertheless, despite Coleridge's importance as one of the chief teachers of the new "Innigkeit," he was by no means the only one. Sampson Reed, the Swedenborgian, whose *Observations on the Growth of the Mind* was published in Boston in 1826, probably suggested to Emerson the stimulating idea that nature "is perfectly adapted to invigorate and strengthen the intellectual and moral man."[26]

Even more influential, however, was the elder William Ellery Channing, a new kind of Unitarian preacher, not afraid of enthusiastic and poetic utterance, whose essay on Milton (published in the *Christian Examiner* in 1826) was described by Emerson as one of the most important essays of its time (*JMN*, 8: 283). Asserting that, to Milton, poetic genius was "a kind of inspiration," Channing continued: "No doctrine is more common among Christians than that of man's immortality; but it is not so generally understood, that the germs or principles of his whole future being are *now* wrapped up in his soul, as the rudiments of the future plant in the seed."[27] Poetry, to Channing, was the first-fruits of that sense of our own immortality. Poetry and religious faith were twin branches of the same stem. Channing was not, however, a religious enthusiast who despised the common powers of the mind. He approved Milton's unorthodox belief that the *prima materia* of creation was of God and that creation was therefore of itself divine: and this led him to the belief that perhaps "the Creator is bound to his works by stronger and more intimate ties, than we now imagine."[28] The corollary of this belief is seen in Channing's *Moral Argument Against Calvinism* (1820), where he argues

25. Emerson et al., *Memoirs of Margaret Fuller Ossoli*, 1: 127–28, 262; Amos Bronson Alcott, *Journals*, ed. Odell Shepard (Boston: Little, Brown and Co., 1938), p. 32.

26. Quoted by Kenneth Walter Cameron, *Young Emerson's Transcendental Vision* (Hartford, Conn.: Transcendental Books, 1971), p. 260.

27. [William Ellery Channing (1780–1842)] review of John Milton, *A Treatise on Christian Doctrine*, trans. Charles R. Sumner (Boston, 1825), (running title: "Milton,") *The Christian Examiner and Theological Review* 3 (January–February 1826): 32. See also Buell, *Literary Transcendentalism*, p. 35, and R. A. Yoder, *Emerson and the Orphic Poet in America* (Berkeley, Los Angeles and London: University of California Press, 1978), p. 14.

28. Channing, "Milton," p. 65.

that Revelation is not our only or supreme source of knowledge and defines Reason as "a prior Revelation," not to be extinguished in the interests of a steadier piety.[29]

There is a considerable distance, of course, between the claim that the presence of universal Reason in human minds reveals to us the existence of a God and the claim that God exists and acts within each one of us. By 1832, however, Emerson felt himself ready to leap this distance. He was no longer satisfied with the conventional view of Scripture, reflected in the early notebooks, that it was "given by heaven" (*JMN*, 2: 191), or that God was its "Author" (*JMN*, 1: 351), or that the ideas of Socrates and Plato, noble as they were, had been entirely swept away by the New Testament revelation, since the Apostles were divinely inspired and Plato was not (*JMN*, 2: 247).

It is true that, as Stephen Whicher shows, Emerson was alarmed by what he heard of German biblical criticism during the 1820s, realizing that if the divinity of Jesus were founded on his miracles, and these miracles were now discovered to have been reported on dubious authority, the New Testament message would lose much of its traditional weight.[30] But there are signs that even as early as 1822 Emerson was beginning to find the religion that resulted from this conventional, "proofs-and-evidences" view of Scripture a rather pallid and almost pagan thing compared to the more fervid Presbyterianism and Calvinism of the South. "An exemplary Christian of today, and even a Minister, is content to be just such a man as was a good Roman in the days of Cicero or of the imperial Antonines. Contentment with the moderate standard of pagan virtue, implies that there was no very urgent necessity for Heaven's last revelation. . ." (*EL*, 1: 128). Jesus must have had some more sublime truth to impart than the conclusions of Plato and Cicero. In 1830, having begun his readings in Sampson Reed and Coleridge's *Friend*, Emerson reached a more satisfactory position: the authority of the New Testament derives not from the church's claim that it is an inspired document but from the agreement or consonance between Jesus' teachings and our inward knowledge of our own moral nature. "Internal evidence," as Emerson put it, "outweighs all other to the inner man." We know that God exists not by proofs but by "consciousness" (*JMN*, 3: 214, 207).

29. Quoted by Francis Otto Matthiessen, *American Renaissance: Art and Expression in the Age of Emerson and Whitman* (London: Oxford University Press, 1941), p. 14, n. 1.

30. Whicher, *Freedom and Fate*, p. 11.

From this it was but a short step to the idea that "God in us worships God" (*JMN*, 3: 273). Emerson had made the transition from a view of the Bible as objective evidence to a view of it as a record of inner experience that speaks to our own inner experience. To remove Scripture to an impregnable and remote fortress of absolute authority, Emerson realized, was to protect it from rationalistic attack only at the price of cutting ourselves off from its liberating influence. We had to see that the same gift of the Spirit which inspired the prophets was also present in those closer to our own time.

> And what shall forbid us to universalize the operations of God & to believe the operation of the Holy Spirit is the same in kind in the prophet Isaiah as in the poet Milton? . . . The prophet in an excited state of mind surrenders himself, or rather I would say, applies himself (for the mind seems to be active & the truth passive) to a more extended thought than other men, & actually sees those things to be true which he utters (*JMN*, 3: 240)

A favourite text of Emerson's during the year he faced an internal and pastoral crisis over the meaning of the Lord's Supper, which led to his resignation from his ministry at the Second Church in Boston, was "Why even of yourselves judge ye not what is right?" (Luke 12:57; see *JMN*, 3: 321, 325). When the unnecessary defences of infallibility and plenary inspiration had been removed, Emerson saw that Jesus' words would become a much more radical challenge to the reader, because they could now be seen as the words of a man who spoke directly to the inner moral nature of humankind, the first prophet to do so unequivocally.[31] This change brought Emerson's view of Scripture remarkably close to that of Blake in the 1790s. Isaiah and Ezekiel, in *The Marriage of Heaven and Hell*, are portrayed as honest men who are "perswaded . . . that the voice of honest indignation is the voice of God," and Jesus as "the greatest man," who "acted from impulse not from rules."[32] Where, for the old world, holiness was enshrined in an external object, the ark of the testimony or the house of the Lord (Exodus 40:3, 1 Kings 7:51), Jesus had overturned the worship of externals and revealed the "ark of God within" (*JMN*, 3: 212), the

31. Modern commentators often emphasize, however, the extent to which OT prophets such as Amos and Hosea appeal to the "moral nature," long before the time of Jesus; see for example Julius A. Bewer, *The Literature of the Old Testament*, 3rd ed., rev. Emil G. Kraeling (New York: Columbia University Press, 1962), pp. 93–94.

32. Blake, *Poetry and Prose*, pp. 38, 42.

actual existence of God within human beings themselves. Every renaissance of Christian faith, from Luther and Fox to Guyon and Swedenborg, was essentially a rediscovery of this truth. Three years after the crisis, Emerson wrote:

> When we catch one clear glimpse of the moral harmonies which accomplish themselves throughout the Everlasting Now & throughout the omnipresent Here how impertinent seem the controversies of theologians. God is before us & they are wrangling about dead gods. What matters it whether the inspiration was plenary or secondary; whether this or that was intended by the Prophet; whether Jesus worked a miracle or no; if we have access inwardly to the Almighty & all wise One, Inspirer of all Prophecy, Container of all Truth & Sole Cause of Causes? All the Godhead that was in either of those ages in either of those men was the perception of those resplendent laws which at this very moment draw me at the same time that they outrun & overwhelm my faculties. (*JMN*, 5: 6)

Emerson's wish to make the celebration of the Lord's Supper a merely commemorative act, not a sacramental one,[33] was intimately connected, then, with his reappraisal of the matter of Jesus' own "inspiration," and the peculiar kind of authority granted to the Bible in traditional theology. If Jesus' proclamation of the moral nature of humankind was truth, and if this truth, once proclaimed, had to be self-evident, why did it continually have to be buttressed by appeals to the *person* of Jesus? Instead of living by the truths Jesus taught, Christians had cultivated a cowardly, superstitious religiosity with Jesus himself as its figurehead. "The whole world holds on to formal Christianity, & nobody teaches the essential truth, the heart of Christianity for fear of shocking &c." (*JMN*, 4: 45). The sacramental interpretation of the Lord's Supper, Emerson felt, stood in the way of an honest and direct promulgation of Jesus' principles, by appearing to ground them in the extraordinary nature of Jesus rather than in their independent and self-subsistent truth. The message that Emerson himself was now driven to preach, the presence of a divinity within, an equal inspiration in each living man and woman, could not be taught alongside a cult of Jesus the person.[34] Jesus "knew what was in man," as Emerson affirmed (quoting John 2: 25; compare *JMN*, 4: 322), but

33. See James Elliot Cabot, *A Memoir of Ralph Waldo Emerson*, 2 vols. (Boston: Houghton Mifflin Co., 1887), 1: 154–58.

34. See Cabot, 1: 211–13.

his followers had bartered what was in them for a mere image of Jesus. "Christ preacheds the greatness of Man but we hear only the greatness of Christ" (*JMN*, 5: 549).

Emerson shared with Carlyle, therefore, a strong distaste for the props and trappings of organized religion. Predictably he found the splendour of ecclesiastical ritual at St. Peter's in Rome, during his visit there in 1833, to have little to do with the Jesus *he* loved (*JMN*, 4: 153), and debates about the various "isms" of theology—what Carlyle scathingly called "pantheisms and pottheisms"—meant nothing to him. Far more than Carlyle, however, Emerson saw himself as announcing a truly *scriptural* doctrine, and as carrying on, like William Blake, a scriptural understanding of inspiration. In this respect, Emerson was much closer to Sterling than to Carlyle, and the similarity of their views about the authority of the Bible goes a long way towards explaining the unusual affinity Emerson and Sterling felt for each other. Both had learned to see the Bible as an invaluable heritage, the most glorious affirmation of spiritual truth ever made, but—for that very reason—not the last nor necessarily the definitive text.[35] "I think the true poetry which mankind craves," Emerson wrote, "is that Moral Poem of which Jesus chanted to the Ages stanzas so celestial yet only stanzas. The Epos is not yet sung" (*JMN*, 5: 186). The Bible, in other words, is not in any sense a closed book. Barely two weeks after returning from his visit to Europe, Emerson recorded his belief that the teacher of the new age "must work in the conviction that the Scripture can only be interpreted by the same spirit that uttered them. And that as long as the heart & the mind are illumined by a spiritual life there is no dead letter but a perpetual Scripture" (*JMN*, 4: 94).

The inspiration of the present hour, rather than the petrified inspiration of a past age, became, then, the driving power which was to fuel Emerson's career outside the Church, as lecturer, poet, and essayist. As William J. Scheick has shown, Emerson developed his own doctrine of the Logos as the creative Word which all may utter: "Like the traditional Logos, the self should continue at every present moment to speak truth into being."[36] Inconsistency is less to be feared than dishonesty or pretension. The Emersonian ideal of the poet-as-oracle,

35. See Cabot, 1: 211.

36. William J. Scheick, *The Slender Human Word: Emerson's Artistry in Prose* (Knoxville: University of Tennessee Press, 1978), p. 89.

speaking not on his own behalf but for the truth revealed to him, is vividly described in a poem of 1833:

> My heart lies open to the Universe
> I read only what there is writ I speak
> The sincere word that's whispered in my ear
> I am an organ in the mouth of God
> My prophecy the music of his lips.
>
> (*JMN*, 4: 90)

The thought that he might now speak the word that was whispered in his ear, without anxious debate as to whether that word conformed to accepted doctrine or not, was undoubtedly a liberating and energizing thought for Emerson. The recollection of his new freedom to be honest could alone fortify him against the virulent attacks of such as Andrews Norton. Yet there was, at the same time, a terrible irony in his new position as self-proclaimed oracle. As Coleridge had discovered (and demonstrated with concise brilliance in "Kubla Khan"), the true state of possession or inspiration was no longer open to the Romantic poet, however much he might admire and court this state. Whicher, adapting an insight of Robert Lowell, has said that after rejecting official Christianity in favour of an "immanentist" faith, Emerson suffered from a kind of split personality, part of him, his "Plotinus," given to oracular utterance, the other half, his "Montaigne," eternally questioning and rejecting.[37] Such a split is only a more acute (or better-articulated) form of the tension that afflicted every writer in the Romantic tradition, from Coleridge to Browning. Inspired utterance could no longer be taken on trust; the poet was obliged to weigh his words before the critics did. The ancients' "deep & universal reverence for poetry," Emerson saw, "indicates a faith in Inspiration" (*JMN*, 5: 109), but could that reverence be reawakened in the nineteenth century? Emerson's answer, in his own case, was to strive always to "say the thing that is fit for this new-born and infinite hour" (*JMN*, 5: 222). Permanent, irrefragable truth was beyond his reach, or rather, in the nature of things, it could not be uttered. Emerson's writings, then, carry always with them the avowal, sometimes implicit, often explicit, that the most "oracular" utterance is an utterance of the moment and should not be received as if graven on

37. Whicher, *Freedom and Fate*, p. 32.

a tablet. Emerson almost *advertizes* the conflict between his inspiration, what the poetic afflatus compels him to say, and his artistry, the controlling and restraining hand of the rhetorician. Such a self-conscious thrusting on the reader of the always-tenuous linkage between one word, one thought, and another, was in fact a significant *part* of that artistry, as Morse Peckham demonstrates (*EESS*, pp. xi–xiv). Any and every assertion Emerson makes is uttered in the full awareness of its opposite.

In addition to this historically conditioned brake on the free flow of inspiration, Emerson also had to deal with what is commonplace in the experience of every orator, lecturer, and preacher: the fact that inspiration often simply does not flow. After a disappointing run of lectures in Boston during the winter of 1839–40, Emerson confided to his notebook, "I have not once transcended the coldest selfpossession. I said I will agitate others, being agitated myself. I dared to hope for extacy & eloquence" (*JMN*, 7: 338); and the recognition that truth is something which can be grasped only momentarily and intuitively is implicit in the statement, in the 1841 essay "Intellect," that one must choose between truth and repose; one cannot have both (*EESS*, p. 282). Nevertheless, it was a constant goal of Emerson's endless seeking to discover a rationale for what might be called the phenomenon of inspiration.

Though the explanation given in the comparatively late essay "Inspiration" (1853) has a naturalistic sound to it—Emerson listing such mundane helps to creative genius as fresh air, exercise, conversation, and letter-writing—it does not amount to a thoroughgoing naturalistic explanation, which is what Whicher takes it to be.[38] What has happened, I believe, is that Emerson's attitude towards the divine source of inspiration has changed from the sublime confidence expressed in *Nature* and the "Divinity School Address" to an agnostic or existential view. Emerson is not quite guilty of the bad faith found in him by Whicher: of acting "as if the change made no difference and his discovery of the God within had never been."[39] The worst that can be said (and it should be said) is that the older, more sceptical Emerson did not sufficiently respect the Plotinian avowals made by his younger self.

While inspiration is certainly seen, in *Nature*, as "a literal influx of

38. Whicher, *Freedom and Fate*, pp. 99–100.
39. Whicher, *Freedom and Fate*, p. 127.

the divine,"[40] this doctrine has to be understood within a context in which nature itself is seen as being perpetually shaped, moulded, and altered by Spirit (*N*, p. 79; compare *JMN*, 5: 182). Nature constantly "speaks of" Spirit, and from her we learn the symbols and vocabulary by which we grasp spiritual realities (*N*, pp. 65, 31). This form of transcendentalism has little to do with *transcendence*: it emphasizes rather what it sees as God's immanence in creation. The view of the universe put forward in *Nature* might profitably be compared with that evoked in a Blakean Song of Innocence such as "Night," "A Dream," or "The Lamb": a universe so ordered that divine care and benevolence surround the young soul at every turn. "We must trust the perfection of the creation so far as to believe that whatever curiosity the order of things has awakened in our minds, the order of things can satisfy" (*N*, pp. 10–11). It is, note, "the order of things" that both awakens curiosity and satisfies it in this harmonious universe, so that there is no need to go outside the order of Nature, if it were even possible to do so, to find the sources of inspiration. The knowable power within us, the ground of our being, is continuous with the universal Spirit that grounds the changing world we look on, if indeed it does not itself *create* that universe, as is implied in the second and more overtly "idealist" half of the book. In an important transitional passage, Emerson reflects: "Man is conscious of a universal soul within or behind his individual life, wherein, as in a firmament, the natures of Justice, Truth, Love, Freedom, arise and shine. This universal soul he calls Reason. . . . That which intellectually considered we call Reason, considered in relation to nature, we call spirit. Spirit is the Creator" (*N*, p. 33).

Poetry, for Emerson, is the vehicle of Reason (*JMN*, 5: 51), so that poetic inspiration becomes, on this view, the creating, shaping Spirit of Nature speaking as "Reason" through a human mind and voice, deep calling to deep. The famous "transparent eyeball" passage, in which Emerson describes himself as a reborn Orphic bard, all consciousness of self and all "mean egotism" transcended, is nothing less than an attempt to evoke the state of possession and ecstasy: "the currents of the Universal Being circulate through me; I am part or parcel of God" (*N*, p. 16).

Nature is a prose Ode to Inspiration, rather than a philosophical treatise or even a discursive essay. The book invokes a state of being

40. Yoder, *Emerson and the Orphic Poet*, p. 7.

(comparable, I have suggested, to Blake's "Innocence"), rather than analysing mental powers or debating a strictly philosophical question such as the relation of mind to nature, and it is only with considerable difficulty that it can be read for its doctrine. Nevertheless, several early critics did read *Nature* as a philosophical treatise, and not surprisingly found it inconsistent. The "Berkeleian" second half of the book, observed Francis Bowen acidulously, neutralizes the first half—which is concerned with the effect of natural appearances on the mind—by denying the reality of Nature. The *nexus* that was meant to provide the vital link between mind and Nature did not do so; Emerson had failed to make a satisfactory case for what he called "Reason." "Our assertion," wrote Bowen, "is, that the argument for the existence of a God, or the immateriality of the soul, is tested by the same power of mind that discovered and proved any proposition in Euclid."[41] Before such criticisms are dismissed as the attempt of sour old age to clip the wings of youth's spirit of delight we should perhaps ask whether Emerson displayed in *Nature* the control of form and implied context which is the key to the greatness of Blake's *Songs*, or of Wordsworth's *Lyrical Ballads* and "Lucy" poems.

Emerson's "Address Delivered before the Senior Class in Divinity College, Cambridge" returned to the theme of "a perpetual Scripture," but with a closer control of form and tone than was the case in *Nature*. Here the image of the inspired man is entirely unified with the central theme of Emerson's oration, the need for a renewal of the spirit that filled the biblical prophets and poets. "The stationariness of religion; the assumption that the age of inspiration is past, that the Bible is closed; the fear of degrading the character of Jesus by representing him as a man;—indicate with sufficient clearness the falsehood of our theology. . . . The true Christianity,—a faith like Christ's in the infinitude of man,—is lost" (*DSA*, p. 142; compare *JMN*, 5: 492).

As Emerson had noted in "The American Scholar" (1837), the impulse to canonize inspired utterance, an admirable impulse in itself, leads to the tyranny of texts over the human spirit. "The sacredness which attached to the act of creation, the act of thought, is transferred

41. [Francis Bowen,] review of *Nature* (1836) (running title: "Transcendentalism"), *Christian Examiner* 21 (January 1837): 372, 384. Part of this review is reprinted in Milton R. Konvitz, ed., *The Recognition of Ralph Waldo Emerson* (Ann Arbor: University of Michigan Press, 1972), pp. 3–6.

to the record" (*AmS*, p. 90). Such tyranny can be ended only by freeing the texts themselves from their false canonized position and at the same time regaining the Christlike "faith . . . in the infinitude of man." The Scriptures have no "epical integrity"; rather, they are still incomplete, the first stanzas of an Ode of which the Epos is not yet sung (*DSA*, p. 148). Like the Israelites who preferred that Moses should speak with God for them, rather than that they should speak with God themselves (Exodus 20:19), we demand to be *protected* from the visitations of the Spirit, distrusting our own ability to bear such an influx of the divine (*EESS*, p. 64).

Emerson realized that it was not the existence of the Scriptures which constituted the problem, but the prevalent attitude of self-abasement before them, the attitude which assumed that revelation was at an end and (as one of Emerson's own early journals put it) that the human race travels daily further and further away from its source (*JMN*, 1: 62).

Not the Bible itself, then, but a certain deadened and deadening attitude towards the Bible was the main object of Emerson's attack in the "Divinity School Address." He adopted the tone of a Jeremiah denouncing an establishment religion of external observances.[42] Coleridge's description of a Gothic church as "petrified religion," quoted by Emerson in *Nature* (p. 49), concisely conveys the double message of the "Divinity School Address": what was once created in the name of religion—however beautiful, however expressive—must not be mistaken for the last, definitive or supreme achievement of the human spirit. "Refuse the good models," Emerson exhorts, "even those which are sacred in the imagination of men. . . . Yourself a newborn bard of the Holy Ghost, cast behind you all conformity, and acquaint men at first hand with Deity" (*DSA*, p. 143).

Though Emerson's language is less extravagant and Plotinian in the "Divinity School Address," there is considerable similarity between the view of the world implied in the "Address" and that outlined at greater length in *Nature*. The mind has the power to read the eternal deep; one's own soul is wiser than the whole external world. An essential harmony between mind and nature is implied, especially in the opening paragraph. Emerson had still not met, however, the chal-

42. See Carol Johnston, "The Underlying Structure of the Divinity School Address: Emerson as Jeremiah," *Studies in the American Renaissance, 1980*, ed. Joel Myerson (Boston: Twayne, 1980), p. 42.

lenge of his critics: to show convincingly why the renewal of inspiration he pleaded for was not a prescription for "a battle field for enthusiasms . . . a discord of obstinate and irresponsible wills."[43] Andrews Norton, representing or misrepresenting Emerson's first principle as simply that "the mind must be its own unassisted teacher," was distrustful of Emerson's belief that the word whispered in his ear—and in those of his disciples—would be a redemptive, truthful word.[44] Yet some contemporary theological thought *was* moving towards the view that the human mind *as normally constituted*, and in its ordinary daily operations, must be held to be susceptible to the influence of a divine power.

John Brazer, in his "Essay on the Doctrine of Divine Influence," published in the *Christian Examiner* in 1835, took issue with the orthodox Calvinist view that divine influence was necessarily supernatural in character. "We observe that this Divine Influence is not *supernaturally* imparted. There is no evidence to prove that there is any thing *miraculous* in the methods in which it is vouchsafed to the mind. . . . The influences of the Spirit . . . are not, in themselves, *distinguishable* from the ordinary operations of the human mind."[45] Just as, in the 1820s, the Calvinist doctrine of the Atonement had come to seem, in the eyes of many devout people, incompatible with the idea of a loving and merciful God, so now the idea of a divine influence that worked *only* by miraculous means (and Brazer was constrained to admit a distinction between the miraculous powers scripturally promised to the Apostles and the "non-miraculous aids" promised to every follower of Jesus)[46] appeared no longer compatible with the idea of an omnipotent and omnipresent Deity.

Emerson was not by any means remote from at least the more avant-garde wing of the Unitarian Church, therefore, when he argued that

43. R[ichard]. M[onckton]. M[ilnes], review of *Nature* (Boston, 1836), etc. (running title: "Emerson's Discourses"), *The London and Westminster Review* 33 (October 1839–March 1840): 364.

44. Andrews Norton, "On the Divinity School Address," in Konvitz, *Recognition of Emerson*, p. 7.

45. [John Brazer,] "Essay on the Doctrine of Divine Influence," *The Christian Examiner and Theological Review* 18 (March–May 1835); 50, 238. For attribution, see Buell, *Literary Transcendentalism*, p. 38.

46. [Brazer,] "Essay on the Doctrine of Divine Influence," *Christian Examiner* 17 (January 1835): 326.

all minds were potentially open to the influx of the divine. If the visible world is merely the "terminus" or "circumference" of Spirit, as the Plotinian Emerson had asserted in *Nature*, then there is every likelihood that the mind, too, is constantly fed by the streams of the shaping Spirit (*N*, p. 40). In *Essays*, 1841, Emerson tried to give a more precise account of the mechanisms through which inspiration reaches the mind of the individual and to justify his belief that such inspiration is necessarily benign—that "the relations of the soul to the divine spirit are so pure that it is profane to seek to interpose helps" (*EESS*, p. 54). Principally, Emerson believes that the mind shares with the universe around us the attribute of Being, and if Being is good, as he also believes, then that which comes from it must be good. There is simply more of Being in a virtuous thought or act than in a vicious thought or act. "We first share the life by which things exist, and afterwards see them as appearances in nature, and forget that we have shared their cause. Here is the fountain of action and the fountain of thought. Here are the lungs of that inspiration which giveth man wisdom, of that inspiration of man which cannot be denied without impiety and atheism" (*EESS*, p. 53).

In "The Over-Soul," however, Emerson concedes a significant point when he agrees that the actual origins of our thoughts are always concealed from us. "Always our being is descending into us from we know not whence" (*EESS*, p. 222). We cannot, then, *know* that the promptings of the spirit will in any particular case be benign. We simply trust that they are, given our conviction or faith that Being itself is good. It is the Over-Soul that excites in human beings every kind of creative mood, from "extasy and trance and prophetic inspiration" in the highest degree to the "glow of virtuous emotion" in the lowest, yet the Over-Soul itself cannot be interpreted, cannot be "spoken for" (*EESS*, pp. 233, 223).

Since Emerson emphasizes the unconscious part of the mind's activity in bringing to fruition the impulses of the Over-Soul some modern critics have suggested a similarity between Emerson's doctrine and Jung's hypothesis of the "collective unconscious."[47] Despite superficial resemblances, however, there is a radical difference between the *ontological basis* of Emerson's Over-Soul and that of Jung's collective

47. J. Russell Reaver, *Emerson as Mythmaker* (Gainesville: University of Florida Press, 1954), p. 27.

unconscious. Spirit, for Emerson, is not a purely human possession (despite the flirtation with idealism in the second part of *Nature*), and the truth of inspired utterance is not guaranteed, in any sense, by its correspondence with what others have thought or said, but by its grounding in the universal Reason, which we did not make but which rather made us. The inspiration of a Pindar, a Moses, or a Zoroaster was still available to moderns, according to Emerson, not so much because of our shared humanity but because, as human beings, they, like us, were "open on one side . . . to all the attributes of God" (*EESS*, pp. 23, 225).

With the concession that his belief in the Over-Soul and its benevolence rests on faith rather than knowledge, however, Emerson takes a significant step towards the reduced, more sceptical philosophy which characterized his later years. The Plotinian affirmations of the 1830s give way to a form of organized innocence in which the relative precariousness of the mind's healthful relationship with nature is recognized. Emerson concedes, in "The Poet," the need for a skilled interpreter of the mixed and sometimes disturbing signals we receive from the natural world. The poet is, of course, this skilled interpreter. All of us, Emerson says, receive rays or "appulses" from nature, but "the poet is the person in whom these powers are in balance, the man without impediment, who sees and handles that which others dream of, traverses the whole scale of experience, and its representative of man, in virtue of being the largest power to receive and to impart" (*EESS*, Second Ser., pp. 6–7).

This more limited definition of the poet's role, one more in the tradition of Wordsworth (the Wordsworth of the 1800 "Preface") than of Shelley, though still stressing the poet's redemptive or liberating role, is matched by a corresponding unwillingness on Emerson's part to define too precisely the "ineffable cause" which prompts poetic utterance. All our human attempts to find names for Being, and ways of addressing it, are now admitted to have fallen short. Various different traditions have named it "Fortune," "Minerva," "Muse," "Holy Ghost"; and philosophers and prophets symbolize it variously as water, air, Νοῦς, fire, or love (*EESS*, Second Ser., p. 79). The causes of inspiration remain unknown, then, but whereas in the 1830s Emerson had been inclined to stress the likelihood that these causes, being invisible, must be divine, he now emphasizes rather the ephemeral nature of any explanations or mythologies constructed around our ignorance of ultimate causes. The origin and the destination of the human soul, as the essay "Experience" sets out to demonstrate, are alike hidden from us.

Naturally this change—from a conception of the poet as a man unified at the deepest levels of mind with spiritualized nature to a conception of the poet as a man among men, subject to a distinct human law—was reflected in the poetry Emerson wrote. The enthusiastic poet of the early "Woodnotes" (first published in 1840) embraced a High Romantic, Schellingian idea of the poet's function. The poet's utterance is godlike because it is impelled by that same divine *nisus formativus* or *Bildungstrieb* which thrusts through all nature. Though disguised as the Greek god Pan (with a Protean ability to elude capture by shape-shifting), the creating Word, in this poem, is unmistakably the same as the "striving-for-form" hypostatized by the *Naturphilosophen.* In the words of Emerson's pine tree:

> "Onward and on, the eternal Pan,
> Who layeth the world's incessant plan,
> Halteth never in one shape,
> But forever doth escape,
> Like wave or flame, into new forms
> Of gem, and air, of plants, and worms."
>
> (*EP*, p. 56)

"Woodnotes" is a brave attempt to put off our years, to escape self-consciousness and tap the pure wells of ancient oracular poetry—"When holy were the haunted forest boughs." But its blend of animism and *Naturphilosophie* fails to convince us that a nineteenth-century poet can quite so straightforwardly overleap history. Where Keats makes poignant use of his sense of belatedness, bringing his "Ode to Psyche" to the borders of elegy, Emerson appears to refuse even to recognize belatedness as a problem—although history does obtrude on the poem in such inapposite images as "Caesar of his leafy Rome / There the poet is at home" and " 'The least breath my boughs which tossed / Brings again the Pentecost' " (*EP*, pp. 43, 52). The eye altering alters all: a pine tree seen by the nineteenth-century poet on furlough from lecturing in Boston is not the same as a pine tree seen by a shepherd of Arcady or by an Iroquois. Newness cannot be collected like water from a spring. Moreover, there is a confusion of modes here: pastoral is uncomfortably blended with High Romantic organicism. If Pan is a mischievous shape-shifter, can he *at the same time* personify the natural order as understood by the natural philosophers of the nineteenth century?

In a sense, Emerson says too much in "Woodnotes" and other early poems. He makes us aware of his escape to the woods much more as a flight *from* something than as a discovery *of* something. When "safe in my sylvan home," he assures us in "Goodbye,"

> I laugh at the lore and the pride of man,
> At the sophist schools and the learned clan;
> For what are they all, in their high conceit,
> When man in the bush with God may meet?
>
> (*EP*, p. 38)

The unfortunate casualness of "man in the bush with God may meet" undermines the poem's satiric animus and at the same time is too unwarily self-assured to hit the true Wordsworthian note of cautious trustfulness. In proclaiming so proudly the sylvan sources of his inspiration, Emerson really just betrays his own distance from them.

Where the poet is more doubting of his inspiration, as in "The Poet" (begun in 1831 or earlier, and still unfinished when Emerson laid it aside over twenty years later), the counterbalancing reassurance is more convincing. Fearful of losing the inspiration granted him, the poet addresses a "Chorus of Spirits," who answer:

> "See, all we are rooted here
> By one thought to one same sphere;
> From thyself thou canst not flee,—
> From thyself no more can we."
>
> (*EP*, p. 262)

This perception—that "spirit" is not a visitor from a remote sphere but is closer to the poet than his own five senses and shares in the "ebb and flood" of human thought—deserved more attention than the elusive wood-gods invoked in "Woodnotes," "The Apology," and elsewhere. Naturalizing the Muse does not of itself make the poet's calling any easier, since the poet remains what he always was: a mutable, mortal seeker, who sees by glimpses, not by the full glare and splendour of revelation.

In the poems of the 1840s there is less emphasis on what the poet *knows*, less emphasis therefore on inspiration, and much more on the poet as fabulist, reconciler of differences, creator of "the mid-world that is best."[48]

"Merlin" (written and published in 1846) portrays not the ecstatic prophet, but the legislator: "Merlin's mighty line / Extremes of nature reconciled . . ." (*EP*, p. 108). Nature still lends the poet a helping hand by providing numerous *exempla* of balance and harmony (the keys of statecraft, as well as of poetry). "Perfect-paired as eagle's wings / Justice is the rhyme of things . . ." (*EP*, p. 110). But the poet knows himself set apart from nature. There is "Law for man, and law for thing" (*EP*, p. 73). To know the "truths" of nature is not, now, to worship the *Bildungstrieb* under the appellations "Pan" or "Proteus," but to know the uses of the "herbs and simples of the wood" ("Blight," *EP*, p. 122) or to emulate the farmers in their cunning use of element against element, harnessing beast, bird, wind, and river to grow and harvest their crops:

So, year by year,
They fight the elements with elements,
(That one would say, meadow and forest walked,
Transmuted in these men to rule their like,)
And by the order in the field disclose
The order regnant in the yeoman's brain.
("Musketaquid," *EP*, p. 126)

The poet of "Musketaquid" is much more man among men than the poet of "Woodnotes." Cultivating his own garden (and orchard) Emerson has a more wary respect for untamed nature, upholds an order which is distinctively *human* (not read out from nature in any straightforward way), and has abandoned the proud independence of the prophetic poet resolved on nothing short of ecstatic utterance. Submission and plain-dealing wisdom are the new keynotes. The poet's strength is that of the willow, in knowing when to bend.

The gentle deities
Showed me the lore of colors and of sounds,
The innumerable tenements of beauty,
The miracle of generative force,
Far-reaching concords of astronomy

48. Yoder, *Emerson and the Orphic Poet*, pp. 7, 51.

Felt in the plants and in the punctual birds . . .
                                        still
I am a willow of the wilderness
Loving the wind that bent me. All my hurts
My garden spade can heal.

(*EP*, p. 126)

The echo of Coleridge's "Fears in Solitude" ("I walk with awe, and sing my stately songs, / Loving the God that made me!—"[*PW*, 1: 263]) emphasizes the transition Emerson successfully negotiates here from a poetry of prophetic affirmation to a poetry of limited aims and local attachments. Though even in "Musketaquid" Emerson does not achieve Thoreau's particularity, he is there closer in spirit to Thoreau than to Coleridge. Inspiration has become the natural byproduct of a useful life; almost the simple produce of the common day.

In the 1853 essay "Inspiration," then, without actually retracting his earlier affirmations, Emerson represents inspiration as something that can be worked for and cultivated (just as in "Man, the Reformer" he encourages his audience to be practical, to do the work that lies to hand). Emerson sounds almost like Thoreau as he announces, brusquely, "Every youth should know the way to prophecy as surely as the miller understands how to let on the water or the engineer the steam" (*LSA*, p. 258). Health, letter-writing, willpower, solitary walks, and conversation with congenial friends are listed as promising ways of opening the sluice-gates of inspired thought. So demythologized, inspiration becomes one of the necessary accomplishments of manhood, a mystery in the medieval sense of "craft, profession," not an outlandish and often terrifying power. The correspondence between mind and nature, on which inspiration ultimately depends, is still a theme, though Emerson implicitly recognizes that this correspondence is itself a result of a healthy disposition, the organized innocence of the poet, and is not bestowed equally and permanently on all human beings. In a journal entry of 1839, Emerson had in a sense anticipated this picture of the ideal poet as one who "cannot see a natural phenomenon which does not express to him a correspondent fact in his mental experience," and who "is made aware of a power to carry on and complete the metamorphosis of natural into spiritual facts" (*LSA*, p. 257). Yet the earlier passage had made much larger claims: "The poet the true naturalist for example domesticates himself in nature with a sense of strict consanguinity. His own blood is in the rose &

the appletree. The Cause of him is Cause of all. The volcano has its analogies in him. He is in the chain of magnetic, electric, geologic, meteorologic phenomena & so he comes to live in nature & extend his being through all: then is true science" (*JMN*, 7: 181–82).

The essay "Inspiration," while holding out the poet's invigorating sense of a universal harmony as a goal and a criterion of our "happier" moments, emerges from a comparison with the journals of the 1830s as saying, in effect, "cherish your best thoughts, but remember your humanity." It is this more temperate Emerson that has most in common with the new humanism of Margaret Fuller, Walt Whitman, and the Thoreau who wrote, "To perceive freshly, with fresh senses, is to be inspired."[49]

Some of the special characteristics of the Romantic and Coleridgean heritage express themselves more clearly in Emerson than in any other nineteenth-century writer. Lacking Coleridge's acute sense of the transcendent (which, I have argued, was never wholly eclipsed, even during Coleridge's protracted and arduous study of Schelling and *Naturphilosophie*), Emerson tried to account in immanentist fashion for the phenomenon of inspiration and to provide a natural history of inspiration which would augur well for the new literature of an emergent nation. The solution given in *Nature*, stressing that nature itself is constantly shaped and permeated by Spirit and that "inspiration," therefore, is simply a state of extraordinary receptiveness to omnipresent Spirit, is an attractive one in many respects; but it is vulnerable in the same way in which Wordsworth's "chearful faith that all which we behold / Is full of blessings" is vulnerable. The eye altering alters all. The state of ecstasy invoked in the "transparent eyeball" passage is discovered, in the light of later experience, to have depended on an inherently unstable harmony between the self and the world.

If this first formulation was over-optimistic, however, Emerson does not make the mistake of over-correcting himself by denying that inspiration in any sense is possible. Inspiration appears to be a function of spiritual health: the order regnant in the brain must correspond with the order sometimes (not always) discernible in the universe. Let

49. Quoted in Joel Porte, *Emerson and Thoreau: Transcendentalists in Conflict* (Middletown, Conn.: Wesleyan University Press, 1966), p. 141. The phrase "new humanism" is used of Margaret Fuller's thought by Kathleen Dierdre Guerin, SND., "Margaret Fuller d'Ossoli, Modern American Humanist," Ph.D. diss., University of Minnesota, 1975, p. ix.

that state of health, then, be the poet's ideal goal. The poet may still perceive "The miracle of generative force, / Far-reaching concords of astronomy": such perceptions are earned by his self-discipline, his acceptance of human limitations, and they are no guarantee of divine favour.

This reduced view of poetic inspiration is in one sense an end, in another sense a beginning. The immanentist faith of *Nature* survives only as an attractive but untenable hypothesis or as a Plotinian expression of youthful joy. But the later perception of Emerson, that Spirit—if it speaks to human minds at all—can communicate only through human experiences and in human modes, brings us to a new sense of the poet's role.

Espousing Emerson's desire to see the poet as microcosm, as reconciler of contraries, the poet may enlarge the sphere of his own being to embrace everything that Emerson comprehended under the terms "Nature" and "Spirit." This is Whitman's way, in "Song of Myself." Whitman is to be, in his own person, the reincarnation of all the old gods, and their best interpreter,

> Accepting the rough deific sketches to fill out
> better in myself . . . bestowing them freely
> on each man and woman I see.[50]

Or the poet may return—doubtingly, it may be, and with a complexly questioning rather than a straightforwardly affirming stance—to the figure in whom many generations have found the only compelling expression of God's commitment to humankind, the figure of Christ. This solution—or rather (since it is not so much a solution as an opening-up to exploration, a choice of choices) this reorientation towards a promise of transcendent love—is Browning's response to the failure of pantheisms and natural religions, his way of glimpsing "How heaven's high with earth's low should intertwine!"

50. Walt Whitman, *Leaves of Grass*, ed. Harold W. Blodgett and Sculley Bradley (New York: New York University Press, 1965), p. 75.

Bibliography

WORKS BY COLERIDGE

Manuscripts

Toronto. Victoria University Library MS BT 30. "Fly-catchers," nos. 1–3. Transcribed by two unknown hands, with notes by Henry Nelson Coleridge and Ernest Hartley Coleridge.

– Victoria University Library MS LT 44. Marginalia in Johann Jahn, *Appendix Hermeneuticae* (Vienna, 1813–15). Transcribed by James Dykes Campbell and unknown hand.

– Victoria University Library S MS 28. "Opus Magnum."

– Victoria University Library S MS 29. "Opus Maximum."

London. British Library. Shelfmark C.126.h.9. Marginalia in F. D. E. Schleiermacher, *A Critical Essay on the Gospel of St. Luke* [translated by Connop Thirlwall] (London: John Taylor, 1825).

Printed Works

Aids to Reflection . . . First American, from the first London edition; with an Appendix . . . together with a Preliminary Essay, and Additional Notes, by James Marsh. Burlington: Chauncey Goodrich, 1829.

Biographia Literaria. Edited by James Engell and W. Jackson Bate. *Collected Works* (Bollingen Series 75), vol. 7. 2 vols. London and Princeton, N.J.: Routledge and Kegan Paul and Princeton University Press, 1983.

Collected Letters. Edited by Earl Leslie Griggs. 6 vols. Oxford: The Clarendon Press, 1956–71.

Complete Poetical Works. Edited by Ernest Hartley Coleridge. 2 vols. Oxford: The Clarendon Press, 1912.

Complete Works. Edited by W. G. T. Shedd. 7 vols. New York: Harper and Brothers, 1853–58.

The Friend. Edited by Barbara E. Rooke. *Collected Works* (Bollingen Series 75), vol. 4. 2 vols. London and Princeton, N.J.: Routledge and Kegan Paul and Princeton University Press, 1969.

Lay Sermons. Edited by R. J. White. *Collected Works* (Bollingen Series 75), vol. 6. London and Princeton, N.J.: Routledge and Kegan Paul and Princeton University Press, 1972.

Lectures 1795 on Politics and Religion. Edited by Lewis Patton and Peter Mann. *Collected Works* (Bollingen Series 75), vol. 1. London and Princeton, N.J.: Routledge and Kegan Paul and Princeton University Press, 1971.

Marginalia. Edited by George Whalley. *Collected Works* (Bollingen Series 75), vol. 12. Vol. 1: Abbt to Byfield. London and Princeton, N.J.: Routledge and Kegan Paul and Princeton University Press, 1980.

The Notebooks. Edited by Kathleen Coburn. Bollingen Series 50. New York: Bollingen Foundation/Pantheon Books, 1957—.

"On Poesy or Art." In *Biographia Literaria*. Edited by J. Shawcross. 2 vols. London: Oxford University Press, 1907.

On the Constitution of the Church and State. Edited by John Colmer. *Collected Works* (Bollingen Series 75), vol. 10. London and Princeton, N.J.: Routledge and Kegan Paul and Princeton University Press, 1976.

The Table Talk and Omniana. Edited by T. Ashe. London: George Bell and Sons, 1884.

WORKS BY OTHER AUTHORS

Abrams, M. H. "The Correspondent Breeze: A Romantic Metaphor." In *English Romantic Poets: Modern Essays in Criticism*, edited by M. H. Abrams, pp. 37–54. London: Oxford University Press, 1960.

Adams, Maurianne Schifreen. "Coleridge and the Victorians: Studies in the Interpretation of Poetry, Scripture, and Myth." Ph.D. dissertation, Indiana University, 1967.

Alcott, Amos Bronson. *The Journals*. Edited by Odell Shepard. Boston: Little, Brown and Co., 1938.

Alexander, Edward. *Matthew Arnold and John Stuart Mill*. New York and London: Columbia University Press and Routledge and Kegan Paul, 1965.

Allen, Peter. *The Cambridge Apostles: The Early Years*. Cambridge: Cambridge University Press, 1978.

Arnold, Thomas. *Sermons Chiefly on the Interpretation of Scripture*. London: B. Fellowes, 1845.

– *Two Sermons on the Interpretation of Prophecy*. Oxford: J. H. Parker, 1839.

Ashton, Rosemary. *The German Idea: Four English Writers and the Reception of German Thought 1800–1860*. London: Cambridge University Press, 1980.

Austin, Alfred. *The Poetry of the Period*. London: Bentley, 1870.

Barfield, Owen. *What Coleridge Thought*. London: Oxford University Press, 1972.

Barth, J. Robert, S.J. *Coleridge and Christian Doctrine*. Cambridge, Mass.: Harvard University Press, 1969.

– *The Symbolic Imagination: Coleridge and the Romantic Tradition*. Princeton, N.J.:

Princeton University Press, 1977.
Beer, J. B. *Coleridge's Poetic Intelligence*. London: Macmillan, 1977.
– *Coleridge the Visionary*. 2nd ed. London: Chatto and Windus, 1970.
Berlin, Isaiah. *Vico and Herder: Two Studies in the History of Ideas*. New York: Viking Press, 1976.
Bewer, Julius A. *The Literature of the Old Testament*. Rev. Emil G. Kraeling. New York: Columbia University Press, 1962.
Blackburn, William. "Carlyle and the Composition of *The Life of John Sterling*." *Studies in Philology* 44 (1947); 672–87.
Blake, William. *The Notebook of William Blake: A Photographic and Typographic Facsimile*. Edited by David Erdman. Rev. ed. N.p.: Readex Books, 1977.
– *The Poetry and Prose*. Edited by David Erdman, commentary by Harold Bloom. Garden City, N.Y.: Doubleday, 1965.
Bloom, Harold. *The Anxiety of Influence: A Theory of Poetry*. London: Oxford University Press, 1973.
– "Coleridge: The Anxiety of Influence," In *New Perspectives on Coleridge and Wordsworth: Selected Papers from the English Institute*, edited by Geoffrey H. Hartman, pp. 247–67. New York and London: Columbia University Press, 1972.
Bostetter, Edward E. "The Nightmare World of the Ancient Mariner." *Studies in Romanticism* 1 (1961): 241–54.
Boulger, James D. *Coleridge as Religious Thinker*. New Haven: Yale University Press, 1961.
[Bowen, Francis.] Review of Ralph Waldo Emerson's *Nature* (running title: "Transcendentalism"). *The Christian Examiner* 21 (1837): 371–85.
Bowra, C. M. *Inspiration and Poetry*. London: Macmillan, 1955.
[Brazer, John.] "Essay on the Doctrine of Divine Influence." *The Christian Examiner* 17 (1835): 311–32, and 18 (1835): 50–84, 230–59.
Brew, Claude. "A New Shelley Text: Essay on Miracles and Christian Doctrine." *Keats-Shelley Memorial Bulletin* 28 (1977): 10–28.
Brisman, Leslie. *Romantic Origins*. Ithaca, N.Y.: Cornell University Press, 1978.
– "Coleridge and the Supernatural." *Studies in Romanticism* 21 (1982): 123–59.
Bruns, Gerald L. "The Formal Nature of Victorian Thinking." *PMLA* 90 (1975): 904–18.
Buell, Lawrence. *Literary Transcendentalism: Style and Vision in the American Renaissance*. Ithaca, N.Y.: Cornell University Press, 1973.
Burlington, Vt. Guy W. Bailey Library, University of Vermont. James Marsh Collection.
Buttrick, George A., ed. *The Interpreter's Dictionary of the Bible*. 4 vols. New York and Nashville: Abingdon Press, 1962.
Cabot, James Elliot. *A Memoir of Ralph Waldo Emerson*. 2 vols. Boston and New York: Houghton Mifflin Co., 1887.
Cambridge. Trinity College. Whewell Collection Add. MSS a 206, a 215.

Cameron, Kenneth Walter. *Young Emerson's Transcendental Vision.* Hartford, Conn.: Transcendental Books, 1971.

Campbell, Joseph. "Bios and Mythos: Prolegomena to a Science of Mythology." In *Myth and Literature: Contemporary Theory and Practice,* edited by John B. Vickery, pp. 15–23. Lincoln, Neb.: University of Nebraska Press, 1966.

Carafiol, Peter C. "James Marsh's American *Aids to Reflection*: Influence through Ambiguity." *New England Quarterly* 49 (1976): 27–45.

Carlyle, Thomas. *Letters of Thomas Carlyle to John Stuart Mill, John Sterling and Robert Browning.* Edited by Alexander Carlyle. London: T. Fisher Unwin, 1923.

– *The Life of John Sterling.* Centenary Edition of Carlyle's *Works,* vol 11. London: Chapman and Hall, c. 1895.

– *New Letters of Thomas Carlyle.* Edited and annotated by Alexander Carlyle. 2 vols. London and New York: John Lane, The Bodley Head, 1904.

Cassirer, Ernst. *The Philosophy of the Enlightenment.* Translated by Fritz A. Koelln and James P. Pettegrove. Princeton, N.J.: Princeton University Press, 1951.

Chadwick, Owen. *From Bossuet to Newman: The Idea of Doctrinal Development.* Cambridge: Cambridge University Press, 1957.

– *The Victorian Church.* 2 vols. Part 5 of *An Ecclesiastical History of England,* edited by J. C. Dickinson. London: Adam and Charles Black, 1966.

[Channing, William Ellery.] Review of Milton's *A Treatise on Christian Doctrine,* translated by Charles R. Sumner (running title: "Milton"). *The Christian Examiner and Theological Review* 3 (1826): 29–77.

[Cheever, George Barrell.] Review of Coleridge's *The Friend. North American Review* 40 (1835): 299–351.

Christensen, Torben. *Origin and History of Christian Socialism 1848–54.* Acta Theologica Danica 3. Aarhus: Universitetsforlaget i Aarhus, 1962.

Coburn, Kathleen. *Experience Into Thought: Perspectives in the Coleridge Notebooks.* Toronto: University of Toronto Press, 1979.

– *The Self Conscious Imagination.* London: Oxford University Press, 1974.

Cooke, George Willis. *An Historical and Biographical Introduction to Accompany "The Dial".* Reprint. 2 vols. New York: Russell and Russell, 1961.

Coulson, John. *Newman and the Common Tradition: A Study in the Language of Church and Society.* Oxford: Clarendon Press, 1970.

Delaura, David J. *Hebrew and Hellene in Victorian England: Newman, Arnold and Pater.* Austin: University of Texas Press, 1969.

de Man, Paul. "The Rhetoric of Temporality." In *Interpretation: Theory and Practice,* edited by Charles Southward Singleton, pp. 173–209. Baltimore: Johns Hopkins University Press, 1969.

Dewey, John. "James Marsh and American Philosophy." *Journal of the History of Ideas* 2 (1941): 131–50.

Distad, N. Merrill. *Guessing at Truth: The Life of Julius Charles Hare (1795–1855).* Shepherdstown, W. Va.: The Patmos Press, 1979.

Duffy, John J., ed. *Coleridge's American Disciples: The Selected Correspondence of*

James Marsh. Amherst, Mass.: University of Massachusetts Press, 1973.
Edinburgh. National Library of Scotland. Sterling Collection, MSS 1765, 1766.
Eliot, George. *Adam Bede*. Edited by Stephen Gill. Harmondsworth: Penguin Books, 1980.
Emerson, Ralph Waldo. *A Correspondence between John Sterling and Ralph Waldo Emerson*. Edited by E. W. Emerson. Boston and New York: Houghton, Mifflin and Co., 1897.
– *Essays* [and] *Essays: Second Series*. Merrill Standard Editions. Columbus, Ohio: Charles E. Merrill Publishing Company, 1969.
– *The Journals and Miscellaneous Notebooks*. Edited by William H. Gilman et al. Cambridge, Mass.: Harvard University Press, The Belknap Press, 1960—.
– *The Letters*. Edited by Ralph L. Rusk. 6 vols. 1939. Reprint. New York and London: Columbia University Press, 1966.
– *Letters and Social Aims*. Riverside Edition of Emerson's *Works*. Vol. 8. London and New York: George Routledge and Sons, 1883.
– *Nature, Addresses, and Lectures*. Riverside Edition of Emerson's *Works*. Vol 1. London and New York: George Routledge and Sons, 1886.
– *Poems*. Riverside Edition of Emerson's *Works*. Vol. 9. London and New York: George Routledge and Sons, 1888.
Emerson, Ralph Waldo, William Henry Channing, and James Freeman Clarke. *Memoirs of Margaret Fuller Ossoli*. 2 vols. Boston: Roberts Brothers, 1881.
Empson, William. "The Ancient Mariner." *The Critical Quarterly* 6 (1964): 298–319.
Engell, James. *The Creative Imagination: Enlightenment to Romanticism*. Cambridge, Mass.: Harvard University Press, 1981.
Evans, C. F. "The Inspiration of the Bible." *Theology* 59 (1956): 11–17.
Feuer, Lewis S. "James Marsh and the Conservative Transcendentalist Philosophy: A Political Interpretation." *The New England Quarterly* 31 (1958): 3–31.
Fish, Stanley. *Is There A Text In This Class? The Authority of Interpretive Communities*. Cambridge, Mass.: Harvard University Press, 1980.
Frei, Hans. *The Eclipse of Biblical Narrative: A Study in Eighteenth and Nineteenth Century Hermeneutics*. New Haven and London: Yale University Press, 1974.
Frothingham, Octavius Brooks. *Transcendentalism in New England: A History*. 1876. Reprint. New York: Harper and Brothers, 1959.
Frye, Northrop. *The Great Code: The Bible and Literature*. Toronto: Academic Press Canada, 1982.
Furst, Lilian. *Romanticism in Perspective*. London: Macmillan, 1969.
Garland, Martha McMackin. *Cambridge Before Darwin: The Idea of a Liberal Education, 1800–1860*. Cambridge: Cambridge University Press, 1980.
Gérard, Albert. "The Systolic Rhythm: The Structure of Coleridge's Conversation Poems." *Essays in Criticism* 10 (1960): 307–19.
Goddard, Harold Clarke. *Studies in New England Transcendentalism*. 1908. Reprint. New York: Hilary House Publishers, 1960.
Goethe, Johann Wolfgang von. *West-Eastern Divan, in Twelve Books*. Translated

by Edward Dowden. London: J. M. Dent and Sons, 1914.
– *West-oestlicher Divan.* Stuttgart: Lottaischer Buchhandlung, 1819.

Goodheart, Eugene. *The Failure of Criticism.* Cambridge, Mass.: Harvard University Press, 1978.

Grant, Robert M. *A Short History of the Interpretation of the Bible.* London: Adam and Charles Black, 1965.

Greenslade, S. L. *The Cambridge History of the Bible: The West from the Reformation to the Present Day.* Cambridge: Cambridge University Press, 1963.

Guerin, Kathleen Dierdre, S.N.D. "Margaret Fuller d'Ossoli, Modern American Humanist." Ph.D. dissertation, University of Minnesota, 1975.

Haney, Janice L. " 'Shadow-Hunting': Romantic Irony, *Sartor Resartus,* and Victorian Romanticism." *Studies in Romanticism* 17 (1978). 307–33.

Harding, Anthony John. "Development and Symbol in the Thought of S. T. Coleridge, J. C. Hare, and John Sterling." *Studies in Romanticism* 18 (1979): 29–48.
– "James Marsh as Editor of Coleridge." In *Reading Coleridge: Approaches and Applications,* edited by Walter B. Crawford, pp. 223–51. Ithaca, N.Y.: Cornell University Press, 1979.
– "Mythopoeic Elements in 'Christabel.' " *Modern Language Quarterly* 44 (1983): 39–50.

Hardy, Thomas. *Jude the Obscure.* Edited by Norman Page. New York: W. W. Norton, 1978.

Hare, Augustus J. C. *Memorials of a Quiet Life.* 12th ed. 2 vols. London: Daldy, Isbister, and Co., 1875.

Hare, J. C. Manuscripts. See Cambridge. Trinity College.
– *The Mission of the Comforter.* 1846. Rev. ed. Boston: Gould and Lincoln, 1854.
– *Thou Shalt Not Bear False Witness Against Thy Neighbour: A Letter to the Editor of the English Review . . . With a Letter from Professor Maurice to the Author.* London: John W. Parker, 1849.

Hartman, Geoffrey H. *Beyond Formalism: Literary Essays 1958–1970.* New Haven and London: Yale University Press, 1970.
– *Criticism in the Wilderness: The Study of Literature Today.* New Haven and London: Yale University Press, 1980.
– *The Unmediated Vision: An Interpretation of Wordsworth, Hopkins, Rilke, and Valéry.* New Haven: Yale University Press, 1954.

Haven, Richard, Josephine Haven, and Maurianne Adams. *Samuel Taylor Coleridge: An Annotated Bibliography of Criticism and Scholarship.* Vol. 1: 1793–1899. Boston: G. K. Hall and Co., 1976.

[Hedge, Frederic Henry.] Review of Coleridge's *Biographia Literaria,* etc. (running title: "Coleridge's Literary Character"). *The Christian Examiner* 14 (1833): 108–29.
– Introduction to *Essays and Reviews By Eminent English Churchmen.* 3rd American ed. New York: Henry Holt and Company, 1874.

Heraud, John Abraham. *A Philosophical Estimate of the Controversy respecting the Divine Humanity*. London: James Fraser, 1831.

Herder, Johann Gottfried von. *Sämmtliche Werke*. Edited by Bernhard Suphan. 33 vols. Berlin: Weidmannsche Buchhandlung, 1877–1913.

– *The Spirit of Hebrew Poetry*. Translated by James Marsh. 1833. Reprint (2 vols in 1). Naperville, Ill.: Aleph Press, 1971.

Hirsch, E. D., Jr. *Validity in Interpretation*. New Haven: Yale University Press, 1967.

Hoffpauir, Richard. " 'Kubla Khan' and the Critics: Romantic Madness as Poetic Theme and Critical Response." *English Studies in Canada* 2 (1976): 402–22.

Hunt, Bishop C. "Coleridge and the Endeavor of Philosophy." *PMLA* 91 (1976): 829–39.

James, William. *The Varieties of Religious Experience: A Study in Human Nature*. London: Longmans, Green and Co., 1928.

Johnston, Carol. "The Underlying Structure of the Divinity School Address: Emerson as Jeremiah." In *Studies in the American Renaissance*, edited by Joel Myerson, pp. 41–49. Boston: Twayne Publishers, 1980.

Johnston, Kenneth R. " 'Home at Grasmere': Reclusive Song." *Studies in Romanticism* 14 (1975): 1–28.

Jowett, Benjamin. "On the Interpretation of Scripture." In *Essays and Reviews*, edited by Frederick Temple et al., pp. 330–433. London: John W. Parker, 1860.

Kessler, Edward. *Coleridge's Metaphors of Being*. Princeton, N.J.: Princeton University Press, 1979.

Konvitz, Milton R., ed. *The Recognition of Ralph Waldo Emerson*. Ann Arbor: The University of Michigan Press, 1972.

Kramer, Lawrence. "That Other Will: The Daemonic in Coleridge and Wordsworth." *Philological Quarterly* 58 (1979):298–320.

Küng, Hans. *On Being a Christian*. Translated by Edward Quinn. N.p.: Collins, 1978.

Lamb, Charles, and Mary Anne Lamb. *Letters*. Edited by Edwin W. Marrs, Jr. 4 vols. Ithaca and London: Cornell University Press, 1975.

Lessing, Gotthold Ephraim. *The Education of the Human Race*. Translated by Fred. W. Robertson. 4th rev. ed. London: Kegan Paul, Trench, Trübner and Company, 1896.

– *Werke*. Edited by Georg Witkowski. 7 vols. Leipzig and Vienna: Bibliographisches Institut, c. 1911.

Long, Orie William. *Frederic Henry Hedge: A Cosmopolitan Scholar*. Portland, Me.: The Southworth-Anthoensen Press, 1940.

McFarland, G. F. "Julius Charles Hare: Coleridge, De Quincey, and German Literature." *Bulletin of the John Rylands Library* 47 (1964): 165–97.

McFarland, Thomas. *Coleridge and the Pantheist Tradition*. Oxford: The Clarendon Press, 1969.

– "The Origin and Significance of Coleridge's Theory of Secondary Imagination." In *New Perspectives on Coleridge and Wordsworth: Selected Papers from the English Institute*, edited by Geoffrey H. Hartman, pp. 195–246. New York and London: Columbia University Press, 1972.

– *Romanticism and the Forms of Ruin: Wordsworth, Coleridge, and Modalities of Fragmentation.* Princeton, N.J.: Princeton University Press, 1981.

Marsh, James. Manuscripts. See Burlington, Vt. Guy W. Bailey Library, University of Vermont.

– *An Address Delivered in Burlington, upon the Inauguration of the Author to the Office of President of the University of Vermont, Nov. 28, 1826.* Burlington, Vt.: E. and T. Mills, 1826.

– Review of di Breme's *Intorno all'ingiustizia di alcuni letterarii Italiani* (running titles: "Present Literature of Italy—Ancient and Modern Poetry"). *North American Review* n.s. 15 (1822), 94–131.

Martineau, James. *Essays, Reviews, and Addresses.* 4 vols. London and New York: Longmans, Green and Co., 1890–91.

Matthiessen, Francis Otto. *American Renaissance: Art and Expression in the Age of Emerson and Whitman.* London: Oxford University Press, 1941.

Maurice, Frederick. *The Life of Frederick Denison Maurice Chiefly Told in His Own Letters.* 4th ed. 2 vols. London: Macmillan and Co., 1885.

Maurice, [John] Frederick Denison. *The Epistle to the Hebrews: Being the Substance of Three Lectures Delivered in the Chapel of the Honourable Society of Lincoln's Inn.* London: John W. Parker, 1846.

– Introduction to *Charges to the Clergy of the Archdeaconry of Lewes, delivered . . . in the years 1843, 1845, 1846*, by Julius Charles Hare. Cambridge: Macmillan, 1856.

[–] *The Kingdom of Christ: or Hints on the Principles, Ordinances and Constitution of the Catholic Church. In Letters to a Member of the Society of Friends. By a Clergyman of the Church of England.* 3 vols. London: Darton and Clark, c. 1837.

– *The Kingdom of Christ; or, Hints to a Quaker, respecting the Principles, Constitution, and Ordinances of the Catholic Church.* 2nd ed. 2 vols. London: J. G. F. and J. Rivington, 1842.

– *The Religions of the World and Their Relations to Christianity.* London: John W. Parker, 1847.

– *Sequel to the Inquiry, What Is Revelation? In a Series of Letters to a Friend.* Macmillan: Cambridge and London, 1860.

– *Theological Essays.* 1853. Reprint. London: James Clarke and Co., 1957.

– *What is Revelation? A Series of Sermons on the Epiphany.* Cambridge and London: Macmillan, 1859.

[– and John Sterling?] "Coleridge and the Germans. A Dialogue." *Athenaeum* No. 101 (30 September 1829): 613–14.

Mellor, Anne K. "Coleridge's 'This Lime-Tree Bower My Prison' and the

Categories of English Landscape." *Studies in Romanticism* 18 (1979): 253–70.

Mileur, Jean-Pierre. *Vision and Revision: Coleridge's Art of Immanence*. Berkeley: University of California Press, 1982.

Miller, R. D. *Schiller and the Ideal of Freedom*. Oxford: The Clarendon Press, 1970.

[Milnes, Richard Monckton.] Review of Emerson's *Nature*, etc. *The London and Westminster Review* 33 (1840): 345–72.

Milton, John. *Poems*, Edited by B. A. Wright. London: Dent, 1962.

Moffat, Douglas. "Coleridge's Ten Theses: The Plotinian Alternative." *The Wordsworth Circle* 13 (1982): 27–31.

Mozoomdar, Protap Chunder. "Emerson as Seen from India." In *The Genius and Character of Emerson*, edited by F. B. Sanborn. 1885. Reprint. Port Washington, N.Y.: Kennikat Press, 1971.

Muirhead, J. H. *Coleridge as Philosopher*. London: Allen and Unwin, 1930.

[Newman, Francis W.] "John Sterling." *Prospective Review* 8 (1852): 1–16.

Newman, John Henry. *An Essay on the Development of Christian Doctrine*. London: Longmans, Green and Co., 1920.

Newsome, David. *Two Classes of Men: Platonism and English Romantic Thought*. London: John Murray, 1974.

Nicolson, Marjorie Hope. "James Marsh and the Vermont Transcendentalists." *Philosophical Reveiw* 34 (1925): 28–50.

Ong, Walter J., S.J. *The Presence of the Word: Some Prolegomena for Cultural and Religious History*. 2nd. rev. ed. Minneapolis: University of Minnesota Press, 1981.

Orr, Alexandra Sutherland. "The Religious Opinions of Robert Browning." *The Contemporary Review* 60 (1891): 876–91.

Palmer, Richard E. *Hermeneutics: Interpretation Theory in Schleiermacher, Dilthey, Heidegger, and Gadamer*. Evanston: Northwestern University Press, 1969.

[Palmer, William.] "On Tendencies Towards the Subversion of Faith." *The English Review* 10 (1848): 399–444.

Passmore, John. *The Perfectibility of Man*. London: Duckworth, 1970.

Pearce, Donald. " 'Kubla Khan' in Context." *Studies in English Literature 1500–1900* 21 (1981): 565–83.

Plato. *Ion*. Translated by Michael Oakley. In *Symposium and Other Dialogues*, pp. 63–77. London and New York: Dent and Dutton, 1964.

– *The Laws*. Translated by A. E. Taylor. London: J.M. Dent, 1934.

Pochmann, Henry A. *German Culture in America: Philosophical and Literary Influences 1600–1900*. Madison, Wis.: University of Wisconsin Press, 1957.

Porte, Joel. *Emerson and Thoreau: Transcendentalists in Conflict*. Middletown, Conn.: Wesleyan University Press, 1966.

Porter, Noah. "Coleridge and His American Disciples." *Bibliotheca Sacra* 4 (1847): 117–71.

Preyer, Robert Otto. *Bentham, Coleridge, and the Science of History*. Bochum-Langendreer: Verlag Heinrich Pöppinghaus, 1958.

Prickett, Stephen. *Romanticism and Religion: The Tradition of Coleridge and Wordsworth in the Victorian Church*. Cambridge: Cambridge University Press, 1976.

Read, Herbert. *Coleridge as Critic*. London: Faber and Faber, 1949.

Reaver, J. Russell. *Emerson as Mythmaker*. Gainesville, Fla.: University of Florida Press, 1954.

Review of Coleridge's *Aids to Reflection*, etc. *Eclectic Review* 5th ser., 1 (1851): 1–22.

Review of Maurice's *The Church a Family*. *Prospective Review* 7 (1851): 25–49.

Review of Coleridge's *Confessions of an Enquiring Spirit*. *The English Review* 12 (1849): 247–71.

Review of Cousin's *Fragmens Philosophiques*. *American Quarterly Review* 10 (1831): 291–311.

Review of Maurice's *The Kingdom of Christ*. *Eclectic Review* 4th ser., 7 (1840): 150–63.

Review of Maurice's *The Kingdom of Christ*, 2nd. ed., etc. *Eclectic Review* 5th ser., 2 (1851): 257–84.

[Ripley, George.] Review of Martineau's *The Rationale of Religious Enquiry*. *The Christian Examiner* 21 (1836): 225–54.

[–] Review of Herder's *The Spirit of Hebrew Poetry*, translated by James Marsh. *The Christian Examiner* 18 (1835): 167–221.

Rosenblatt, Louise M. *The Reader: the Text: the Poem: The Transactional Theory of the Literary Work*. Carbondale: Southern Illinois University Press, 1978.

Roston, Murray. *Prophet and Poet: The Bible and the Growth of Romanticism*. London: Faber and Faber, 1965.

Sanders, Charles Richard. "The Background of Carlyle's Portrait of Coleridge in *The Life of John Sterling*." *Bulletin of the John Rylands University Library of Manchester* 55 (1973): 434–58.

– *Coleridge and the Broad Church Movement*. Durham, N.C.: Duke University Press, 1942.

– "Maurice as a Commentator on Coleridge." *PMLA* 53 (1938): 230–43.

Scheick, William J. *The Slender Human Word: Emerson's Artistry in Prose*. Knoxville: University of Tennessee Press, 1978.

Schelling, Friedrich Wilhelm Joseph von. *Sämmtliche Werke*. Edited by K. F. A. Schelling. 14 vols. Stuttgart and Augsburg: J. G. Cotta, 1856–61.

Schlegel, Friedrich. *Charakteristiken und Kritiken* 1. Edited by Hans Eichner. *Kritische Friedrich-Schlegel-Ausgabe*, vol 7. Munich: Verlag Ferdinand Schöningh, 1967.

Schleiermacher, Friedrich Daniel Ernst. *Der christliche Glaube nach den Grundsäzen der evangelischen Kirche in Zusammenhange dargestellt*. 2nd rev. ed. 2 vols. Berlin: G. Reimer, 1830–31.

– *A Critical Essay on the Gospel of St. Luke.* [Translated by Connop Thirlwall.] London: John Taylor, 1825.

– "*The Hermeneutics*: Outline of the 1819 Lectures." Translated by Jan Wojcik and Roland Haas. *New Literary History* 10, no. 1 (1978): 1–16.

Schneider, Elisabeth. *Coleridge, Opium and "Kubla Khan."* Chicago: University of Chicago Press, 1953.

Schulz, Max F. "Coleridge and the Enchantments of Earthly Paradise." In *Reading Coleridge: Approaches and Applications*, edited by Walter B. Crawford, pp. 116–59. Ithaca, N.Y.: Cornell University Press, 1979.

– *The Poetic Voices of Coleridge.* Detroit: Wayne State University Press, 1963.

Schweitzer, Albert. *The Quest of the Historical Jesus: A Critical Study of its Progress from Reimarus to Wrede.* Translated by W. Montgomery. 2nd English ed. London: A. and C. Black, 1922.

Seybold, Ethel. *Thoreau: The Quest and the Classics.* New Haven: Yale University Press, 1951.

Shaffer, Elinor S. *"Kubla Khan" and "The Fall of Jerusalem": The Mythological School in Biblical Criticism and Secular Literature 1770–1880.* Cambridge: Cambridge University Press, 1975.

Shelley, Percy Bysshe. "A Defence of Poetry." In *Complete Works*, edited by Roger Ingpen and Walter E. Peck, vol. 7. London and New York: The Julian Editions, 1930.

Snelders, H. A. M. "Romanticism and Naturphilosophie and the Inorganic Natural Sciences 1797–1840: An Introductory Survey." *Studies in Romanticism* 9 (1970): 193–215.

Stanley, Arthur Penrhyn. *The Life and Correspondence of Thomas Arnold, D.D.* 3rd ed. 2 vols. London: B. Fellowes, 1844.

Sterling, John. Manuscripts. See Edinburgh: National Library of Scotland.

– *Essays and Tales.* Edited by Julius Charles Hare. 2 vols. London: John W. Parker, 1848.

– *Letters from John Sterling to George Webbe Dasent 1838–1844.* Edited by John R. Dasent. Edinburgh: privately printed, 1914.

– *Sterling's Letters to Coningham.* Edited by William Coningham. 3rd ed. London and Bath: Simpkin, Marshall and Co. and R. E. Peach, 1872.

Sternbach, Robert. "Coleridge, Joan of Arc, and the Idea of Progress." *ELH* 46 (1979): 248–61.

Stewart, Herbert L. "The Place of Coleridge in English Theology." *Harvard Theological Review* 11 (1918): 1–31.

Stoughton, John. *Religion in England from 1800 to 1850. A History.* 2 vols. London: Hodder and Stoughton, 1884.

Strauss, David Friedrich. *Das Leben Jesu, kritisch bearbeitet.* 2 vols. Tübingen: C. F. Osiander, 1840.

– *The Life of Jesus, critically examined.* [Translated by George Eliot.] 3 vols. London: Chapman, Brothers, 1846.

[Tennyson, Hallam.] *Alfred Lord Tennyson: A Memoir By His Son*. London: Macmillan and Co., 1906.

[Thirlwall, Connop.] Introduction to *A Critical Essay on the Gospel of St. Luke*, by Friedrich Daniel Ernst Schleiermacher. London: John Taylor, 1825.

– *Letters Literary and Theological*. Edited by J. J. Stewart Perowne and Louis Stokes. London: Richard Bentley and Son, 1881.

Thompson, Frank T. "Emerson's Indebtedness to Coleridge." *Studies in Philology* 23 (1926): 55–76.

Tuell, Anne Kimball. *John Sterling: A Representative Victorian*. New York: Macmillan, for the Sophie Hart Fund of Wellesley College, 1941.

Vawter, Bruce. *Biblical Inspiration*. London and Philadelphia: Hutchinson, Westminster, 1972.

Warren, Robert Penn. "A Poem of Pure Imagination." *Kenyon Review* 8 (1946): 391–427.

Wasserman, Earl R. *The Finer Tone*. Baltimore: Johns Hopkins University Press, 1953.

Wells, G. A. "Man and Nature: An Elucidation of Coleridge's Rejection of Herder's Thought." *Journal of English and Germanic Philology* 51 (1952): 314–25.

Wheeler, Kathleen M. *The Creative Mind in Coleridge's Poetry*. Cambridge, Mass.: Harvard University Press, 1981.

Whicher, Stephen E. *Freedom and Fate: An Inner Life of Ralph Waldo Emerson*. Philadelphia: University of Pennsylvania Press, 1953.

Whitman, Walt. *Leaves of Grass*. Edited by Harold W. Blodgett and Sculley Bradley. New York: New York University Press, 1965.

Willey, Basil. *Nineteenth-Century Studies*. Harmondsworth: Penguin Books, 1964.

Wilson, Douglas Brownlow. "Two Modes of Apprehending Nature: A Gloss on the Coleridgean Symbol." *PMLA* 87 (1972): 42–52.

Wimsatt, W. K. "Organic Form: Some Questions about a Metaphor." In *Romanticism: Vistas, Instances, Continuities*, edited by David Thorburn and Geoffrey H. Hartman, pp. 13–37. Ithaca, N.Y.: Cornell University Press, 1973.

Winslow, Donald F. "Francis W. Newman's Assessment of John Sterling: Two Letters." *English Language Notes* 11 (1974): 278–83.

Winstanley, D. A. *Early Victorian Cambridge*. Cambridge: Cambridge University Press, 1955.

Wittreich, Joseph Anthony, Jr. " 'A Poet Amongst Poets': Milton and the Tradition of Prophecy." In *Milton and the Line of Vision*, edited by Joseph Anthony Wittreich, Jr., pp. 97–142. Madison: The University of Wisconsin Press, 1975.

Wordsworth, William. *Poetical Works*. Edited by E. de Selincourt and Helen Darbishire. 5 vols. Oxford: The Clarendon Press, 1940–49.

Yoder, R. A. *Emerson and the Orphic Poet in America*. Berkeley: University of California Press, 1978.

Index